The New South Creed

THE
NEW
SOUTH
CREED

A Study in Southern Mythmaking

PAUL M. GASTON

LOUISIANA STATE UNIVERSITY PRESS

BATON ROUGE

ISBN 0–8071–0256–3
Library of Congress Catalog Card Number 70–98640
Copyright © 1970 by Paul M. Gaston
All rights reserved under International and
Pan-American Copyright Conventions
Manufactured in the United States of America
Louisiana Paperbacks edition, published 1976
by special arrangement with Alfred A. Knopf, Inc.

Second Printing (April, 1983)

for my father
and the memory of my mother

Acknowledgments

My interest in the New South movement began a long time ago in the seminar of Fletcher M. Green at the University of North Carolina. Professor Green subsequently directed my dissertation on the subject and this book is an extension and refinement of that study.

Many persons and institutions have helped me in the interval between dissertation and book, and it is pleasant finally to be able to acknowledge their assistance. I have received financial aid from the Southern Fellowships Fund, the Social Science Research Council, the American Council of Learned Societies, the Old Dominion Foundation, and the Wilson Gee Institute for Research in Social Science of the University of Virginia. To all of them I reiterate my gratitude. Two research assistants, John Boles and Holt Merchant, helped more than I had a right to expect. Mr. Boles, with an unerring eye for the relevant, collected a large stack of notes which I have used profitably; Mr. Merchant checked most of the footnotes and offered valuable criticism and welcome enthusiasm. Several friends and colleagues have read all or portions of the manuscript. For their suggestions, encouragement—and time—I thank William W. Abbot, George H. Callcott, John Hammond Moore, Willie Lee Rose, and C. Vann Woodward. My reading of Professor Woodward's essay,

"The Search for Southern Identity," led me to the framework for the study.

My wife types badly and her spelling, punctuation, and proofreading are unreliable; but she persuaded me to pursue the subject in the first place, let few of my paragraphs escape revision, and wrote the passages I like most.

P.M.G.

Contents

The New South Creed

Prologue

The New South
Symbol

Surely the basis of the South's wealth and power is laid by the hand of the Almighty God, and its prosperity has been established by divine law.

—HENRY W. GRADY, 1887[1]

Who can picture the vast, illimitable future of this glorious sunny South? . . . Here is a land possessing in its own matchless resources the combined advantages of almost every other country of the world without their most serious disadvantages. . . . It is beyond the power of the human mind to fully grasp the future that is in store for this country. . . . The more we contemplate these advantages and contrast them with those of all other countries, the more deeply will we be impressed with the unquestionable truth that here in this glorious land, "Creation's Garden Spot," is to be the richest and greatest country upon which the sun ever shone.

—RICHARD H. EDMONDS, 1888[2]

In the spring of 1865 momentous decisions awaited the American people. The old Federal Republic, sundered by the secession of the principal slaveholding states, had existed barely more than seventy years under the Constitution. With victory won, it now had a second chance to vindicate the faith of the Founding Fathers. But the task of mending its torn fabric and revitalizing the principles of which Lincoln had spoken on the Gettysburg battlefield would not be easy. That fabric and those principles had been strained at one time or another before the war by every section of the country, but in 1865 only the memory of the South's apostasy was recalled. Tension caused by the peculiarities of the slave-holding region had been an omnipresent source of national disquietude and, according to the Northern view, the South's determination to perpetuate its anachronistic way of life had been, in some ultimate sense, responsible for disruption of the Union, discredit to the cause of democracy everywhere, and bloody civil war. In the aftermath of Appomattox, then, citizens of the victorious Union believed that the future of the Republic and the success of its mission as exemplar of free government would depend heavily on the extent to which the South could adjust, or be made to adjust, to the national viewpoint.

Meanwhile, the conquered Southerners abandoned

forever their dream of separate nationhood, and having
to share with Northerners the desire to restore the Union,
they wished keenly for that result to come about quickly.
Cherishing memories of the Republic, and proud of their
conspicuous role in creating it, they likewise wished to
see it regain its former glory, and to share in its fame.
But in the agony that arose from their collapse they could
hardly agree that the injuries it had sustained and the
calamity the nation had suffered were all of their doing.
Rather, they expressed reverence for the civilization that
had existed in the South, but conceded that it had passed
irrevocably into history, had become an "Old South" that
must now be superseded by a new order. In time, the
words "New South" became the symbol that expressed
this passage from one kind of civilization to another.

This book is about that symbol. It deals with the
meaning that spokesmen for a new South gave to their
rallying cry, analyzes their program for making it a
reality, discusses the outcome and significance of their
movement in the nineteenth century, and concludes with
an appraisal of the legacy they bequeathed to the twentieth century.

I

Almost from the beginning of its popularity, the term
"New South" has had a blurred and ambiguous meaning.
Historians have not had much success with their efforts
to bring it into sharp focus. For one thing, they have
never agreed on the central characteristics of Southern

history itself, so that different interpretations of the region's past necessarily lead to conflicting accounts of what is new in the New South. Other factors have similarly complicated the historians' job of clarifying the image. For some, New South signifies a doctrine or point of view, not always clearly defined, that has been characteristic of certain groups of Southerners. For others, it has been used to delimit a period of time, with little agreement on beginning or terminal dates. It may mean the South since 1865; since 1877; from 1877 to 1913; since 1900; or simply the South of the present. And some compound the ambiguity by using it to designate both a doctrine and a period of time.

Another reason for ambiguity is that the concept of a New South, unlike the picture of the Old South, has always been a contemporary one, useful as a propaganda device to influence the direction and control of Southern development. Various groups have seized upon the term to symbolize their particular programs and name their publications. A nineteenth-century New South journal championed industrialism, high tariffs, and social Darwinism. A twentieth-century one was the voice of Southern communism.[3] Since its creation in 1944, the Southern Regional Council has published a magazine called *New South* which advocates a South free of racial discrimination; and in Nashville, the Southern Student Organizing Committee's *New South Student* joins to the movement for racial equality a militant antimilitarism and a vaguely defined program for the restructuring of Southern society. Used in these and other ways, "New South" may stand for whatever kind of society adopters of the term believe will serve the region's interests best or promote their own ambitions most effectively.

The common ingredient in these variations is the concept of a *South*—of whatever kind or period it may be. Southerners have shared experiences and circumstances which seem to make it natural, perhaps necessary, for their memories, new ideas, and aspirations to be arranged to fit coherently into some concept of Southernness. The spokesmen for a new South after the Civil War were as influenced by and responded as naturally to this tendency in their society as other Southerners. For this reason it is important in understanding their "New South" to see their ideas not only as a program or new departure but also as elements in a total mythic configuration with a history of its own.

Perception of the reality of both the past and the present is greatly determined for most people by the myths which become part of their lives. Defeat in the Civil War and humiliation in the Reconstruction that followed provided an atmosphere for the growth of two images of the South that, on the surface at least, appeared to have little in common. The defeat and despondency called forth a collection of romantic pictures of the Old South and a cult of the Lost Cause that fused in the Southerner's imagination to give him an uncommonly pleasing conception of his region's past. Increasingly, he came to visualize the old regime as a society dominated by a beneficent plantation tradition, sustained by a unique code of honor, and peopled by happy, amusing slaves at one end of the social spectrum and beautiful maidens and chivalric gentlemen at the other—with little in between. That this noble order had been assaulted and humiliated by the North was a source of poignancy and bitterness for Southerners; but, in the bleak aftermath of defeat, the recollection of its grandeur was also—and more importantly—a wellspring of intense satisfaction and the basis for an exaggerated regional pride.

No amount of nostalgia, however, could gainsay the fact that the South in the generation after Appomattox was desperately poor, alternately despised, ridiculed, or pitied, and saddled with many unwelcome burdens. To find a way out of this syndrome, optimistic young Southerners like Henry W. Grady and Richard H. Edmonds began to talk hopefully of a new scheme of things that would enrich the region, restore prestige and power, and lay the race question to rest. The term "New South" in their lexicon bespoke harmonious reconciliation of sectional differences, racial peace, and a new economic and social order based on industry and scientific, diversified agriculture—all of which would lead, eventually, to the South's dominance in the reunited nation.

Unlike though they were, the picture of the Old South and the dream of a New South were both expressions of the hopes, values, and ideals of Southerners. In time, both became genuine social myths with a controlling power over the way in which their believers perceived reality. The mythic view of the past, already beyond the embryo stage in the antebellum period, was fully articulated in the 'eighties. The New South creed, born to inspire a program of action, expressed faith in the South's ability to bring about its own regeneration in partnership with sympathetic Northerners; but in the 'eighties it began to undergo a metamorphosis and soon came to be a description not of what ought to be or would be, but of what already was.

The presence of myths in and about the South does not, of course, mark the region off as different either from the rest of the country or from other parts of the world,

for every nation or group can be identified in some measure
by the myths upon which it rests. What does distinguish
the South, at least from other parts of the United States,
is the degree to which myths have been spawned and the
extent to which they have asserted their hegemony over
the Southern mind. George B. Tindall, in a recent essay
on the mythmaking penchant of the South, has prepared
a kind of genealogical guide to Southern mythology which
abundantly supports his conclusion that its "infinite
variety . . . could be catalogued and analyzed endlessly."[4]
One of the reasons for the superabundance of Southern
myths is that Southern life has involved such a high degree
of failure and frustration that intellectual and emotional
compensations have been at a premium. Myths have been
equally important as means of making some sense and
order out of the complex, ambivalent patterns of the
Southern experience. The South, as David M. Potter
observes, "has been democratic as well as aristocratic,
fond of 'flush times' and booms as well as of tradition;
it has lusted for prosperity, bulldozers, and progress,
while cherishing the values of stability, religious ortho-
doxy, and rural life." Caught in a painful dilemma,
Southerners "could not bear either to abandon the patterns
of the Old South or to forego the material gains of
modern America."[5]

To harmonize these conflicting ambitions and experiences, Southerners have nurtured their myths to perform
something closely akin to the function of religion—to
unify experience, as Mark Schorer has remarked in
another context, "in a way that is satisfactory to the whole
culture and to the whole personality." Myths, Schorer
writes, "are the instruments by which we continually
struggle to make our experience intelligible to ourselves."

A myth, he continues, "is a large controlling image that gives philosophical meaning to the facts of ordinary life; that is, which has organizing value for experience."[6] For their believers, as C. Vann Woodward writes, myths are "charged with values, aspirations, ideals and meanings";[7] and for the individual involved, as Robert Penn Warren puts it, the myth "defines the myth-maker's world, his position in it, his destiny, and his appropriate attitude."[8] Myths, as these comments attest, are not polite euphemisms for falsehoods, but are combinations of images and symbols that reflect a people's way of perceiving truth. Organically related to a fundamental reality of life, they fuse the real and the imaginary into a blend that becomes a reality itself, a force in history. The distinction between creed and myth, which is important to this study, is one of emphasis. Both concern beliefs, but the former is a conscious statement concerned primarily with how things ought to be, while the latter is more a generalized, unconsciously held belief in how things actually are or were.

Historians have long been aware of dynamic myths in the Southern past but, with a few notable exceptions, they have not focused their studies on myth as a subject of historical investigation. Rather, they have produced a lush and stimulating interpretive literature designed to identify the central theme or themes of Southern history. Fruitful though this approach has been, it is beset by serious limitations. In ordering and simplifying their materials—and investing their conclusions with value judgments—most practitioners of this genre of historical writing have fashioned interpretations that have become little myths themselves, subject to endless critiques by other historians. For example, William E. Dodd wrote early in the twentieth century that the normative South was the South of Jefferson, which he presumed to be liberal and agrarian, not intolerant and hierarchical.[9] But, as Potter observes, Dodd "reconciled his love for his native South and his commitment to democracy, and with very little disclosure of the wishful thinking which was involved, identified the land he loved with the values he cherished."[10] Similarly, in 1930 a group of young Nashville intellectuals, the Vanderbilt Agrarians, projected their hostility to modern industrial America into a generalized picture of the Southern past which portrayed agrarianism as the decisive factor in the region's development. In their view agrarianism had produced a traditional style of life characterized by order, rootedness, and respect for the individual.[11] In literal form, neither Dodd's picture of a democratic agrarian society nor the Nashville group's image of a conservative agrarian society fits with what historians now know about the Southern past, and "the whole idea of the South as an agrarian society," Potter notes, "seems more and more an illusion, nourished by a wish."[12]

Less illusory, and somewhat more durable, is Ulrich B. Phillips's thesis that the central theme of Southern history has been the white man's determination to maintain a biracial society. Southernism, Phillips wrote in 1928, arose from "a common resolve indomitably maintained" that the South "shall be and remain a white man's country." And, he continued, "the consciousness of a function in these premises, whether expressed with the frenzy of a demagogue or maintained with a patrician's quietude, is the cardinal test of a Southerner and is the central theme of Southern history."[13] But even the Phillips thesis has appeared outmoded of late because of the rapid and profound changes in race relations. These and alterations of other aspects of Southern life have caused many scholars to doubt the continuing distinctiveness of the region and have stimulated a new round of assessments of the Southern experience. They have led to C. Vann Woodward's "Search for Southern Identity," to the invocation of Harry Ashmore's epitaph for Dixie, to a reconsideration of the validity and usefulness of the concept of regionalism, and to one writer's proclamation of the "happy truth" that the South has lost its "regional integrity," so that the "writer of tomorrow must take into account another South, a South already born and growing lustily, a rich South, urban, industrialized, and no longer 'Southern,' but rather northernized, Europeanized, cosmopolitan."[14]

Changes, in both the region and the nation, have transformed the reality as well as the image of the South in recent years, but as Edgar T. Thompson remarked a short time ago, "before and since Henry W. Grady used the expression in 1886, every generation of Americans has been told that the South of its day was a 'New South.' "[15] This ongoing concern to discover and explain the significance of a new South, suggested by Thompson's observation, has nearly always required the would-be discoverer to distinguish between the civilization of the Old South and the emerging, or presumably emerging, New South. Deprecating this tendency, W. J. Cash wrote more than a generation ago, in what is probably still the most widely read study of the Southern mind, that "the extent of the change and of the break between the Old South that was and the South of our time has been vastly exaggerated," and he urged his readers to disabuse their minds "of two correlated legends—those of the Old and the New Souths."[16] But Cash's popular theory of historical continuity, as later parts of this study will suggest, was constructed by misjudging the significance of key elements in the Southern experience; and the Old South–New South dichotomy which he minimizes is in fact a crucial one with which every search for the "central theme" of Southern history must come to terms at one point or another.

II

Quests for the essence of Southernism have been greatly aided by the appearance of numerous excellent works on the values and ideals of the antebellum South so that we have today a rich literature in that field.[17] Unfortunately, the same cannot be said for the intellectual history of the postwar South, and because the subject has been neglected generalizations about the ideology of the period and attempts to portray convincingly the Old South–New South dichotomy rest on inadequate monographic foundations.[18] In part, then, this study of the New South creed is designed to narrow one of the gaps that must be closed to permit further advances in the interpretive literature of Southern history. It is also conceived as a study in the history of Southern mythology, a largely unexplored field. As Tindall notes, myths have profoundly influenced the shaping of the Southern character and have had much to do with "unifying society, developing a sense of community, of common ideals and shared goals, making the region conscious of its distinctiveness." Whether he is accurate in predicting that historians may "encounter the central theme of Southern history at last on the new frontier of mythology" remains to be seen, but the prospects are inviting enough to encourage exploration of that frontier.[19]

Neither Southern mythology nor Southern history can be studied intelligently in a regional vacuum. The South, to be sure, has been different from the nation, but to explain the nature and significance of its distinctiveness the successful historian must transcend regional perspectives. For example, Woodward's influential essay, "The Search for Southern Identity," explains how Southern peculiarities appear to be unique only because the South is part of America. American history, unlike the history of other parts of the world, has been characterized by economic abundance and opportunity, success and invincibility, and a legend of moral innocence. The Southern experience, on the other hand, has been shaped by the obverse of these endemically American characteristics: poverty, frustration and defeat, and an ever-present moral dilemma.[20]

To the men of the postwar period who proclaimed the New South creed, these differences were real and painful; and their program, product of a subtle interaction between national ideals and achievements on the one hand and regional aspirations and failures on the other, was designed to obliterate them. How the New South creed was first articulated; how it inspired a program to make the South rich, triumphant, and morally innocent; how it adjusted to and manipulated the myth of the Old South; and how, in the end, it became itself a powerful and enduring social myth are the subjects of the chapters that follow.

1
Birth of a Creed

The pride which we might have felt in the
glories of the past is rebuked by the
thought that these glories have faded away.
It is rebuked by the thought that they
were purchased at the expense of the
material prosperity of the country; for men
of wealth and talents did not combine their
fortunes, their energies, and their intellects
to develop the immense resources of the
land of their nativity.

—DANIEL HARVEY HILL, 1866[1]

The Old South . . . has gone "down among
the dead men," and on its head-stone we
see not the word "Resurgam." For that
vanished form of society there can be no
resurrection. . . . But the New South—its
child and legitimate successor—sits in the
seat of the dethroned king, exhibiting a
lustier life, and the promise of greater
growth and strength, than did its
predecessor.

—EDWIN DELEON, 1870[2]

We can live neither *in* nor *by* the defeated past, and if we would live in the growing, conquering future, we must furnish our strength to shape its course and our will to discharge its duties. The pressing question, therefore, with every people is, not what they have been, but whether and what they shall determine to be; not what their fathers were, but whether and what their children shall be.

— BENJAMIN HARVEY HILL, 1871[3]

H enry W. Grady, the young and ebullient editor of the Atlanta *Constitution*, appeared before the New England Society of New York in 1886 to make a speech that subsequent generations of Southern schoolboys would be required to commit to memory. Surrounded by imposing men of affairs, Grady announced that an Old South of slavery and secession had passed away to be replaced by a new South of union and freedom. The national press reacted jubilantly to the occasion, hailing the optimistic orator from Georgia as the personification and chief spokesman of his region's dynamic movement of regeneration. When he died three years later, still a young man, the New York *Times* lauded him as the "creator of the spirit" that animated the once despondent region. Other contemporaries, in all parts of the country, were similarly impressed by Grady's evangelistic mission and golden words and were extravagant in their praise of him as the first and foremost New South spokesman.[4]

Later generations of Southerners, seldom corrected and sometimes abetted by their historians, continued to look upon Grady not only as the chief apostle of the New South movement—a title he probably deserved—but as its originator as well. It was not so many years ago, for example, that a president of the Southern Historical Association lent his authority to the popular belief that the term "New South," if not actually invented by Grady, was "first put into circulation by him."[5] Grady himself, however, never claimed either to have coined the phrase or to have been the first to popularize it. He had used it as early as 1874, in an editorial in the Atlanta *Daily Herald*, but he knew that others had used it before; and by the time of his widely publicized New York address the term was already household knowledge.

I

Twenty-four years before the New York speech, and three years before Lee surrendered to Grant, the term New South made its debut. A Union officer, exhilarated by his army's capture of the sea islands of South Carolina and Georgia, apparently had visions not only of victory but also of a new and better order to come. On March 15, 1862, Captain Adam Badeau edited the first number of *The New South*, a newspaper designed to serve the Federal troops in the Port Royal area. Less than a year after the war had begun, at nearby Fort Sumter, Port Royal was the scene of a rehearsal for the later reconstruction and it seemed appropriate that the newspaper serving the lush and once opulent sea islands should adopt a name symbolizing the inauguration of a new era.[6]

Despite the title, however, the journal gave little indication of what shape the postwar order might take, for neither Badeau nor his editorial successor, Joseph H. Sears, spelled out a comprehensive program for the region. The newspaper was heavily military in tone and coverage, exuding contempt for the South's aspiration to independence and frequently emphasizing Badeau's declaration in the maiden issue that the Federals were able and determined to restore the "civil union at any cost." Partly because of wartime circumstances and partly because of its peremptory, hostile tone, the Port Royal newspaper was read by relatively few Southerners and even fewer looked to it for instruction and encouragement. Not surprisingly, then, the first effort to introduce the term "New South" into the lexicon of Southerners faded from memory and Badeau's creation earned no place in the movement that was to adopt its name.

It would be five years after Appomattox before the term was to be used positively as the symbol for a specific and indigenous movement of social, economic, and intellectual regeneration. During the first half-decade after the war Southerners responded in a variety of ways to the crushing defeat they had sustained and to the revolutionary consequences of emancipation which suddenly faced them. Some, filled with hatred and belligerence, hoped to restore the old order as perfectly as possible by assigning the Negro to a status of near-slavery and by refusing to abandon their agrarian economic and social order and the static value system it had spawned. Others, despairing of all programs to save the region, proposed mass emigration, convinced that the Confederate ethos could be preserved only in a foreign land, untainted by the progressive doctrines of the nineteenth century. Persuaded that the society they cherished could never be revived, these fatalists spoke naturally of an "old" South that now belonged to history. To most Southerners, however, total resistance to change or flight from their country were unsatisfactory solutions. They, too, recognized the passing of an era and undoubtedly many of them used the term "new" South to suggest, however vaguely, the inevitability of change.

Gradually, out of the attempt to give form and direction to a new order, the New South movement of the next decade emerged.

The need for a new material basis and a new intellectual rationale for Southern society was obvious and acute in the early postwar period. Before the Civil War the South had worked out an intricate material and social system, elaborately rationalized by an intellectual and moral creed that viewed the Southern way of life as fundamentally different from and superior to that of the North. When cotton culture spread across the older regions of the South and then into the newer lands of the Southwest, staple-crop agriculture became more firmly established than ever before. At the same time, and as a product of the same dynamic, a new and more aggressive plantation aristocracy was grafted onto the older one to dominate society and dictate the course of its development. Slavery, which had shown some signs of being moribund before the cotton revolution, rapidly came to be regarded as a vital and immutable condition of both staple-crop agriculture and plantation aristocracy. These three intertwining economic and social interests—staple-crop agriculture, plantation aristocracy, and Negro slavery—produced a formidable defense mechanism that frustrated industrial and urban developments capable of undermining their foundations. The value system that grew naturally out of this order was inevitably hostile to the increasingly pragmatic and utilitarian cast of mind of nineteenth-century liberal development and suspicious of its notable shibboleths and achievements: economic individualism, urbanism, industrialism, and mass culture.

During the three decades prior to the war all facets of the Southern system were bitterly attacked as a consequence of the crusade against slavery. Attack produced response, and the best minds of the South labored for more than a generation to fashion a damning critique of free society and an ingenious rationalization of slavery as the only sound basis for the development and preservation of republican virtue, constitutional rectitude, and class harmony. Hostility to the forces of industrialism and urbanism was greatly augmented, and in the contest with antislavery polemicists the planters and their theoreticians identified the North, and especially New England, with virtually all of those evils inimical to the peace and prosperity of the South. Hostility combined with fear quickly led to the erection of a "cotton curtain" to diminish the flow of hostile ideas from the outside and to protect the orthodox viewpoint from erosion within.

By the time Lincoln called for 75,000 troops to suppress the disorders at Fort Sumter, the most popular slogan in the South was the exuberant cry, "Cotton is King." The boast meant not only that the Confederacy was unbeatable, but also that the Southern monarch had produced a near-idyllic society ready to prove its superior quality in warfare. Enthusiasm for the Confederate cause burgeoned into euphoria at the outset of the conflict, and for this reason the frustrations and defeats that soon came struck with unusual force. The war completely destroyed the myth of invincibility and made it increasingly difficult to retain the corollary myth of superiority, for failure to meet the test of endurance inevitably raised doubts about the quality of the defeated society. To many Southerners, then, sober second thoughts came in 1865; the result was dissipation of the antebellum unity of mind that had unquestioningly accepted the social, economic, and intellectual structure of Southern civilization.[7]

There was, to be sure, no mass repudiation of Southernism in 1865, or at anytime thereafter. On the contrary, nostalgia, despair, pride in the defeated soldiers, and pathos—mixed with a generous measure of relief—combined to produce a mood of ambivalence. Few Southerners neatly sorted out their conflicting sentiments and certainly few of them suffered a real crisis of faith. Their mental dilemmas were resolved simply by paying homage to the gallantry and honor of the old regime without letting that ritual interfere excessively with an examination of the problems of the present and the future—even when that examination led them, as it must, to search for the flaws in the old closed system of staple-crop agriculture, planter domination, and Negro slavery.

Although it never appeared with clarity in the first years after the war, what the South set off in search of was a new modus operandi with a harmonizing rationale to supply the same kind of fraternal unity that the creed of the Old South had furnished. The task was formidable. For one thing, it could not be achieved without substantial material and spiritual aid from the North; and yet pride could be restored and confidence built only if the movement were, or at least appeared to be, indigenous in origin and control. Moreover, with the power of the planter destroyed, there was no group within the region that could wield the kind of moral and social power that the deposed class had enjoyed. For this reason proposals for self-reconstruction often lacked focus and authority and crystallized slowly. Finally, the more violent and dramatic contest over Congressional Reconstruction, centered on the status of the Negro and the locus of political power, both diverted energies from programs of self-reconstruction and virtually eliminated the possibility of intersectional harmony necessary to their achievement.

Nevertheless, during the immediate postwar years a beginning was made. Dozens of proposals, having little or nothing to do with the more publicized issues of the main Reconstruction, appeared in speeches, newspapers, magazines, and reports; and, despite the turmoil, a program began to take shape. Increasingly, hope was expressed that old errors could be corrected and new courses charted. A former Confederate colonel, member of an aristocratic South Carolina family, put the necessity simply: "We must," said Ben Allston, "begin at the beginning again. We must make a new start."[8]

II

No more likely place for launching the new start that Allston called for could be found than *DeBow's Review*, the journal which published his speech. Before the war, J. D. B. DeBow's New Orleans magazine had combined an intense Southern nationalism with an equally fervent call for industrialization. The journal ceased publication during the war, but DeBow revived it in 1866. In the maiden issue of the "After the War" series, he roamed broadly over the problems of the South. "The vast mineral resources which geological surveys have divulged," he wrote, were as yet untouched by the "hand of industry," and the limitless number of rich manufacturing sites dazzled the imagination, so that the South now faced her moment of greatest opportunity. "If there ever was, then, a period in the history of a people, when it became necessary for them to be aroused as one man into action," DeBow declared, "and to put their shoulders to the wheel, and with energy and spirit and determination to make a giant and master struggle, that period has come for the South." Meeting the challenge and seizing the opportunity which now lay before her, he promised, the South would quickly resume "her place in the mighty empire of States" and "no son of hers will have reason to be ashamed of her place in the picture."[9]

In June 1866, DeBow published an essay by Matthew Fontaine Maury, promoter of a Confederate colonizing effort in Mexico.[10] DeBow understood the sense of despair which had caused the exodus, but though he confessed that "the clouds are dark," he wrote in the introduction to Maury's article that he was "not yet despondent. We have the nerve yet to endure and wait."[11] This cautious mood, based largely on his suspicions of the Radical element in Congress, was but a minor motif in the *Review*. Characteristically, like the New South prophets who would follow him, DeBow wrote extravagantly of the boundless resources whose exploitation would make emigration a senseless surrender. Typical of the pieces he published—and a striking contrast to Maury's somber article—was an ecstatic essay by A. P. Merrill, who believed that the unparalleled advantages of the South would make "Nineveh, Babylon, Rome, and Britain, with all their boasted wealth and dominion, sink into insignificance."[12]

In an essay on South Carolina, DeBow confessed that much had been said and written about the underdeveloped resources of the South, "but there are very few who are informed as to the peculiar advantages or special aptitudes of any particular section." He therefore proposed, as "one of the first and most practicable steps that can be adopted to revive the former prosperity of these States," a project "to disseminate reliable information regarding the opportunities for profitable employment offered by the specialities of each section."[13] The present flow of population was westward, DeBow noted, but he believed that this could not continue indefinitely. Once the true possibilities of the South were understood a mighty immigration movement would begin. Happily, he believed the South was now ready to remove the "dykes and barriers and invite the inundation."[14]

To seize the opportunities that lay before them, Southerners were told by *DeBow's Review* that the region must industrialize, diversify its staple-crop agricultural system, seek immigrants and capital from the North and from Europe, and infuse the region with a new spirit of business enterprise. DeBow saw, perhaps more clearly than some of the later New South prophets, that the shortage of capital and skilled labor, combined with difficult marketing problems, presented severe obstacles; but he wrote confidently that they would be overcome once a genuine effort got underway. Industrial development was the first necessity. Designating manufacturing as the South's "true remedy," he wrote:

We have got to go to manufacturing to save ourselves. We have got to go to it to obtain an increase of population. Workmen go to furnaces, mines, and factories— they go where labor is brought. Every new furnace or factory is the nucleus of a town, to which every needed service is sure to come from the neighborhood or from abroad. Factories and works established establish other factories and works. Population, we repeat, is one of the sorest needs of the South; immigration only can supply this. We can surely obtain that by providing our labor with diversified employment.

Capital, to the extent that the South shall have occasion to borrow, will, by a law of economy that never fails, flow here to erect, equip, and start every manufacturing establishment as fast as it can profitably be run.[15]

DeBow's plea for manufacturing was supported by numerous contributors to the *Review*. Robert M. Patton, a former governor of Alabama, writing in 1867 of a "New Era of Southern Manufacturers," stressed the importance of cotton textile development. With increasing uncertainties in the cotton field, owing, he thought, to the unreliability of Negro labor, Patton argued that a shift of capital from cotton growing to cotton manufacturing would provide employment for thousands of war widows and orphans. Moreover, the advantages of the South in textiles—favorable climate, abundant water power, nearness to the raw material—especially suited the region to the industry.[16] Another contributor, repeating many of Patton's arguments, added the happy thought that the textile industry could be built on the cheap labor of poor whites. Housed in mill villages, where common schools would be practicable, they would become better educated, more industrious, happy, and responsible citizens.[17] So important was industrial development to the material welfare of the region that another contributor pleaded for support from the region's state legislatures. "The capital of the State and its credit," he wrote, "should be employed to aid in establishing certain leading manufactures of iron and cotton." State aid to manufacturers was necessary and justifiable, he argued, "on the same principle that States aid [is] . . . in building ways of transportation. The reasoning is precisely the same, with this special and conclusive reason. The State must build a poor-house and a prison, or a cotton factory in every county or parish."[18]

DeBow's main emphasis was on industrial development, which he believed would go far toward bringing balance to the Southern economy. But his analysis also led him to attack vigorously the notion that the South should continue to place most of its agricultural capital into production of staple crops. Farming, he recognized, would continue to be the backbone of the economy for some time, but the region would not prosper until it created a new, diversified agriculture. Farmers, he frequently wrote, should take advantage of the long growing season to produce numerous and varied crops for ever widening markets. A contributor from New Orleans stated the dogma of the *Review* when he wrote that cotton was no longer king, that a revolution of "great magnitude" had taken place, and that it would be the essence of folly to attempt to resurrect an agricultural system that had caused such woe.[19]

The attraction of capital and skilled labor from the North and from Europe was a critical element in DeBow's program. To lure them he proposed, first, that the South begin its industrial development earnestly, using the resources immediately at hand; and, second, that the leaders of the region undertake a massive campaign to advertise its rich potential. With a faith that capital would come in naturally as a result of proper dissemination of information, and despairing of the reliability of Negro labor, DeBow and his contributors devoted most of their energies to designs for attracting non-Southern whites to supply the shortage of skilled labor. Proposals were made for the promotion of immigration societies and states were urged to form immigration bureaus. One contributor, like DeBow, urged that the state take the leadership in breaking up large plantations in order to make land available to immigrants. The hope was that such a scheme would offset the competitive advantage which the Homestead Act had given the West.[20] To assure potential non-Southern investors and laborers of a friendly reception, the *Review* ran several articles in 1866 on the theme of sectional reconciliation. One optimistic contributor, writing in the first issue, pronounced the end of sectionalism. Sectional questions, he wrote, "are *settled;* and settled forever. We all, North, South, East, and West, have *one country, one destiny, one duty.*"[21]

DeBow died in 1867, and his magazine survived him only a short while. William M. Burwell, the new editor, was a loyal disciple and the *Review* continued, until its demise in 1870, to develop the program DeBow had worked out in 1866. In his statement of purpose, Burwell summarized the goals to which his predecessor had been committed and pledged his support to them. He would oppose sectionalism, advocate protection of Negro rights, encourage programs to entice labor and capital into the region, and impress upon all Southerners their "paramount duty" to work "silently, resolutely, honorably for the social and industrial reconstruction of the South."[22]

In the same year that DeBow revived his *Review,* former Confederate general Daniel Harvey Hill had published the first number of his new magazine in North Carolina. The name Hill chose, *The Land We Love,* suggests nostalgia and recrimination rather than optimism and innovation; and editorial pronouncements from a former Confederate general—even one as irascible as Hill—might well be expected to excoriate prophets of a new order. But, in the beginning at least, Hill offered his readers a fare strikingly similar to DeBow's. In May 1866 he began his personal crusade to remake the South, warning that Southerners had better change their "minds upon many subjects, else our very name and nation will be taken away."[23] To begin with, Hill called into question the pride which blinded men to the deficiencies of the old regime:

The pride which we might have felt in the glories of the past is rebuked by the thought that these glories have faded away. It is rebuked by the thought that they were purchased at the expense of the material prosperity of the country; for men of wealth and talents did not combine their fortunes, their energies, and their intellects to develop the immense resources of the land of their nativity. What factories did they erect? What mines did they dig? What foundries did they establish? What machine shops did they build? What ships did they put afloat? Their minds and their hearts were engrossed in the struggle for national position and national honors. The yearning desire was ever for political supremacy, and never for domestic thrift and economy. Hence we became dependent upon the North for everything, from a lucifer match to a columbiad, from a pin to a railroad engine. A state of war found us without the machinery to make a single percussion cap for a soldier's rifle, or a single button for his jacket.[24]

Hill's first editorial, a broad-ranging survey of the South's problems, was entitled "Education." The title was revealing because Hill believed that the planters' failure to produce a flourishing and balanced economic system was intimately related to a value system that scorned material progress. Thus, the educational task of the postwar South was to retrain its people and particularly to educate them in the ways of thrift and industry and instill in them a respect for manual labor. Men needed to learn that the effete, aristocratic educational values of the Old South were both cause and consequence of the economic failures the South had sustained. The needs of the present, he felt, were clear:

Is not attention to our fields and firesides of infinitely more importance to us than attention to national affairs? Is not a practical acquaintance with the ax, the plane, the saw, the anvil, the loom, the plow, and the mattock, vastly more useful to an impoverished people than familiarity with the laws of nations and the science of government? What will a knowledge of the ancient classics, of metaphysics and belles-lettres do to relieve our poverty? What will it add to our prosperity? We want practical learning, not scholastic lore. We want business men with brain and hand for work, not the recluses of the library or convent.[25]

Building on a new appreciation of the value of work, inculcated by an educational system attuned to the needs of the region, the South's next step in regeneration, Hill believed, led to a broadly diversified agricultural system to replace the old regime of staple-crop agriculture, and an imaginative, aggressive industrial system that would fully exploit the rich natural resources of the region. For two years the magazine developed these themes. In contrast to DeBow, whose emphasis was on industrial growth, Hill was more interested in diversified, scientific farming. Successive issues not only exhorted farmers to break away from the old system, but also supplied abundant practical and technical advice on such subjects as soil types, fertilizers, truck farming, and the economic management of small enterprises.

In 1868, Hill's tone changed abruptly. For reasons that are not entirely clear—but which probably relate to his growing enmity toward the unfolding program of Congressional Reconstruction—he began to retreat from many of his previously expressed views. He continued to preach agricultural reform, as he would throughout the rest of his life, but he said no more about the benefits of industrialism. Instead, he wrote vehemently about its evils. By May 1868 he was in full attack on the grasping drive for material success which he felt abounded in the nation. In this vein he wrote that rapid industrialization was producing a new industrial oligarchy "a hundred-fold less respectable and venerable, than the landed aristocracy which the spirit of the age has swept away."[26] Never returning to his early views, he was scornful of the New South movement when it materialized. Speaking to a veterans group in 1887 he referred sarcastically to the movement that had built on his own early ideas. Southerners, he said, are proud of the label New South; they "brag about it, and roll it as a sweet morsel under their tongues." For his part, he told the veterans, he would rather talk about the Old South.[27]

If D. H. Hill retreated from the New South movement before it had fairly begun, there were other Southerners with an audience who showed more tenacity, less squeamishness. Across the region the ideas expressed by DeBow and Hill were repeated with increasing emphasis. In Charleston in 1869, William Lee Trenholm told the city's Board of Trade to accept the fact of defeat, banish animosities toward the North, and turn to new patterns of development. Respect for the Old South, he said, was natural and proper, but the economic theories of that era should be abandoned so that the region might pursue the "Northern ideal" (by which Trenholm meant industrial development) while at the same time cultivating the best that was indigenous.[28] In Virginia, in the same year, the Richmond *Whig* declared that nothing was more important to the South than the establishment of factories and workshops. The editor had a vision of Richmond as the region's leading manufacturing center and pledged the newspaper "to hasten the realization of that destiny."

He closed with an admonition to the people of the South to cast aside "all men wedded to old systems, dogmas and prejudices, and take up progressive men, with enlarged and liberal views, who draw their inspirations from the present and the future, and not from the past."[29]

III

Until 1870, the "progressive men, with enlarged liberal views," to whom the Richmond *Whig* looked for leadership, had set forth their program of regeneration without the benefit of an appropriate and inspiring slogan. In April of that year Edwin DeLeon published what may have been the essay that gave the name "New South" to the incipient movement which he attempted to define and encourage. A native South Carolinian of good lineage, DeLeon was an author, diplomat, and former Confederate propagandist.[30] The title of his article, published in *Putnam's Magazine*, was "The New South: What It is Doing, and What It Wants." The Civil War, DeLeon wrote, marked a great divide in the history of the South. "Four years of war wrought mighty changes internally on the society," he wrote, "and Reconstruction completed what the war [had] begun, utterly overturning the old system." Out of the debris of the old order, he continued, there arose "a New South, whose wants and wishes, ends and aims, plans and purposes, are as different from those of 1860, as though a century instead of a decade only, divided the two."[31] No despondent prophet of gloom, DeLeon surveyed the developments of the previous half-decade, with special emphasis on Virginia, to find that the South was turning to constructive measures of reform, despite the turmoil of Reconstruction.

Encouraged by industrial and railroad developments and by immigration movements into the region, DeLeon foresaw two related prospects which augured well for the South's future. First, he was convinced that increasing numbers of Southerners were coming to realize that a New South program of industrial progress, diversified agriculture, and cooperation with the North was the only hope for the region. Second, he believed that the opportunities in the South were now sufficiently recognized by those outside the region that the influx of labor and capital already in evidence would inevitably be multiplied many times in the next few years. "Whatever the case may be as regards the political affinities of the two sections," he noted, "there can be no doubt of the rapid fusion and assimilation of the social and material elements," for "each successive day blends and binds more intimately together the lives and fortunes of the two, owing to the movement of Northern men and capital southwards."[32] The outcome of this new union was bound to be mutually beneficial, he believed:

> The Northerner will carry South his thrift, his caution, his restless activity, his love of new things; the Southerner will temper these with his reckless liberality, his careless confidence, his firey energy, and his old-time conservatism; and both will be benefited by the admixture.[33]

Three years later DeLeon made an extended tour of the region and published his observations in a series of long articles in *Harper's Magazine*, *The Southern Magazine*, and *Fraser's Magazine*. The *Harper's* piece, the only one entitled "The New South," was widely read, and after its publication the term "New South" appeared regularly as the recognized name of the emerging movement.[34]

A year after the appearance of DeLeon's first New South essay, Benjamin Harvey Hill told the Alumni Association of the University of Georgia that "thought is the Hercules of this age," and he urged his listeners to turn their minds to the task of "cleaning out the Augean stables of accumulated social errors." In strong, bold fashion Hill recounted those social errors which had made the civilization of the Old South a terrible failure. Certain that it would be foolish to attempt to resurrect "theories and systems" that had been "swept down by the moving avalanche of actual events," he declared that Southerners could "live neither *in* nor *by* the defeated past." The over-riding question for his generation, Hill warned, was not what Southerners had been, "but whether and what they shall determine to be; not what their fathers were, but whether and what their children shall be." The South stood at one of those rare moments in history when "one civilization abruptly ends and another begins." The test of greatness for the new civilization, he said, would lie in men's ability and courage to "correct the real cause of this, our failure in the past."[35]

Like Daniel Harvey Hill, to whom he was not related, B. H. Hill was a former Confederate general. He had opposed secession, but served loyally once Georgia had left the Union. After the war he was one of the state's leading opponents of Congressional Reconstruction. By 1870, however, he had moderated his stand and in July 1871, when he spoke to the Alumni Association, he was under suspicion as a man much too friendly with the invading Republicans.[36] Partly for this reason the speech, which was widely circulated, produced a mild storm of controversy in the Georgia press. Outside the state, in the national magazines, it gave rise to extended discussion and analysis of the emerging New South doctrine. And Henry Grady, soon to become the major spokesman of the doctrine, read and admired the speech and later declared that Hill, more than anyone else, had provided him with the ideas and the inspiration which he carried into his crusade.[37]

For the most part, Hill's speech dwelt on the baneful effects of slavery on the South. Combining simple analysis with extravagant language, Hill declared that a thoughtful observer of 1787 would have foreseen greater material advancement for the South than for any other part of the country. This reasonable prediction was not borne out, Hill felt, because of the total commitment the region subsequently made to a system that demanded the perpetual ignorance of the laboring class. For two generations, he declared,

> Southern progress, Southern development, and Southern power have been in bondage to the negro; and Southern failure, Southern dependence, and Southern sorrow are the heavy penalties we suffer for that bondage. For more than thirty years Southern genius, with all its glorious natural spirit of Promethean daring and venture, has been chained by some offended god of jealous vengeance to this solid rock of slavery, and vultures have preyed upon it.[38]

In the closing section of his address, and in subsequent speeches and essays, Hill challenged his fellow Southerners to look upon emancipation primarily as the opportunity to free the white South from the bondage of an outmoded, stultifying economic system. The region now had the chance, he believed, to exploit fully its many resources by

constructing a balanced industrial system to be complemented by a diversified, scientific agriculture. Essential
to the success of this program, he stressed, would be the
proliferation of new institutions of learning to train men
in the ways of industry, and the strengthening of established universities to impart the new doctrine. The educated men of the South, he told the university alumni
audience, must be responsible for the future of the South.
Should the South's leaders respond to the challenge, Hill
promised, "we shall soon find that only our fetters have
been broken, and the day of unequaled greatness and
prosperity will dawn and brighten to glorious and lasting
noon in the South."[39]

Hill did not use the term "New South" in his 1871
speech, but the ideas he expressed would, in time, form
the nucleus of the New South ideology. One of his re-
viewers, William D. Trammell, wrote ecstatically of the
speech in *The Southern Magazine* and, two years later,
published a trite novel, entitled *Ça Ira*, in which he applied
the term "New South" to Hill's program.[40] One of his
characters took words almost directly from the Hill address, asking "why should we look back? We have neither
time nor strength to waste in defense of theories and
systems that have been forever swept away by the progress
of actual events. They must learn that we cannot live
by the defeated past."[41] Making its way into fiction, the
new doctrine also began to appear in poetry, once the
stronghold of the romance of the Old South.[42] Margaret
J. Preston, another Hill enthusiast, intoned:

> *Not a word of the Past! It has perished,*
>   *Gone down in its beauty and bloom:*
> *Yet because it so proudly was cherished,*
>   *Shall we sigh out our years at its tomb?*

Entitling her poem "Gospel of Labor," the poetess admonished Southerners to be done with the effete ways of the past, to give honor to the laboring man, and to cherish "the clink of the artisan's hammer."[43]

IV

In 1874, DeLeon published his extensive series of New South articles. The immediate and enthusiastic response to them, far surpassing the reception his 1870 article had received, indicates that both the term and the movement were catching hold. Their rising popularity, in fact, increased in direct proportion to the declining enthusiasm for the program of Congressional Reconstruction. For Southerners, it was difficult to focus on programs of self-reconstruction when, as so many felt, immediately pressing demands of the duel with the Radicals required all of one's energy. Henry Watterson, whose Louisville *Courier Journal* would soon rival Grady's *Constitution* as an organ of the New South movement, recalled later that "there was in those days but a single political issue for the South. Our hand was in the lion's mouth, and we could do nothing, hope for nothing, until we got it out."[44] To Grady it seemed almost impossible for the movement to gain real momentum until "redemption" from alien rule was achieved. To celebrate restoration of home rule in Georgia he wrote his first editorial under the title New South. "Freed from organized bands of robbers and bayonet rule," he wrote, Georgia and the South would have the opportunity to accept and act on new programs.[45]

Francis W. Dawson's early career as New South editor

further illustrates the delaying influence which Reconstruction had on the movement. As a young man, Dawson left his native England to join the Confederacy. Only twenty-five when the war ended, he moved to Charleston, where he soon became the city's leading newspaper editor —first of the *News* and then of the combined *News and Courier*. Continuing to pay fealty to the honor and justice of the Confederate cause, Dawson nonetheless scored those who let memories of the past interfere with programs for the future. "Respect for ourselves and our fathers requires us to reverence the past," he wrote in criticism of a fellow editor, "but we cannot rebuild the fallen structure, and it would be simply foolish in our people to spend the fleeting years of opportunity in lamentation."[46]

To make the postwar South better, Dawson was an early advocate of all those ideas advanced by DeBow, the two Hills, and DeLeon. He invented the slogan "Bring the Cotton Mills to the Cotton" and used it effectively in numerous editorials in the 'seventies. Campaigning for any factory "which would turn the South's natural resources into finished products in their native environment," he was also an avid promoter of the commercial development of Charleston, which he hoped would one day become the "Liverpool of America."[47] But Dawson was also an intensely political editor, and the files of the *News and Courier* reflect his absorbing interest in the issues of Reconstruction. The most articulate critic of Radicalism in his state, he labored first to moderate the impact of Reconstruction and later to overthrow Republican rule. As a consequence, his advocacy of agricultural and industrial reform was partially sacrificed to the cause of Reconstruction politics.

While not all of the advocates of change were as

deeply involved in Reconstruction politics as Dawson, they were inescapably bound up in the antagonisms which it engendered. Fully aware that reconciliation between the sections, based on a liquidation of the Reconstruction program and the spirit that undergirded it, was essential to their movement, they naturally applauded the triumph of each new home-rule movement. With equal pleasure they noted the waning enthusiasm in the North for Radicalism as a happy portent for the New South movement.

Coincidentally with the waning of enthusiasm for Reconstruction, and a major reflection of it, was a new image of the South that began to be projected to Northern readers by a spate of journalists who traveled through the region, beginning in the early 'seventies. *Scribner's Monthly* played a leading role by sending Edward King on trips which resulted in a series of widely read articles, later assembled in a large book entitled *The Great South*. When the last of the articles in the series appeared, *Scribner's* editor Josiah G. Holland commented:

> It is with no ordinary pride and satisfaction that we thus record the completion of a task undertaken with the desire to enlighten our country concerning itself, and to spread before the nation the wonderful natural resources, the social condition, and the political complications of a region which needs but just, wise, and generous legislation, with responding good will and industry, to make it a garden of happiness and prosperity.[48]

Other books which had originally appeared in Northern periodicals or newspapers included Robert Somers, *Southern States Since the War* (1870); James S. Pike, *The Prostrate State* (1874); and Charles Nordhoff, *The Cotton States in the Spring and Summer of 1875* (1876). These and numerous other works began to revise drastically Northern opinions of the former enemy. They argued that sectional bitterness was on the wane in the South and would vanish as soon as unreasonable and hostile legislation ceased to come from the North. Much sympathetic understanding of the South's allegedly cruel plight was expressed, and hope was voiced that Northerners would come to realize that Southerners understood the Negro question and, if let alone, would deal fairly with the former slave. Finally, these journalistic outpourings were highly optimistic in reporting the abundant resources of the region and in designating the South as the section of the country in which great economic advances of the future were to be made.

Despite the growing popularity of the New South idea and the optimistic paeans to reconciliation there were still many persons in all parts of the country who remained skeptical. Albion W. Tourgee, removed from Ohio after the war to become a North Carolina jurist and author of political novels, was exceedingly dubious about the prospects for change in the basic character of the South. As Tourgee viewed the situation, the South was in the process of winning the peace despite defeat in war. Rallying together with greater unity than they had shown in the war itself, Southerners were dedicated to the one "great and holy aim" of expelling all Yankee influence. They desired, Tourgee wrote, to perpetuate Southern isolation from the mainstream of American development, protect white supremacy from all attacks, and preserve the old social order with as little alteration as possible.[49] Reconstruction, despite all the grand designs in the beginning, was nothing but "a fool's errand," based on the disastrously false assumption that defeat would cause the South meekly to mend its ways and adopt a Northern view of life. Nothing, says the hero of one of Tourgee's novels, could be more wrong: "The sick man cannot cure himself. The South will never purge itself of the evils which affect it."[50]

Tourgee's bitter complaints, though inaccurate in some particulars, correctly forecast the abandonment of Reconstruction. As the North became wearied of its experiment and increasingly attuned to the music of the New South prophets, it chose to ignore the warnings from Tourgee and others like him. Increasingly it appeared that Northerners were searching for a suitable rationale to justify the end of an era of Yankee reform in the South, and the New South movement appeared perfectly tailored to meet that need. It promised respect for the rights of the Negro and, more important, invited an invasion of Northern men and capital into the region on terms that seemed to be unusually advantageous to the invaders. To the Southerners, the process of self-reconstruction could begin only when the alien Reconstruction ended. Their obvious preference for the former included the ironic invitation to a new kind of Northern invasion, but at the outset the prospects for mutual benefit seemed too bright to cause them to wonder if a New South reconstruction might, in time, bring them to a point of subjugation quite as serious as the one they were trying to escape.

None of these long-range issues was in focus in the mid-'seventies, however, and the infant movement was still struggling for a wider acceptance. The withdrawal of federal troops and the official end of Reconstruction in 1877 made the struggle easier, but the movement experienced no sudden triumph. For one thing, the South —along with the rest of the nation—was still in the grip of a severe depression, and hard times did not disappear until the end of the decade. The depression over, some contemporaries felt that the election of 1880, involving the "honest" defeat of a Democratic presidential candidate,

acted as a catalyst. Josephus Daniels of North Carolina
drew the moral that "out of political defeat we must work
. . . a glorious material and industrial triumph."[51] Both
he and Grady, convinced that the South had put too many
false hopes in politics as a salvation, urged their fellow
citizens to work more and politic less. Grady's editorial
comment on the election results opened with the opinion
that "the defeat of Hancock will be a blessing in disguise
if it only tends to turn our people from politics to work."
In a passage that would be quoted frequently in the future,
he declared that the South needed "fewer stump-speakers
and more stump-pullers." The old order was passionately
devoted to politics, Grady wrote, but the power and plenty
of the new order must be based on hard work and a
single-minded devotion to business enterprise. "Let us
let politics alone for a while," he admonished, so that a
new orientation might make the South "thrill and swell
with growth until it has compassed the full measure of the
destiny for which God intended it."[52]

With Grady's rhetoric and boundless enthusiasm the
program outlined over a decade earlier by DeBow and
D. H. Hill began to take on the aspects of a creed of
salvation. As older men passed from the scene, Grady
would shortly be joined by a band of young men with
an evangelistic commitment equal to his so that the New
South doctrine would become, in the 'eighties, the South's
major intellectual and moral issue. The subject of numerous books and pamphlets, endless articles, commencement
addresses, and sermons, it finally came into its own. By
the time Grady made his address before the New England
Society of New York, in 1886, it had outdistanced all of
its rivals and was on the verge of achieving the hegemony
once enjoyed by the creed of the Old South.

2
The Opulent South

The record of the south for the past ten
years is equal to that of the west. We
predict that for the next ten years it will
surpass the record made by the west.
The time will come when there will be an
amendment to the shibboleth "Westward
the star of empire holds its sway."

—HENRY W. GRADY, 1884[1]

Wealth and honor are in the pathway of the
New South. Her impulses are those which
are impelling the advance of civilization
and the progress of wealth and refinement
throughout Christendom; and as her
resources . . . are greater and more
diversified than those in the possession of
any other people of equal numbers . . .
[she will soon] resume her once proud
position in the van of civilization's advancing
column. She is the coming El Dorado of
American adventure.

—WILLIAM D. KELLEY, 1887[2]

It is the young men . . . who are making
the South of today. They ask no favors.
Worthy sons of worthy sires, gifted with
the best treasures of Anglo Saxon brawn,
brain, courage and energy, they are resolved
to make "Dixie" the Canaan of the new
world. They are filled with an enthusiasm
that cannot be dampened. They are bold,
earnest, energetic, and above all, they have
a faith in the South's future that
cannot be weakened. All honor to the
young South.

—RICHARD H. EDMONDS, 1889[3]

P erhaps you know that with us of the younger generation in the South," the poet Sidney Lanier wrote to his brother, "pretty much the whole of life has been merely not-dying."[4] Lanier's melancholy estimate of his own postwar experience echoed the lament of a generation of Southerners, including the young New South spokesmen who grew to maturity in the circumstances he decried. Their world was one of crushing poverty and heartbreaking disillusionment—powerful reminders that the inherently weak and static civilization of the Old South was no match for the dynamic and powerful North that had smashed the Southern bid for independence and saddled the region with unwelcomed burdens. Moreover, the victors had devised no modern Marshall Plan to spark economic recovery and soon "The Prostrate South" became a common nomenclature for the region, popularized by the hordes of observers who came to report on life in the former Confederacy.

The poverty and industrial lethargy that hung over the South in the years after the war were sufficient in themselves to cause despair and lead to programs for self-reconstruction. They take on added significance, and indeed can only be understood properly, when one recalls that they existed in a country envied for nothing more than its fabled wealth and opportunity. As David M.

Potter has shown in his brilliant study of the effects of economic abundance on the national character, Americans had been a people of plenty from early colonial days. This happy circumstance shaped their institutions and beliefs and made possible the success of their democratic experiment.[5] Widespread poverty, coupled with and reinforced by fettered opportunity, seemed a strange anomaly in mid-nineteenth-century America; and thoughtful Southerners, as they pondered their own misfortune, could scarcely help but reflect that they were plagued by what C. Vann Woodward would later call a "quite un-American experience with poverty."[6]

The striking and enduring contrast between Southern poverty and American opulence dates most obviously from the devastation of the Civil War era. But even before the war the peculiar structure of the Southern economy had put the South at a disadvantage within the union. Plantation slavery made fortunes for many men, of course, but, as Douglas C. North points out, the income received in the South from the export of staple crops had "little local multiplier effect, but flowed directly to the North and West for imports of services, manufactures and foodstuffs."[7] Whether or not Eugene D. Genovese is correct in characterizing plantation slavery as technologically backward, self-defeating, incapable of reform, and incompatible with genuine industrialism,[8] there is no doubt that Southerners became increasingly aware of their dependence on—and inferiority to—the North. This awareness was revealed in the frantic and abortive campaigns to achieve economic independence and in the bitter denunciation of special economic legislation presumed to favor Northern interests at the expense of the South. As Thomas Prentice Kettell correctly saw, Southern wealth was systematically converted into Northern profits.[9]

One of the purposes of secession was to invigorate Southern economic growth and destroy the colonial dependence on the North. Not only, of course, were these objectives not realized, but the smashing victories of the Union troops seemed to symbolize the hopelessness of the venture in the first place. Concentrating on the development of their own strength, Union leaders greatly expanded productive capacity and appeared almost to ignore manpower losses, instead of playing cautiously on their enemy's weaknesses. In many ways it seemed to be a story of the rich beating the poor; or so it appeared, in any case, to many disillusioned Southerners in 1865.

The lesson of the war, then, seemed clearly to demand the reconstruction of the Southern economy. Postwar developments reinforced this lesson by widening even more the disparity between the two sections. As the South languished during the Reconstruction era, the North boomed ahead. The war had wrecked Southern productive capacity while vastly stimulating and advancing Northern development and after the war, as Eric F. Goldman vividly portrays it, "everybody and everything certainly seemed on the move"—except "in the battered South." "In the East, a rampant prosperity touched every venture with the magic of anything-is-possible. In the West, the tide of migration swept out in proportions unequaled in all man's restless history. West and east, virtually every index of activity . . . showed a wild surge upward."[10] But in the South, as Lanier recorded, "merely not-dying" was the major concern of the day. Thus it became increasingly and painfully clear that the South did not share in the historic American experience of opulence; and, as that experience was on the verge of becoming fantastic beyond belief, fear mounted that the South might be forever left out.

I

The principal spokesmen for the emerging New South movement, with but one notable exception, were all born in the 1850's. Too young to serve in the war, they passed through childhood and adolescence under its influence and reached maturity during the Reconstruction era.[11] Thus their formative years coincided with the period of their region's greatest failure. Quite naturally, the perspective which this experience gave them sharpened their criticisms of the Old South and led them to look to the North in their search for those variables which accounted for Southern poverty in a land of plenty.

Henry Woodfin Grady, the most famous of the New South spokesmen, was born in Athens, Georgia, in 1850. The Athens of Grady's youth was the trading center for surrounding farms and plantations and Grady's father was a prominent local merchant, co-owner of the firm of Nicholson and Grady, a notable mercantile establishment in the community. On the eve of the Civil War the elder Grady sold his share in the firm, invested heavily in real estate, and retained half-ownership in the store building, a gas works, and a saw mill.[12] It was an environment admirably suited for the future New South prophet. Commercial in its essence, young Grady's world was built on bustle, energy, and shrewdness, and he experienced none of the genteel leisure allegedly characteristic of the planter class which had led his region into war.

In the wake of the havoc wrought by the war, Grady secured a college education at the University of Georgia, followed by a year of postgraduate study at the University of Virginia. When he left Virginia he began the career in journalism that was to be his life work. During the 1870's he was associated with several Georgia newspapers and served as Georgia correspondent for a number of Northern papers, beginning with the New York *Herald* in 1876. It was also in 1876 that he joined the staff of the Atlanta *Constitution*, the journal that he would mold into the major organ of the New South movement. Four years later, on the strength of a $20,000 vote of confidence from Cyrus W. Field, he bought a quarter-share in the *Constitution*. From then until his death in 1889 he preached the gospel of the New South in editorial columns and in frequent public addresses in both the South and the North.[13] When he died, the nation's press hailed him as the most effective leader of the New South movement and the New York *Times* declared that he was both the symbol and the creator of the dynamic spirit in the South.[14]

Born a year after Grady, in 1851, Daniel Augustus Tompkins had roots in the plantation South. One of his grandfathers, a first cousin of John C. Calhoun, lived in a "fine country home," while the other, who had been a captain during the Revolutionary War, owned a North Carolina plantation. His father was a wealthy South Carolina planter, owning two thousand acres of land and forty slaves.[15] The war, and Tompkins's restless spirit, severed his connection with the plantation, and he rapidly began to plan a career as publicist and industrialist.

After undergraduate training at the South Carolina College, Tompkins studied in the Rensselaer Polytechnic Institute at Troy, New York, and worked later as a machinist at the Bessemer Steel Works in Troy and then with the Bethlehem Iron Works in Pennsylvania. While employed by Bethlehem Iron he traveled to Germany to take part in the construction of an iron plant there. He was in Missouri next, with the Crystal Plate Glass Works and Crystal Railway Company, but he moved to Charlotte, North Carolina, in 1882, where he was to make his reputation as a promoter and exemplar of the New South creed. As an industrialist he quickly rose to prominence as the principal proprietor and president of three large cotton mills, director of eight others, and stockholder in many more. In addition to his conspicuous role in the cotton-mill industry, and as the father of the cottonseed oil industry, he became a chief publicist of the New South movement as owner of three newspapers—of which the Charlotte *Observer* was the most influential—author of innumerable pamphlets, contributor to manufacturing journals, and popular after-dinner speaker.[16]

The longest-lived of all the New South prophets, and a man who was still writing fervent New South editorials during the administration of Herbert Hoover, was Richard Hathaway Edmonds. Born on a Virginia farm in 1857, Edmonds later claimed that his boyhood experience there had exercised a direct influence upon his mature thinking. The farm was small, he recalled, and there was too little money for hired help to free the youngster from heavy labors. "I worked, and worked hard," he said, "and it was in my opinion the best experience which I ever had, and it has influenced my life for good ever since." It was from this experience, Edmonds believed, that he derived the "gospel of work" that was to form a central part of his later teachings.[17] In fact, Edmonds was probably captured by his own later propaganda and consequently exaggerated the significance of his boyhood labors. His uncle recalled Edmonds as a fragile youth on whom even the slightest amount of work would have made a profound impression.

Later in life the uncle observed that Edmonds was "totally unable to drive a nail," and in the uncle's opinion Edmonds's program derived from his keen and inquiring mind rather than from his farm experience.[18]

In 1871 the Edmonds family moved to Baltimore, where the future New South spokesman was to distinguish himself. During the next decade he pondered the economic problems of the South, traveled widely in the region, and concluded that the depressing poverty of a people living in a land richly endowed in natural resources was the greatest scandal of his day. Determined to reorient what he considered the misguided economic policies of the region, he wrote that the South's basic problem was its lack of industries and cities; the way to create them, he believed, was to organize an informed and effective movement of enlightenment. He rejected politics as the least hopeful approach and put his faith in journalism. The journal that he founded, the *Manufacturers' Record*, began its career in 1881 and soon was widely recognized as the leading industrial periodical of the South. Edmonds turned it into a missionary journal, and its pages fairly bristled with glowing descriptions of the industrial future of the region.[19]

Of all the New South spokesmen, Walter Hines Page was easily the most gifted and the most complex. Born in Cary, North Carolina, in 1855, Page came from a respected family of self-reliant small proprietors, leaders in their community, but not dominant figures in the state. From his mother he learned to love books and from his father he learned to respect enterprise and honesty. He also learned from his father to be suspicious of Southern shibboleths, for the elder Page had had misgivings about slavery, was an opponent of secession, and even during

the war had spoken openly of the inevitability of the restoration of the Union. But it was Page's grandfather who
made the most lasting impression on him. The ideas he
gathered from the patriarch of "The Old Place" were
those he later described as "the background of my life."
"My grandfather," he once wrote, "did not even know the
sectional feeling that the war had aroused." With memories running back to the first years of the Republic, the
grandfather instilled in Page the image of a South innocent
of bitter sectionalism, dedicated to a broad, optimistic
nationalism. This was a vision Page never lost, and he
always referred to the civilization of the Jeffersonian
era as the authentic Southern heritage.[20]

At fifteen, Page left home to begin his college training,
first for a short stay at Trinity College and then for a
longer period at Randolph-Macon College. At Randolph-
Macon his interest in the classics was intensified and he
made the decision to pursue them further in graduate
study. The Johns Hopkins University was a natural choice
and Page studied there for two years under the direction
of Basil Gildersleeve. But, disenchanted with the prospects
of an academic career, he left Hopkins in 1878 and within
a short time had started on a career as a journalist. Soon
he would be back in North Carolina, editing a newspaper
and launching his mission as one of the region's most
persistent and intelligent critics.[21]

The only one of the major New South spokesmen who
grew to maturity in the prewar years of sectional strife
was Henry Watterson, born in Tennessee in 1840. The
Wattersons came to Tennessee when the state was in its
infancy, and Henry's grandfather shortly became a wealthy
planter. Harvey, his father, turned to law and then to
politics. In addition to imbuing his son with the virtues

of the Democratic Party, Harvey Watterson was an advocate of Southern industralization and preached to his son
many of the "New South" ideas which Henry himself was
later to popularize. Lacking sympathy for slavery, the
Wattersons were almost as hostile to the Southern fire-
eaters as they were to Northern abolitionists. As the crisis
of the 1850's wore on, both father and son stood out as
strong Union men and Henry Watterson, remaining in
Washington until after First Bull Run, was torn in his
loyalties by the outbreak of war. His decision to join the
Confederacy was not easily reached, but, like many others
in his plight, he was resolute once the choice had been
made.[22]

As a youth Watterson developed a flair for journalism
that aided him well during the war. He served only briefly
in various military capacities, making his primary contribution as editor of *The Rebel*, the most widely read
newspaper of the Confederacy. In editorial columns he
paid homage to Southern nationalism, but the nation of
which he dreamed was one which would repudiate plantation agriculture to dedicate itself to diversified farming
and industrial upbuilding. "Smoky cities and blue over-
alls," his biographer writes, "promised more for the South,
he believed, than white Grecian porticoes and crinolines."[23]
At war's end, Watterson took up the editorship of the
Nashville *Banner*, urging reunion and forgiveness. Before
long he was in Louisville, and in the 1880's his *Courier-
Journal* became second in importance only to Grady's
Atlanta *Constitution* as a daily organ of the New South
movement.

II

As they grew up in, and pondered, the depressed state of the South in the postwar years—and as the burgeoning wealth of the North was incessantly thrust before them as evidence of their backwardness—the New South prophets were early persuaded that their plight was not the result of the war itself (as so many Southerners believed) but that it was a natural consequence of those conditions which had led to defeat in the first place. The essential lesson which they learned and then translated into the first plank of the New South program was that wealth and power in the modern world flowed from machines and factories, not from unprocessed fields of white cotton. To make the region rich, then—to bring into existence the opulent South—they became in the first place proponents of industrialism and urbanism.

In an ironic sense, they welcomed the desolation and poverty that confronted them, for it created inescapably the necessity of rebuilding the Southern economy; and, in rebuilding, they would persuade the region to reconsider its ancient prejudices and redirect its energies into new paths. Edwin Lawrence Godkin, assessing the chances of the program from his perspective as editor of *The Nation*, wrote in 1880 that the conversion of the South to the "industrial stage of social progress" would not be a more difficult task than that which the abolitionists had undertaken, ultimately with success. For one thing, Godkin pointed out, there was in the new situation a large body of indigenous opinion sympathetic to the conversion. But Godkin recognized that there would be difficulties in prying the Southern mind from its agricultural precepts.[24]

Among the New South advocates themselves there was also a keen awareness of the weight of tradition that would be against them, and as late as 1900, when their ideology had captured large segments of the population, Tompkins sadly acknowledged that "long training as an agricultural people has brought to us a certain abiding degree of prejudice against manufactures and commerce."[25]

To dislodge this "prejudice" and to enlist public spirit and funds in their program, the spokesmen of the New Order knew that more was required of them than a positive program of regeneration. Before they could feel secure in advancing the industrial argument, they had to elaborate a damning critique of the institutions of the Old South. It was not enough, they reasoned, that the old system had been wrecked; it had to be so thoroughly discredited that no one would wish to revive it, in however altered a form.

One of the most outspoken critics of the old regime— a man who played a major role in formulating the New South creed—was a Pennsylvanian whose first desire to reform the South found outlet in the abolition movement. William Darrah ("Pig Iron") Kelley, congressman and industrialist, traveled widely in the South, urging, scolding, and advising the region. During his first visits, shortly after the war, his life was threatened at least once.[26] But, as time passed and as native Southerners began to praise the work of this radical Republican and erstwhile abolitionist, increasingly sympathetic audiences listened to his devastating critique of the old regime.

As he reflected on the poverty of the South, he dismissed the common view that the war had caused it. That it may have been the "proximate cause," he conceded, but the fundamental reason lay in the "economic opinions and industrial system" that had dominated the South before

1860. The root of the difficulty, Kelley explained, was to be plainly seen in the way the "peculiar institution" had enslaved the South. With the perfection of the cotton gin, slavery had become so embedded in Southern life that to challenge it was regarded as a treasonable act. The real disloyalty to the region, though, lay in perpetuating the institution, for slavery wedded the South to a staple-crop agrarian system that ruthlessly militated against the growth of industry and urban centers. Cities were regarded by the leaders of the Old South as "great sores"; and yet, without urban development, there could be no stimulus to develop the bountiful natural resources of the land.[27]

Kelley regarded the "aristocrats" who perpetuated the central institutions of the old regime as conspirators involved in "darkening the minds" of the South's laborers and "protecting her borders from innovations of every kind." Worst of all, he felt, the "fatally vicious economic and agricultural theories" of the old regime had not died with the war. Writing in the 1880's, he hailed the advance of industry where he saw it but called attention to the large areas where the spirit of the Old South persisted. In these places, he wrote, the people were as poverty-stricken as ever—"Yes, the poverty and ignorance that characterized the 'poor whites,' the 'low downs,' the 'clay eaters,' and the 'crackers' of the Old South still prevail" and would continue to exist until the South fully purged itself of past sins and redirected its thinking along the lines charted by the New South program.[28]

The native Southerners in the movement praised Kelley's colorful analysis and eagerly solicited more of it. Edmonds, in particular, was especially obliging in opening to him the columns of the *Manufacturers' Record*, where he became a frequent contributor. The Southerners added an abundance of detail to Kelley's critique, but the essential pattern was the same. The starting point in all arguments was the institution of slavery and the evils it had engendered. Tompkins, lamenting the "estrangement" that slavery had caused between the sections, believed that the failure of Southerners to abolish it themselves had been responsible for the Civil War and the violent, unplanned termination of the institution. The subsequent paralysis of Southern society, it followed, was not due primarily to the war itself but to the errors inculcated by slavery and to the shock of its sudden disappearance.[29]

The shock, however, was necessary to bring the region to its senses, and one of the happiest discoveries of the New South spokesmen was the finding that the destruction of slavery was a great event not because it freed the blacks, although that was important, but because it liberated the whites. As Grady put it, "the shackles that held . . . [the South] in narrow limitations fell forever when the shackles of the negro slave were broken." The Old South, he explained, "rested everything on slavery and agriculture, unconscious that these could neither give nor maintain healthy growth."[30] Emancipation—the first requisite of "healthy growth"—was thus the white man's passport to prosperity.

No one put the new dogma more succinctly than a Virginia contributor to Edmonds's *Manufacturers' Record*. The white man of the Old South, declared John W. Johnston, "was a slave" and "the chains that encumbered him were as inexorable as those that bound the colored race." Contemplating the full extent of the white man's bondage, Johnston waxed eloquent:

> The negro was a slave to him [the white man], and he was a slave to the situation. He could not abandon it

without disastrous results to himself, to the negro, to the State and the world. If ever man were impelled by an irresistible force, it was the Southern white man. What did it matter to him if the earth beneath his feet was loaded with all the minerals which contribute to the wealth, convenience or enjoyment of mankind, or that the stream running by his door had waterpower enough to turn a thousand wheels? He could not utilize them; he was bound hand and foot—bound to his slaves, bound to his plantation, bound to cotton, to his habits of life, to the exigencies of the situation.[31]

In the light of these sentiments, it was no wonder that Kelley should dedicate his vigorously New South book to "The Emancipated South."[32]

To document the baneful effects of slavery on Southern economic growth, Tompkins turned to the census data of 1810. According to his interpretation of those data, the South of 1810—not yet fully committed to cotton and still willing to doubt the wisdom of slavery—was in the process of sound economic development. The census data, he wrote, showed that "the manufactured products of Virginia, the Carolinas and Georgia exceeded in value and variety those of all New England." As late as the 1820's the South Carolina railway, "one of the most important engineering enterprises in the world," demonstrated again the "relative advantage" which the South enjoyed over the North. But all of the South's advantage was swept aside when the impetus to cotton culture, made possible by the perfection of the cotton gin, extended slavery westward, firmly embedded the institution in Southern life, and brought to an end the burgeoning sentiment for industry as well as the notable antislavery sentiment that had previously existed. The result, Tompkins felt, was

catastrophic, not only because of the destruction and loss
of life, but because those things were made inevitable by
the adoption of erroneous policies in the first place.[33]

Like Tompkins, Edmonds stressed the encouraging
features of the Southern economy in the early nineteenth
century. He was also convinced that the slavery and
cotton combination had worked powerfully to thwart
healthy economic growth, but he believed that the appeal
of industry had been too great even for slavery to frustrate
it entirely. He pointed out, for example, that the falling
price of cotton in the 1840's caused Southerners once
again to pay attention to industrial pursuits, and he paid
homage to the band of industrial publicists who struggled
for that cause in the twenty years before the war. The
results of their efforts, he believed, were not negligible.
Between 1850 and 1860, he observed, the railroad mileage
of the South more than tripled, iron production increased
markedly, $12,000,000 was invested in cotton mills, and
the manufacture of steam engines and other machines
increased notably. The war, he felt, interrupted this work
—a work that was already revealing the grave defects of
slavery and staple-crop agriculture.[34]

To reinforce their sweeping condemnation of the old
regime, the New South prophets carried their analysis
into the present to argue, first, that those who continued to
hold to old ideas and old systems courted personal ruin
and, second, that those who resisted the new appeals to
reason and progress were guilty of a great disservice to
their region. Tompkins spoke frequently to the first point.
In a piece published in the *Manufacturers' Record* he
noted that "the condition of civilization" that had grown
up on "the basis of the institution of slavery is dying and
fading away." But not everyone recognized his good for-

tune because of the change. "There are tenacious people of fine education who are living in the dying conditions of ante-bellum life," Tompkins lamented. "They are as a rule growing poorer day by day and will continue to grow poorer until the most tenacious of them pass out of life, and with them will go the system to which they persist in adhering."[35]

To hasten the day of their departure, and with it the system they wished to perpetuate, no New South spokesman was more mercilessly critical than Walter Hines Page. The disenchanted classics scholar began his career as critic of the opponents of progress with an article in the *Atlantic Monthly* in 1881. Fixing on Hillsborough, North Carolina (which was but thinly disguised in the essay), as a "typical" Southern borough, Page drew a picture of the community that none of its first citizens could have been expected to admire. In Europe, Page began, one observed both old and new civilizations, side by side, through architecture. In the South two distinct civilizations existed, but the difference was social, not architectural. "It lies at the very heart of the people," he wrote, "and comes to view only after a study of their history and their life." In Hillsborough the new elements in society were powerless to effect change, so entrenched were the powers of the old regime. The typical Southern community, he wrote, was all but completely out of touch with modern science, art, and thought—and yet the local inhabitants felt it was God's chosen place on earth. It was a discouraging sight to a young reformer, and the prospects for change appeared dim.[36]

A few years later Page expanded his "Southern Borough" attack into a full-scale assault. After some absence from the region, he turned homeward in 1883 to become editor of the Raleigh *State Chronicle*. Aware of the weight of tradition that faced him, he was bolstered by a youthful enthusiasm and apparently expected to remain permanently in North Carolina as a crusading editor. Riding southward on the train, he reflected on the region that unfolded before him and pondered its difficulties. Ironies abounded. Those who had built the South and fought for its independence in 1861–1865 had regarded it as "the crown of civilization." But Page saw only worn-out land, poverty-stricken inhabitants, and directionless Negroes. White men were caught up in "hopeless inertia" and "the earth itself seemed to revolve slowly."[37]

Taking up his editorial cudgels, Page flailed North Carolina for two years with a brand of criticism and prodding that was fresh and novel. "Pungently, wittily, mercilessly," and in English that was "scholarly, clear and dignified," he jarred, instructed, and, on occasion, entertained the state.[38] But the inertia would not yield, at least in his judgment, and he despaired of breaking the hold of the past on the present. Writing years later of his experience in Raleigh, he recalled his view that efficiency, thrift, and imaginative thought were stifled because "only old thoughts were acceptable." There was no change, he wrote, because "society's chief concern was to tolerate no change." For the young crusader it was a "smothering atmosphere."[39]

After two years of crusading, filled with frustration and discouragement, Page resigned from the *State Chronicle* and left the South. His last contribution to the newspaper was a series of "Mummy Letters," published by the new editor, Josephus Daniels.[40] More a Jeremiah than an optimistic prophet of change at this stage of his career, Page was "utterly discouraged" in his hope for the regeneration of North Carolina and of the South. Control of all phases of life, he wrote, was in the hands of

those who looked through rose-tinted glasses to the past—
the Mummies, he called them—and allowed their idealized
vision of the old regime to stand in the way of progress.
There was no intellectual stimulation; it was forbidden.
The gifted men (like Page himself) were driven into exile.
Granting that there had been some "material advancement" since the end of Reconstruction, Page wrote that
it was accompanied by "no appreciation of scholarship, no
chance for intellectual growth." The cause "at the bottom
of all this," he believed, was "the organization of society,
of trades, of professions—of everything—against improvement." Was there hope for a change? Page did not
think so:

> It is an awfully discouraging business to undertake
> to prove to a Mummy that it is a Mummy. You go up
> to it and say, "Old Fellow, the Egyptian dynasties crum-
> bled several thousand years ago: you are a fish out of
> water. You have by accident or the providence of God
> got a long way out of your time. This is America. The
> Old Kings are forgotten, and this is the year 1886, in the
> calendar of a Christ whose people had not even gone to
> Egypt when you died." The old thing grins that grin
> which death set on its solemn features when the world
> was young; and your task is so pitiful that even the
> humour of it is gone.
>   Give it up! It can't be done. We all think when we are
> young that we can do something with the Mummies.
> But the Mummy is a solemn fact, and it differs from all
> other things (except stones) in this—it lasts forever.[41]

Sixteen years later, with the emotional trials of the
State Chronicle days well behind him, Page retained es-
sentially unchanged his criticism of the party of reaction.
Writing in 1902, he singled out three historic deterrents

to progress in the South. The first was slavery, which had "pickled" Southern life at about 1830. The second was the politician; and the third, the preacher. "One has for a hundred years proclaimed the present social state as the ideal condition," he wrote, "and, if any has doubted this declaration, the other has told him that this life counts for little at best." Thus "gagged and bound," Page concluded, "Southern rural society has remained stationary longer than English-speaking people have remained stationary anywhere else in the world."[42]

Page was more pessimistic in his appraisal of the forces of progress than were most of the New South spokesmen. Grady, for example, reprinted some of the North Carolinian's pieces on the tradition-bound and priest-ridden South but then disagreed strongly with the emphasis of Page's criticisms, arguing that his examples were scarcely typical now that the New South crusade was fully launched. Progress, Grady said, was evident more frequently every day.[43] But if Page was less convinced of the reality of progress than were typical New South spokesmen, his essential message was not fundamentally different from theirs: slavery and a spirit of anti-industrialism and anti-urbanism had been responsible for the South's great failure; the New South must root out all remnants of that heritage.

III

Assailing the errors of the past and denouncing their perpetuation in the present, the New South spokesmen turned confidently to the positive aspects of their blueprint for an opulent South. The commanding feature of their plan, of course, was the design for an industrial society. But the South in the 1880's continued to be overwhelmingly rural and agrarian, and it required no great insight to see that a program for the reconstruction of the Southern economy could not neglect agriculture. Despite their passion to erect an industrial utopia, then, the New South spokesmen also drafted a program for a renovated agricultural system infused with the values of business enterprise. Moreover, the vital connection between a sound farm economy and dynamic industrial growth was quickly perceived and assiduously worked out. The spirit of Hamilton and Clay was much alive in Edmonds when he wrote that a "harmonious relationship between industry and agriculture would make the South, with its vast natural resources and human power, 'the garden spot of the world.' "[44]

Sidney Lanier, the pre-eminent poet of the region, was especially hopeful about the future of Southern agriculture. In a famous essay entitled "The New South," published in *Scribner's Monthly* in 1880, he acknowledged and saluted the revolutionary changes which he believed had taken place since the war. The New South which he saw emerging was characterized by political, social, moral, and aesthetic developments that augured well for the future of the region. But, most important of all, he believed, "The New South means small farming." As he interpreted the statistics of land tenure, Lanier concluded that plantations were giving way to farms and staple-crop agriculture to diversified pursuits. An economic democracy in the countryside was in the making.[45]

In "Corn," one of his better poems, Lanier turned his views into a meter-making argument for the new agriculture. The farmer whose life he depicts is driven to ruin by his persistent dependence on cotton. The soil becomes depleted and the farmer impoverished; escape from this vicious circumstance can be found only by migrating, and so he leaves the South, finding a new home in the West. Thus, the tyranny of cotton drives the sturdy men out of the region, depleting not only the land but the human resources as well. To diversify the crops and divide the land, Lanier implies, would solve the problems of the farmer and of the region.[46]

Cotton's dominion was the great *bête blanche* of the New South spokesman and its tyranny occupied a central position in their economic and promotional writings. Edmonds filled column after column in the *Manufacturers' Record* with blasts at "the all-cotton curse" and Grady railed against the "all-cotton plan" with dependable regularity in his editorials and elsewhere.[47] "It is time for an agricultural revolution," Grady announced in one editorial. "When we once decide that southern lands are fit for something else besides cotton, and then go to work in earnest to multiply and diversify our products and industries, independence and wealth will be the certain reward of our intelligent and industrious farmers."[48] Cotton's tyranny, according to the New South view, was all-pervasive. For the region as a whole it retarded economic growth and thus per capita income by frustrating industrial development. It put the farmer at the mercy of a capricious international market and tied him to a credit system that drove him deeper into debt each year. With a lien on his crop and a mortgage on his home he failed to realize that much of the profits from the cotton crop went out of the region, never to return, and it never occurred to him to grow crops which might be marketed locally;

or, if it did, he lacked either the knowledge or the credit, or both, to undertake new systems.

To break this unhappy syndrome, the New South spokesmen early became advocates of agricultural diversification. Over and over again the farmer was told to cut his cotton acreage in half and plant the other half in smaller crops. The possibilities for agricultural diversification were without limit, or so it must have appeared to readers of Grady's optimistic essays on the variety of crops suitable for Southern agriculture. In the North, he noted, farmers concentrated on "small grains, grasses, truck farming, fruit growing, stock raising, and dairy farming," among other things, and all of these enterprises, he believed, were eminently suited for the South.[49] Truck farming held special appeal for him, as it offered profits that were "simply wonderful." The truck farm, Grady wrote,

> should also be a fruit farm, and the fruit that cannot be marketed at good rates should be dried by the new processes. This would give employment throughout the entire season, and at the end of it the fortunate farmer would have before him the assurance that diversified crops and a never-failing market alone afford, with no guano bills to settle, and no liens past or to come to disturb his mind.[50]

The newly diversified farmer, the beau ideal of the New South movement, was to replace the large planter. In the fashion of Lanier, Grady wrote that "the old plantation is a thing of the past." The small farmer, he believed, must press to the front, and "the ambition which covets large areas must be content with a holding small enough for every acre to produce profits. Necessity over-

rides either sentiment or policy here, and necessity will
have its way."[51] Unlike the planter of the Old South, the
New South's small farmer was expected to be thoroughly
scientific in his application of new agricultural imple-
ments and knowedge. More important, he was to be
thoroughly businesslike in his planning. The cash nexus
would drive out the last remnants of an unprofitable
patriarchal system.[52]

With the disappearance of the planter and the "all-
cotton plan" which he had created, the New South spokesmen foresaw also the end of the inherited enmity between
agriculture and industry. Planter hegemony in the Old
South had demanded stringent control of the pace of
industrialization and opposition to anything beyond its
modest development as an adjunct to the plantation
economy.[53] The rise of the small farm and the adoption
of diversified pursuits in the new era, according to the
New South spokesmen, could be achieved only as the
region made a full-scale conversion to industrialism. As
Edmonds put it, "every manufacturing establishment
planted in the South marks the progress towards the time
when diversified agriculture will be the rule throughout
the section."[54]

To Grady, the issue was a simple one of markets.
The only difference between agricultural prosperity in
the North and agricultural poverty in the South was that
industrial development in the North provided a substantial
market for diversified products.[55] Only by developing
a balanced industrial-urban complex could the South hope
to provide the foundation for a prosperous farm economy.
In an editorial penned shortly before he delivered his
famous New York address, Grady wrote that the creation
of a home market for truck crops, added to the region's

cotton monopoly, would make the South "the richest agricultural country in the world." But the key element in
agricultural development was industrialization. More
"than all things else combined," Grady wrote, manufacturing would "bring prosperity to the southern farmer
and high value to his lands."[56]

Important as the agricultural renascence was to the
New South spokesmen, it always occupied a minor place
in their blueprint for the future. The crusade for an urban,
industrialized society was their absorbing concern. Indeed,
so extensive was the emphasis on industrial propaganda
that one observer, writing at the end of the century, concluded that "the program of the New South . . . has not
taken the direction of agriculture. It is through its urban
development only that the section has justly earned its
sobriquet."[57]

That the South was ideally suited to lead in the modern
world of industry none of the New South spokesmen
doubted. With endless repetition they asserted that the
rich endowment of natural resources which the region
enjoyed gave it unparalleled advantages. In a piece entitled
"Nature's Wonderful Blessings to the South," Edmonds
rejoiced in his belief that "truly, everything seems to
be combined to add to the wealth of this section."[58]
There was, of course, a painful irony in this realization,
for the resources were nothing new. Grady dwelled on this
point when he declared it a "curious fact" that three
fourths of the manufacturing wealth of the country was
produced in a narrow strip of land between Iowa and
Massachusetts, comprising only one sixth of the nation's
area, "distant from the source of raw materials on which
its growth is based, of hard climate and in a large part
of sterile soil." He could think of only two reasons why

this Northern region prospered while the South languished: the Yankees had early rid themselves of slavery, thus paving the way for enterprise and capital; and, once committed to industrialism, they had benefitted from the salutary influence of protective tariffs. With the South now emancipated from the errors of the past—and blessed with bounteous raw materials, mild climate, and fertile soil—the way was clear for an almost incredibly rapid development.[59]

While they explained the industrial reticence of the Old South purely on institutional grounds, the New South spokesmen apparently saw no inconsistency in believing, as it was often their habit to do, that resources alone would almost automatically ensure the industrial revolution. Writing of Gadsden, Alabama, "one of the most promising towns in that marvelously endowed state," Edmonds called attention to its mineral wealth, agricultural advantages, favorable location on the Coosa River, and concluded that "its future is assured."[60] Kelley, lamenting mismanagement and lack of progress at South Pittsburgh, Tennessee, assured his readers that the setbacks were temporary because "the agricultural and mineral resources" of the community were so great, "and her location so admirable, that no such mistakes as have been permitted to occur . . . can permanently impair the prospects." His faith in the city's prosperous future, he declared, "rests solidly on my knowledge of the abounding supplies of materials for widely diversified manufactures" found there.[61]

"Abounding supplies" was a phrase that was to permeate the literature of the New South movement. Edmonds was one among many in insisting that nature had "more richly endowed the South than any other section

of the country," so that it could appropriately be designated " 'Creation's Garden Spot.' "[62] The Reverend John
C. Calhoun Newton shared this view and was applauded
when he based his faith in the success of the New South
crusade on his belief that no other part of the country
could rival the South's natural endowments.[63] Not un-
naturally, a petty pride entered into the discussion of the
South's resources and no opportunity was lost to tell of
their extent. One such occasion involved Kelley's story
of how a piece of marble sent to contribute to the building
of the Washington Monument was initially rejected because its unusual beauty obviously identified it as Italian.
Apparently it took the testimony of the governor and
several congressmen to prove its Alabama origins.[64]

It was partly to dramatize the abundant supplies of
the South and partly to stir Southerners out of their
lethargy that Grady conceived his famous "funeral" oration. In different forms the story had been related during
the industrial campaigns of the antebellum era, but in the
new setting it took on a special significance. Speaking of
the burial of a fellow Georgian, Grady wrote:

> They buried him in the midst of a marble quarry: they
> cut through solid marble to make his grave; and yet a
> little tombstone they put above him was from Vermont.
> They buried him in the heart of a pine forest, and yet
> the pine coffin was imported from Cincinnati. They
> buried him within touch of an iron mine, and yet the
> nails in his coffin and the iron in the shovel that dug his
> grave were imported from Pittsburg. They buried him
> by the side of the best sheep-grazing country on the earth,
> and yet the wool in the coffin bands and the coffin bands
> themselves were brought from the North. The South
> didn't furnish a thing on earth for that funeral but the

corpse and the hole in the ground. There they put him away . . . in a New York coat and a Boston pair of shoes and a pair of breeches from Chicago and a shirt from Cincinnati, leaving him nothing to carry into the next world with him to remind him of the country in which he lived and for which he fought for four years, but the chill of blood in his veins and the marrow in his bones.[65]

Optimistic about the potential of the resources in the South and anxious to launch the industrial revolution based on them, the leaders of the movement did not fail to recognize disadvantages they suffered. Capital was scarce and labor was largely unskilled. Awareness, however, was never translated into discouragement. On the contrary, certain that others would share their optimism, they fervently proclaimed that the things in which they were deficient would come pouring in from the North and from Europe; and, to facilitate this inward flow, the New South prophets launched a vigorous crusade for outside capital and immigration.

Spending the winter of 1880–1 in New York to advertise the South, Grady wrote back to Georgia that once the industrial program were fairly begun—once the South had shown itself ready to carry out its "platform of liberation and progressive development"—then it was certain that Northern capital would be seen "seeking southern investments with eagerness and the stream of immigration turned toward Georgia."[66] Returning to Georgia, he devoted countless editorials to the subject of Southern opportunity and the advantages it held for Northern capital. In 1883 he announced that "northern capital has been coming into the south very rapidly for several years," but the next year he lamented that "capital has been kept out of the south by prejudice." The prejudice was costly to Northerners who invested their money at 4 per cent in the North while "the south offered 8 per cent with the best security, and opportunities for safe investment that would pay twice as much." Recurrent financial panics on Wall Street, he predicted, would cause money to come South, "where climate, resources and opportunity all invite." By 1885 he was ready to declare that, in so far as Atlanta was concerned, there was no longer real need "of advertising the attractions." And just before he died he proclaimed that "from Virginia to Texas the woods are full of New England capitalists hunting investments, and you can hardly fire a gun without killing one. . . . The whole of New England appears to have stampeded. . . . So it goes, and the good Lord only knows where it will end."[67]

Like Grady, Edmonds painted attractive pictures of the boundless opportunity in the South and then attempted to clinch his case—and attract more capital—by reciting endless stories of successful Northern investments in the region. In 1886 he noted the move of a New York manufacturer to Birmingham and cited the instance as "the strongest evidence that could be given of the unequalled advantages of the South for manufactures." Typical of scores of Edmonds's editorial comments was the statement that "the profits to be reaped from investments in the South . . . appear to be fabulous to all who are not familiar with the logic of experience." Let men of wealth come South, he promised, "and with anything like discretion in the matter of management, returns upon capital ventured will be double, triple, and in many cases quadruple what can be obtained upon equal outlays upon safe ventures in the North and the older sections of the West." There was no disguising the fact, he wrote, "The El

Dorado of the next half century is the South. The wise recognize it; the dull and the timid will ere long regret their sloth or their hesitancy."[68] Striking off a pamphlet in 1890, he announced that "capitalists in Europe and America are looking to the South as the field of investment." Improving on Greeley, he declared that the cry should no longer be "Go West, Young Man," but "Go South."[69]

To translate optimism into reality—to make the Southern mecca a truly hospitable region for Northern capital—the New South spokesmen bombarded state legislatures with requests for the enactment of tax-exemption schemes and, when possible, for the provision of building sites. The press was advised to create a friendly atmosphere by playing down social conflict and radical movements. Edmonds believed that the "disreputable attempts" sometimes used to frighten Northern capital and labor stemmed from purely "demagogical reasons," and he wanted it known that the South was "prosperous and contented, devoting her energies to the development of her unequalled resources, and to the education of her citizens, white and black." Southern editors, he advised, should "reduce to the minimum their record of local crimes and should demand that news suppliers send them other matters," particularly "industrial information."[70]

This "industrial information" was eagerly gathered and disseminated throughout the country and abroad in a gigantic promotional undertaking. The task of promoting the South to outsiders was one that every small chamber of commerce undertook, each vying with the other for success. Pamphlets, articles, brochures, and books by the hundreds were sent out across the land to tell non-Southerners where they should come to make their fortunes.[71]

M. B. Hillyard's *The New South*, a book full of optimistic statistics, was published by Edmonds and, at his direction and expense, copies were placed in hotel reading rooms, public libraries, and on board passenger ships plying the seven seas. The inquiring reader would find a volume "richly bound in the finest Russian leather, with gilt edge and gilt title."[72] Individual cities were often singled out for special attention in the promotional campaign, as in the case of Anniston, Alabama. Edmonds invited Kelley to do an article on this "model city of the South," declaring that it "would be read over the country, and would be worth many thousands and tens of thousands of dollars." Kelley was happy to oblige, and "Anniston: A Romance of the New South" appeared in the 1887 columns of the *Record*.[73]

Another favored device frequently used to advertise the promise of the South was the industrial and agricultural exposition. New South spokesmen reacted with pleasure to Atlanta's International Cotton Exposition in 1881, and the October 5 issue of the *Constitution* was a special, record-breaking thirty-two page edition celebrating its opening. The next month Grady wrote that the South had never previously had such an opportunity to make its advantages known.[74] As the exposition device caught on, national attention focused on it and the leading periodicals published friendly descriptions. A correspondent for the *Century Magazine* reviewed the New Orleans exposition of 1885 in a two-piece article and concluded that everyone could now plainly see that "there are vast and inviting fields to the south of us waiting to be conquered for our industries and our commerce." Impressed by the region's rapid recovery from the ravages of war, this correspondent believed that the South stood "in the portal of a great industrial development."[75] Two years later, Grady pronounced the Piedmont Exposition a great success, explaining that "within its commodious exposition halls are to be found the raw materials side by side with the finished products, all the result of the energy and enterprise of the new south."[76] Energy, enterprise—and opportunity: these were the charming allurements the expositions were designed to reveal to the prospective investor in the South's future.

Outside capital was essential to the inauguration of the Southern industrial revolution and there was, therefore, a compelling logic to the pleas of the New South spokesmen for Northern investments. The expositions and the promotional campaigns of which they were a part were also, however, intended to attract a great influx of labor into the region. And, as one contemporary observer accurately reported in 1883, "there is, indeed, everywhere in the South, the strongest desire for immigration from the North."[77] In fact, the campaign to attract outsiders had begun immediately after the war with German-born John A. Wagener of South Carolina setting future patterns as that state's commissioner of immigration. By the time the New South movement was in full swing, in the 1880's, immigrants were eagerly sought by state immigration agencies, various regional immigration organizations and conventions, and by individual planters, speculators, railroads, and business organizations.[78]

Agreed that their program of agricultural renascence and industrial development required large-scale immigration, the New South spokesmen turned naturally to propaganda as the device for attracting immigrants. Edmonds noted on one occasion that "the outside world may know something of the matchless resources of the South," but he felt that substantial numbers of persons would not come to the region "until by persistent work the matter has been forced day after day upon their attention."[79] The "persistent work" Edmonds desired was enthusiastically undertaken by Southern promoters, who received a favorable hearing in the Northern periodicals. Repeatedly the point was made that the South's opportunities were unmatched by those in any other part of the country, and the promoters were frequently at pains to make invidious comparisons with the West. As Grady asked rhetorically once, "why remain to freeze, and starve, and struggle on the bleak prairies of the northwest when the garden spot of the world is waiting for people to take possession of it and enjoy it?"[80] A Eufaula, Alabama, resident made the same point by insisting that cheap land and guaranteed returns could be expected in the South, "where schools and churches are already established." With these advantages, he asked, "why go to the harder climate and less profitable crops of the West?" The same writer, attempting to woo prospective farmers into the South, extolled the sharecrop system as an ideal device for those who had no capital with which to purchase a farm. "This is a most admirable plan," he wrote. "The tenant's risk is small, support is certain, and almost always there is something besides to begin another year on."[81]

When the New South spokesmen wrote in specific terms about the kinds of immigrants they preferred (which was not frequent) they commonly selected what Grady called "the better class of immigrants."[82] By this they meant Northern farmers and artisans of Anglo-Saxon stock, first of all. When they thought in terms of tapping the growing supply of foreign immigrants into the nation, logic moved them to favor the attraction of any hard-working individual, whatever his nationality; but inherited

enmities and prejudices caused them to turn their backs
on the mass of immigrants from southern and eastern
Europe—the very men who made up the great bulk of
the immigration of the late nineteenth century. Grady
felt, for example, that the immigration conventions which
sought to tap this flow were not seeking "the kind of
immigration most desirable for the south."[83] Edmonds
was more concrete—and more belligerent. He opposed
"all schemes looking toward the colonization of large
numbers of ignorant foreigners." He wanted settlers, to
be sure; and he believed that there was room "for thousands, even millions of industrious people." But the new
arrivals of the late 'eighties were "not composed of the
character of people desired by the South." Too many of
them were "socialists and anarchists," he explained, and
"we do not want that kind."[84]

Thus favoring immigration but reluctant to welcome
those immigrants in largest supply, the New South spokesmen were driven increasingly into vague generalizations
about the wonders of the region, studding their remarks
with assertions that "the need of a tide of immigration
is greater in the South than in any other section of the
country" in order to make the region "as fruitful and
as prosperous as nature intended it should be."[85] This
kind of appeal was frustrated by the actual conditions
of the region. There were already more farmers in the
region than could establish themselves on a self-supporting
basis—as witnessed by the growing rate of tenancy. And
the paucity of factories combined with the flight of Southern farm whites into the mill villages meant that there
were few opportunities in industry. Nonetheless, the cry
for immigration continued, based on what one historian
has recently called "the illusory belief that factories would
follow labor."[86] Somehow, they sensed, men must be

attracted to fill up the unoccupied land and develop the
generous resources, and so they rested their faith in the
future, once again, on the bounty of nature, confident that
things would work themselves out once the good news
were known.

IV

With bountiful resources, confidence in the acquisition
of capital, and faith that labor adequate to develop the
region would be attracted, the New South prophets found
their greatest pleasure in describing the nature of the
future. They envisioned a balanced, diversified, dynamic
economy that would produce incalculable riches. Cotton
would continue to exert its magical powers, but diversification and the application of scientific, businesslike principles would end its debilitating effects on the region.
More important than the agricultural renascence, an
industrial and commercial revolution was planned and
anticipated as the true salvation of the region. With
absolute confidence, Grady wrote, one could expect "the
certain and steady shifting of the greatest industrial centers of the country from the north to the more favored
regions of the south."[87] The vast forests of the region
would support a great lumber and furniture industry;
the mineral resources would lead to coal, iron, and steel
production unmatched. anywhere. Older industries, like
tobacco manufacturing, were expected to see great expansion. And, of course, by bringing "the factory to the
fields," the New South promoters would create a cotton-

mill industry that would become a Southern monopoly. "This," Grady declared, "is a result that cannot long be delayed. Those who oppose such a movement are merely fighting one of the invincible forces of nature."[88] With the expansion of railroad track and the multiplication of banking facilities, the region would have a transportation and commercial system more than adequate to facilitate agricultural and industrial prosperity.

The full fruit of the New South program would be riches such as neither the South nor the nation had ever seen before. A Vanderbilt theology professor looked forward to the appearance of numerous millionaires who would use their wealth to develop the land, and he waited confidently because "the white man of the South . . . has set himself to work in earnest; and on the grave of the Old South, aided now by colored freemen instead of slaves, he is building a New South that will be far grander than ever the Old South was or could have been."[89] Virginia, once the proud "mother of presidents," was to become the "mother of millionaires."[90] Edmonds believed that the South was "simply rising to her manifest destiny of advancement,"[91] while Grady was certain that the Deity himself was on her side. "Surely the basis of the South's wealth and power," he declared, "is laid by the hand of the Almighty God, and its prosperity has been established by divine law."[92] Kelley, foreseeing illimitable wealth and honor "in the pathway of the New South," implored the Almighty to "speed and guide her onward progress."[93] The South, Edmonds knew, "was to be the richest country upon the globe."[94] And those riches would lead to grander victories; would recoup the losses of the past and, in the end, create a triumphant South.

3
The Triumphant South

You wish me to talk to you about the
South. The South! The South! It is no
problem at all. I thank God that at last we
can say with truth, it is simply a
geographic expression. The whole story
of the South may be summed up in a
sentence: She was rich, and she lost her
riches; she was poor and in bondage; she
was set free, and she had to go to work;
she went to work, and she is richer
than ever before.

—HENRY WATTERSON[1]

The South whose gaze is cast
No more upon the past,
But whose bright eyes the skies of promise
sweep,
Whose feet in paths of progress swiftly leap;
And whose fresh thoughts, like cheerful
rivers run,
Through odorous ways to meet the morning
sun!

—MAURICE THOMPSON[2]

With a population of 80,000,000 active, virile people, unvexed by the arbitrary laws of differing nationalities as in Europe, the foremost in general education, the foremost in wealth, the foremost alike in manufactures and agriculture of all the nations in the world, man never before conceived of such possibilities as the future holds out to us. Well may the people of the South rejoice that it is in their power to make this section hold a dominating position in this, the dominant power of the world.

—RICHARD H. EDMONDS[3]

As he reflected on the progress of the New South movement, Amory Dwight Mayo related it to major themes in American history, one of which was that "every one who is fit for American citizenship has the right to believe that all things are possible in a republic like our own."[4] The statement raised two questions for which the New South spokesmen were to have ready answers. First was the implied query: Are Southerners fit for American citizenship? Second, if they were, was there anything that should prevent them from sharing in the historic sense of optimism and triumph that rightfully belonged to every American?

Between 1861 and 1865 Southerners had fought to dissociate themselves from American citizenship. When capitulation was forced upon them they renounced their former ambitions, pledged fealty to the Union, and expected to resume the role they had enjoyed prior to hostilities. Their conqueror, however, was reluctant to concede that they were so soon "fit for American citizenship." In the minds of many Northerners, as Paul Buck writes, the South continued to be regarded as a threat to those things for which the Republic stood. It was, in many Northern eyes, a region guilty of manifold sins—"the sin of causing the war, the sin of slavery, the sin of seeking the life of the Union"—and, equally reprehensible, it "was still a South in which the evil consequences of wrong exerted a baneful influence."[5]

Thus rudely excluded from the full benefits of American citizenship, the South was also denied that sense of "anything-is-possible" that was deeply imbedded in the minds of other Americans. "Nothing in all history had ever succeeded like America," Henry Steele Commager writes. "As nature and experience justified optimism, the American was incurably optimistic. Collectively, he had never known defeat, grinding poverty, or oppression, and he thought these misfortunes peculiar to the Old World. Progress was not, to him, a philosophical idea but a commonplace of experience."[6] Clearly, the American of whom Commager writes was not a Southerner, or at least not a Southerner who grew to maturity after 1830. The Southerner's experience in the nineteenth century had been, in many essentials, precisely the opposite of that of other Americans.[7] Rewriting Commager's assessment to make it apply accurately to the South, one would have to say that "as experience did not justify optimism, the Southerner was incurably pessimistic. Collectively, he had known defeat, grinding poverty, and oppression, and he did not think these misfortunes peculiar to the Old World. Progress, to him, was more an illusion than a reality."

It is also clear that the prophets of a New South did not cherish these peculiarities of their region. They did not wish to be cast in the common lot of mankind elsewhere, but they aspired to fulfill the American success story in all of its ramifications. The New South creed was designed to point the way toward that achievement. It embodied a fervent gospel of union and brotherhood, to facilitate full acceptance into the union, and tailored its notions of both individual and collective success to the dominant American pattern.

I

When Edward Atkinson, New England cotton-mill magnate and friend of the New South spokesmen, came to Atlanta in 1881 to promote the International Cotton Exhibition, he told a group of receptive Georgians what they themselves would soon be making standard doctrine. The "greatest need of the present time," Atkinson said, was "that the citizens of the two sections . . . should visit each other, learn the respective methods and opportunities of each State, and become convinced that in this mutual inter-dependence is the foundation of their true union."[8]

In the years before Atkinson's address there were those, including Southern men of prominence, who had similarly pleaded for the cessation of sectional animosities. Lee himself had tried to lead the way by declaring that all was not lost and by insisting that Southerners seek to rebuild their shattered society within the framework of a broad nationalism. Other former leaders of the Confederacy added their authority to Lee's in the 'seventies. Benjamin Harvey Hill urged North and South to "unite to repair the evils that distract and oppress the country" and implored, "let us turn our backs upon the past, and let it be said in the future that he shall be the greatest patriot . . . who shall do most to repair the wrong of the past and promote the glories of the future."[9] L. Q. C. Lamar, in his famous eulogy of the once-hated Sumner, declared: "My countrymen! *Know* one another, and you will *love* one another."[10] Henry Watterson chanted, "war or no war, we are all countrymen, fellow citizens."[11] And Wade Hampton urged that the curtain be dropped on the war and that every citizen "look beyond to the

future, when through all time that [American] flag shall
float over a true and prosperous and reunited country."[12]

These ringing pleas, while they were supported by
men in all sections of the country as the Reconstruction
experiment underwent successive failures, made only in-
substantial progress before the 1880's. The lingering suspicions and enduring dissensions between the sections
made the goal of reconciliation seem almost beyond reach.
To convert the effort into a brilliant success became a
cardinal ambition of the New South prophets in the
'eighties and 'nineties. They plunged into this mission with
the same enthusiasm they had applied to the crusade for
economic regeneration and, in the process, they created
a gospel of union that became an integral part of the
New South creed.

No one was more zealous in the mission than Henry
Grady. Early in his career he designated "this miserable
sectional strife" as the most formidable obstacle in the
way of Southern progress, and for ten years he developed
the theme in editorials, feature stories, and speeches.[13]
In 1880 he charged that the sectional spirit was kept alive
in the North, apparently for selfish reasons, and he maintained that there was not in the South "a single spark
of that peculiar sectional madness which is now rampant
at the North."[14] In the next year he wrote warmly and
sympathetically about President Garfield, praying for his
recovery, praising his personal qualities, and finally lamenting his death as the loss of a man who would have
been a friend to the South.[15] Later in 1881 he welcomed
the arrival of Atkinson to the Cotton Exhibition, praising
in particular his nationalist message.[16] By 1884 he was
writing that "the better the masses of the north and of
the south know each other the better it will be for all,"

explaining that "we have a common country, which is working out a common destiny and in which we have common pride and interest."[17]

These and other editorials, coupled with Grady's optimistic nature and friendly disposition, brought to him a matchless opportunity to send his message of reconciliation vibrating through the nation. The New England Society of New York, determined to have a Southern speaker for the 1886 banquet at Delmonico's, wanted a man who would speak for reconciliation and who would, at the same time, command the respect of all parts of the country. Grady was a natural choice. Growing up since the war, he had no Confederate background, and he was known primarily as a journalist and not as a politician. His record as a spokesman for progressive economic policies and section reconciliation was already well known, and his oratorical abilities similarly commended him.[18]

The atmosphere at Delmonico's would almost surely have frightened, or antagonized, a man who came without confidence—and a purpose. The 360 seats were filled, for the most part, by wealthy, conservative businessmen eager to hear of a South that had mended its rebellious ways and was prepared to offer a stable and suitable climate for Northern investments. On the speaker's platform General William Tecumseh Sherman sat in prominence. At the end of his short address the band played "Marching Through Georgia." It was then that the young editor from Atlanta was introduced.[19] His opening paragraph was destined to become the most famous passage in the literature of the New South movement:

"There was a South of slavery and secession—that South is dead. There is a South of union and freedom—

that South, thank God, is living, breathing, growing
every hour." These words, delivered from the immortal
lips of Benjamin H. Hill, at Tammany Hall, in 1866,
true then and truer now, I shall make my text to-
night.[20]

The Northern businessmen could now relax; the speaker
they had imported from the South was apparently going
to play his role well.

Appealing further to the theme of national unity,
Grady rapidly wove into his speech—which was not made
from a prepared text—a criticism of one of the earlier
speakers, who had stated that the country still had to look
forward to the appearance of the "typical" American.
On the contrary, Grady declared, the man who had directed the victory of the Union over the Confederacy was
the typical American. Abraham Lincoln embodied the
best of the "Puritan" and the best of the "Cavalier"; in his
simple, sublime life were all the elements that summed
up America. National admiration for the great Lincoln
should unify former enemies and still leave ample room
for reverence of "your forefathers and . . . mine."[21]

With the tone of his speech thus set in a harmonious
chord, Grady invited the audience to consider the plight
of the South in the two decades since Appomattox. He
described the war-weary veteran coming home from the
terror of battle only to find his house in ruins. Ruined
homes were symbolic of the condition of the whole region.
But the veteran did not fret—he worked. Sherman—a
general slightly careless with fire, Grady remarked to the
amusement of his audience—had left Atlanta in ashes,
but from those ashes was raised a "brave and beautiful
city," and "somehow or other we have caught the sunshine

in the bricks and mortar of our homes, and have builded therein not one ignoble prejudice or memory."[22] With the stops all out, the audience now alternated between discrete weeping and loud cheering.

Trying next to sum up the essence of the New South that he said had now been built, Grady continued:

> But what of the sum of our work? We have found out that in the summing up the free negro counts more than he did as a slave. We have planted the schoolhouse on the hilltop and made it free to white and black. We have sowed towns and cities in the place of theories, and put business above politics. We have challenged your spinners in Massachusetts and your ironmakers in Pennsylvania. We have learned that the $400,000,000 annually received from our cotton crop will make us rich when the supplies that make it are home-raised. We have reduced the commercial rate of interest from 24 to 6 per cent., and are floating 4 per cent. bonds. We have learned that one Northern immigrant is worth fifty foreigners; and have smoothed the path to southward, wiped out the place where Mason and Dixon's line used to be, and hung out our latchstring to you and yours.[23]

With Mason and Dixon's line "wiped out" the rest could only be anticlimactic. He spoke of the achievements of the South in the previous decade and of the failures of the Old South, of the justice tendered the Negro by Southern whites, and of the unqualified acceptance in the South of defeat in the war. In recognizing misguidance in the past—and in accepting the decision of the sword—he nonetheless made it clear that the South had nothing to take back, no fundamental apologies to make, only promises for the future made credible by the actions of the present. In the tradition of Lee and Grant at Appomattox, he explained, the South was prepared to grasp hands with its Northern brethren and resume the joint task of building a great America.[24]

No isolated and unimportant incident, Grady's address created a veritable "tidal wave of New South sentiment." In the North, South, and West the press was enthusiastic and extensive in its reporting.[25] Grady would live but three years after he returned triumphantly from Delmonico's, but in that time he rode the crest of his fame and fanned the sentiment for reconciliation wherever he went. Speaking before the Boston Bay State Club in December 1889, in his last public address, he told his New England friends that his son, the "promise" of his life, could find no better place to learn "the lessons of right citizenship, of individual liberty, of fortitude and heroism and justice" than on Plymouth Rock.[26] Less than a week later, just short of his thirty-ninth birthday, Grady was dead. Joel Chandler Harris, his close friend and associate on the *Constitution*, had a memorial volume on the market before another year had passed and, in the memory of "our Messenger of Peace," he dedicated the book to the "Peace, Unity and Fraternity of the North and South."[27] It was as a pacificator, more than anything else, that Harris liked to remember his old friend.

In his role as "pacificator" Grady had clearly seen that there were two groups which needed to be pacified: the doubters in the North and the doubters in the South. When he spoke in New York he was concerned primarily to allay Northern fears—hence the wiping out of Mason and Dixon's line. When he spoke to Southern audiences he enlarged on the minor theme introduced in New York —that the South had nothing to take back—and promised

his listeners that the authentic Southern heritage of nationalism was one that guaranteed a bright future to the
region.

The announcement of the death of sectionalism in the
South was present in virtually every discussion of the
New South movement. The literature is cluttered with
overblown phrases like those of Robert Bingham, a North
Carolina educator, who proclaimed that "the past of the
South is irrevocable, and we do not wish to recall it.
The past of the South is irreparable, and we do not wish
to repair it," all because "the greatest blessing that ever
befell us was a failure to establish a nationality."[28] Out-
sider observers incessantly reported the new sentiment.
Charles Dudley Warner noted in 1885 that "the South
has entirely put the past behind it, and is devoting itself
to the work of rebuilding on new foundations."[29] Two
years later he wrote that "if I tried to put in a single sentence the most widespread and active sentiment in the
South today, it would be this: The past is put behind us;
we are one with the North in business and national
ambition: we want a sympathetic recognition of this
fact."[30] The editor of *The Century Magazine*, whose devotion to Southern topics was unrivaled by Northern journalists of the 'eighties, observed in 1885 that "the South
believes no longer in slavery, no longer in secession. Some
ex-rebels said not long ago: 'We are glad we were
whipped, and we are in to stay! Now let us see Massachusetts try to get out of the Union!' "[31]

The reporting by non-Southerners accurately reflected
the New South spokesmen's celebration of defeat and the
arrival of a second chance in a stronger nation. Bishop
Atticus Greene Haygood, florid stylist and orator as well
as energetic supporter of the New South movement,

thanked the "gracious Providence that overrules the nations" for the failure of the Confederacy.[32] The extent of
the sentiment was poignantly confirmed in 1889 when the
University of South Carolina conferred an honorary degree
on Edward Atkinson, the New Englander whose first
contact with the South had been in helping to equip John
Brown's raiders with Sharp's rifles.[33] It was further demonstrated by the candid declaration of a twenty-four-year-
old University of Virginia law student. "I yield to no one
precedence in love for the South," Woodrow Wilson
wrote. "But *because* I love the South, I rejoice in the
failure of the Confederacy."[34]

II

To rejoice in the failure of the South's most absorbing
mission required of the New South prophets not only
that they supply a salve for the bitter wounds of defeat,
but also that they offer a vital substitute for the dream of
independence and self-determination; a substitute that
embodied an even nobler vision of the future than the
abandoned Confederate utopia. Fortunately for the New
South spokesmen, the ingredients of such a vision were
already present, though long dormant, in the Southern
mind. To vitalize them required a new appreciation of
the Jeffersonian era when Southerners had been ardent
nationalists and, at the same time, masters of their own
destiny. Spokesmen like Watterson and Page were guilty
of no hypocrisy and hid no duplicitous motives when they
acknowledged and praised this heritage. When Watterson
wrote that "what we really need in the South, above all

else . . . is identity with things national,"³⁵ he could recall
his opposition to both slavery and secession in the years
immediately before the war. Page grew up with the doctrine of nation above section and he never forgot his
grandfather's injunction to serve the nation—a nation of
which the South was but one part.³⁶

Other New South spokesmen were genuinely attached
to the creed of nationalism, but their writings reveal
motives and values which betray a less unreserved dedication to it than they were willing to admit. Underlying
the professions of nationalism, in short, were calculations
of concrete gains for the region. To put it another way,
the nationalism that the New South prophets preached
had as its basic goal the recouping of the losses the South
had incurred because of her long commitment to militant
sectionalism.

Among the most obvious and distressing of those losses
was the self-determination of racial policy that had begun
to be eroded in the 1820's. The victorious principle of
union completed the process and carried with it not only
the abolition of slavery but the constitutional requirement
of Negro equality as well. The New South spokesmen
were honestly relieved to be done with slavery, but to have
the terms of racial equality dictated by the North was
more than they would tolerate. The full implications of
their racial policy will be explored in the next chapter, but
here it should be noted that a vital connection existed
between the professions of nationalism, on the one hand,
and the calculated policy to achieve self-determination in
racial matters, on the other.

George Washington Cable, the New Orleans author
and ardent defender of civil rights, perceived this purpose
behind the New South posture and ridiculed it in rhyme
on the occasion of Grady's New York address:

You've probably heard of one, Grady,
A speech to New Englanders made he.
  They thought it delightful
  Becuz he wa'n't spiteful
And they're what they call "tickled" with Grady.

He was eloquent, also, was Grady;
Patriotic! and bright as a lady.
  But on MEN'S EQUAL RIGHTS
  The darkest of nights
Compared with him wouldn't seem shady.

There wasn't a line, good sirs, bless ye,
Of all that he chose to address ye,
  That touched the one point
  Where his *South's out of joint*
For it wasn't his wish to distress ye.[37]

    The pattern that Grady worked out in his New York speech was followed in subsequent addresses, and in all of his forays into the North it was evident that he did not wish "to distress." Asked by the Boston Merchants' Association to discuss the Negro problem, he began by scolding the New Englanders for meddling in Southern racial policies. In their overzealousness for Negro rights—and in their ignorance of the nature and character of the Southern Negro—they had unwittingly created intense and debilitating racial friction. To stop the discussion here might have distressed, but Grady was just warming up to his subject. He noted that the unsettled conditions resulting from these misguided sentiments had alarmed capitalists throughout the North and had frightened them away from Southern investments. Since the end of Reconstruction, however, native white Southerners had taken charge with the result that the Negro prospered and social conditions were peaceful. Moreover, the economic opportunities in the South cried out for Northern capital, offering automatic and stupendous returns. But the North remained suspicious, fearful that abandonment of coercion had been a mistake—hence the recurrent talk of new civil rights legislation. The wise men of the North, however, would realize that the race problem was virtually solved and that conditions could remain peaceful only if the South were left alone. By this reasoning, then, a Northern hands-off policy was insurance for the safety of Northern capital in the South. With these essential points made, Grady moved easily into an eloquent peroration to the Union, looking to the creation of a "Republic compact, united, indissoluble in the bonds of love," a Republic "serene and resplendent at the summit of human achievement and earthly glory."[38]

In addition to the quest for racial self-determination, the nationalist creed was also, as the above examples suggest, inseparably bound up with the industrial argument so that nearly every New South declaration of loyalty to the Union was also an appeal for Northern capital. Watterson, for example, understood the need for Northern participation in the economic development of the South and made it a theme in numerous speeches and editorials. To disarm Southern reactionaries who feared Northern interference of any sort, he commonly made his appeal to reliable conservative interests in the North. Scolding them for harsh judgments imposed on the South, he would, at the same time, invite their sympathy and their capital.[39]

Speaking before the American Bankers' Association in 1883 he began with the assertion that the South was "simply a geographic expression" and no longer the home of militant sectionalists. The old notion that a different species of person lived below Mason and Dixon's line, he said, was a product of "morbid minds." "We are one people," he told them; and that solid fact, he declared, "gives a guarantee of peace and order at the South, and offers a sure and lasting escort to all the capital which may come to us for investment. . . . We need the money. You can make a profit off the development."[40] On another occasion Watterson made clear how important it was to correct false Northern notions about the South in order to encourage a flow of capital into the region. Writing in 1882, he insisted that the "philosophic observer" of the North would see in the South not a "huddle of lazy barbarians, composed in large part of murderers and gamblers," but, rather, "a great body of Christian men and women, who have had a hard struggle with fate and fortune, but who have stood against the elements with fortitude that contradicts the characteristics formerly imputed to them."[41]

The patterns worked out in the early 'eighties by Grady and Watterson were assiduously applied by the other New South spokesmen. Edmonds, for example, when he proclaimed the "unparalleled industrial progress of the South," stressed the interdependence of the sections and noted pointedly that Southern advancement guaranteed Northern wealth.[42] Summing up the mission of his journal in 1924, he wrote that the objective had always been to build up "the nation through the upbuilding of the South," and he repeated with Kelley's authority the belief that "the development of the South means the enrichment of the nation."[43] Examples could be multiplied to the point of tedium, but without them one can readily agree with Buck that the spokesmen's message was de-

signed "to advertise a New South of progress and reconciliation" and that "no concept was more often transmitted
to the North in the 'eighties than that the South had buried
its resentments and had entered a new era of good feeling
based upon an integration of material interests."[44]

Edwin Lawrence Godkin had said in 1880 that the
conversion of the South to the "ways and ideas" of the
"industrial stage of social progress" was really what was
required to make the region peaceful.[45] He did not spell
out what he meant by "peaceful," but a fair inference
would be that an industrial South would mean the end
of a distinctive South and that with the end of distinction
rancorous sectionalism would dissolve. Seizing upon this
idea, the New South spokesmen fashioned the image of a
harmonious nationalism as the direct product of the industrialization and consequent enrichment of the South. Grady
put it bluntly in one editorial when he wrote that "sectional and political feeling is not likely to make itself
heard when people are busy stuffing their pockets with
dollars."[46] Tompkins, somewhat less bluntly, declared in
a Fourth of July address that the anniversary of American
independence should be celebrated as never before because
"for the first time in a hundred years, the institutions and
interests of the American people are identical and common." The primary reason for the new identity of purpose,
he believed, was that manufacturing was once again
spreading itself across the South.[47] And Walter Hines
Page, less given to wishful thinking than his fellow New
South advocates, wrote that the transformation stimulated
by their movement would surely mean the disappearance
of the old Southern borough he had described in his youth
so that it would soon be "very like a thousand towns in
the Middle West."[48]

Reflecting on the nationalist creed in the New South movement early in the twentieth century, the Southern historian Samuel C. Mitchell remarked that "common interest is a strong amalgam in a modern government" and went on to observe that "whatever tends to equalize economic conditions in different sections of our country promotes similarity of view and identity of purpose. The cotton-mill owner in South Carolina and the iron master in Alabama are, perforce, responsive to the laws of trade as they operate throughout the whole republic. To industrialize is, therefore, to nationalize the South." Taking a broad view of the nationalist movement, with particular emphasis on the Italian and German experiences, Mitchell wrote that consolidation was one of the major forces at work in the nineteenth century. Southerners, he believed, had simply found out "God's plan" for their generation and had "fallen in line."[49]

Falling in line with God's plan did not, of course, mean that the South was to embrace the national will only to remain a colonial, dependent stepchild. On the contrary, the nationalism to which the New South prophets subscribed was pictured as the sure road to Southern prominence in the nation. This is especially apparent in the ambivalent quality of the Southern quest for Northern capital. Frantically seeking Northern money to build the Southern industrial utopia, and applauding every new investment that was made, the New South spokesmen resented any suggestion that the South they were creating was a product of foreign or outside elements. It was "southern brains, and southern enterprise, and southern energy and courage" that had "inaugurated and sustained the booming development of southern soil and resources," Grady boasted.[50] Edmonds castigated those who used the term New South to mean "something which has been brought about by an infusion of outside energy and money"; it was, he said, an "improper use of the term, or, rather, an abuse of it."[51] This jealous regard for Southerners' claim to the laurels of creation is indicative of the deeper sentiment and root motivation of the New South movement which Grady pointedly expressed in his New York address. The new departure, he declared, had brought to the South "a fuller independence . . . than that which our fathers sought to win in the forum by their eloquence or compel in the field by their swords."[52] Northern aid and participation, but Southern self-determination —this was, in the last analysis, the *raison d'être* of the New South spokesmen's dedication to American nationalism.

III

James Phelan, a forgotten and unimportant Congressman from west Tennessee, was surprised and embarrassed in the summer of 1886 when a Tipton County farmer approached him and said "I am not certain that I know exactly what is meant by the phrase 'New South.' They say you are a progressive Democrat—a man of the 'New South.' Now tell me what this means."[53] Phelan recovered from his shock, drew on the confidence which being a "man of the New South" was meant to impart and, a few days later, delivered a speech in answer to the farmer's question. The reply he gave is important because it underscores the inclusiveness and breadth of the New South

creed. At its core were the ideas of economic regeneration, national reconciliation, and adjustment of the race
question. But, radiating from these central concerns was a
plethora of other ideas that helped to supply a vision of
regional and individual success substantial enough to
replace the creed of the Old South.

The New South, Phelan began, could not be easily
defined, for it meant no one thing. It embodied the idea
of the "social and industrial changes" that had come since
the war; it meant a "spirit of enterprise" which had per-
fected those changes; guiding it was the "liberalized state
of mind which recognizes that a new order of things has
come." Put succinctly, it was "the manifestation in all
walks of life and in all undertakings of the progressive
spirit. It means new methods and . . . modes of thought
and action."

Turning to the specific application of the broad generalizations, Phelan detailed the meaning of the New
South idea for each individual in Southern society. To the
farmer it meant better tools, improved methods, diversified crops, the reading of agricultural journals, a liberal
treatment of hired labor, education for his children, and
an "honest pride of character." To the lawyer the New
South spirit should impart a sense of the grandeur of
his profession; it should cause him to rise above the
pedestrian study of dull cases, inspire in him a love of the
literature of his profession, and cause him to cultivate its
philosophy and its history. To the doctor the New South
issued a call to break the shackles of the past, keep abreast
of modern discoveries, and turn medicine from a "Black
Art" into a true science. To the merchant the New South
should mean a "strict sense of enterprise," the development of new trades, and the widening of business horizons.

To the Negro the New South meant a recognition of his freedom and the acceptance of him as a "fellow citizen," with rights protected honestly and zealously. Those rights, however, were political and economic, not social. The Negro must be trained in the ways of industry and in court he should be given a fair hearing, but God had put between the social relationships of white and black a wide river that forever prohibited social intercourse. Finally, to the Democrat of the South it should mean all these things and more. "In him it should find its highest and most practical exponent." He should be the "Knight of the New South." His leadership should be that of the "practical" statesman of hard work, free from verbiage and empty promises.[54]

Amory Dwight Mayo, an educator and clergyman, was typical of the new breed of Northern reformers who muted or abandoned whatever abolitionists and radical sympathies they might once have had and allied themselves with the spokesmen of the New South. Born in Massachusetts in 1823, Mayo served the Unitarian Church as both minister and professor of church polity in the Meadville Theological Seminary. In the last two decades of the nineteenth century, as a private citizen, he traveled some 200,000 miles in the South, studying conditions in the region, advising on educational matters, and applauding the work of the New South spokesmen.[55] In an article published in 1893 he took an especially broad view of their work. The New South, he wrote, meant urbanization and industrialization and reconciliation with the North—these things were axiomatic. Beyond this it meant the uplifting of "our brothers in black," a logical and just solution to the race problem. Intellectually, it meant the growth of cosmopolitanism, the renunciation of the intense

Southern provincialism which isolated the South from the nation and the world. For the masses it implied a broadening participation in public life, undergirded by education, economic opportunity, and political equality. These changes assured the downfall of the old aristocracy and would lead the South to prominence in a new America based on a new American nationalism.[56]

Among Southern clergymen and educators who carved conspicuous places in the New South movement none was better known than Atticus G. Haygood. Born in Georgia in 1839, Haygood spent his life there and was a staunch admirer of Henry Grady. His father was an attorney and active lay worker in the Methodist Episcopal Church, South. His mother was a committed school teacher. The son combined qualities of his parents to become president of Emory College from 1875 to 1884 and a bishop in the Methodist Episcopal Church, South, in 1881. From this background he was able to speak with an authority that wide segments of Southern society were accustomed to respect.[57]

In the early 'eighties Haygood was probably best known for his attempt to fit the Negro into the progressive ideology of the New South, a subject that will be discussed in the next chapter. But it was on Thanksgiving day, 1880, that he first came into prominence as a New South spokesman. The sermon he preached on that occasion to the students of Emory—*The New South: Gratitude, Amendment, Hope*—launched him on what Judson Ward has called a "tempestuous and controversial career as a social philosopher of the New South."[58] Ten thousand copies of the sermon were printed, at the expense of a New York financier, to spread Haygood's message.[59] Essentially humanitarian, Haygood spoke in broad, hopeful phrases about the future of the region, while pointing to recent changes to justify his optimism. But as a prophet of progress he listed four ills that required attention. The region was intensely provincial; it did not feel the "heart beat" of the outside world. Isolation, he declared, had been a decisive factor in permitting the war to occur; it must be abolished to bring the South into its full development. Illiteracy was a second ailment; great masses of the population must be elevated by a broad program of public education. Thirdly, he lamented the absence of a flourishing literature and found this subject too "painful to dwell on." Finally, he deplored the backwardness in manufacturing, cited the abundant natural resources of the South and exhorted his fellows to take full advantage of them.[60]

Jabez Lamar Monroe Curry was especially sympathetic to Haygood's plea for an end to illiteracy, and more than any other Southerner of the 1880's he sought to make public education the South's number one concern. Born in Georgia in 1825, Curry was trained in law at Harvard and during his Massachusetts residence he was profoundly impressed by Horace Mann, the nation's leading advocate of universal education. Returning to the South, he practiced law in Alabama and served the Confederacy as both legislator and military officer. He was ordained a Baptist minister in 1866, but education remained his enduring concern. After resigning the presidency of Howard University, in Alabama, he accepted a professorship in Virginia, at Richmond College, and in 1881 was appointed General Agent of the Peabody Education Fund, a philanthropy established in 1867 to improve Southern education.[61]

Already a prominent national figure by the 1880's, Curry spoke widely on the needs of the South and, except for a brief period as ambassador to Spain (1885–8), he regularly recorded his support of the standard New South programs. Unlike the notable New South spokesmen, however, Curry placed primary emphasis on public education, the area in which he worked most actively. In addition to his position as General Agent of the Peabody Fund he became chairman of the Committee on Education of the Slater Fund for Negro education in 1890, and was an officer or moving force in every Southern educational organization of consequence until his death in 1903.

Curry crusaded for education in part because he believed in that way he could best discharge his duty to the region, for "the free school is the corner-stone of any New South."[62] He also looked upon state-supported education as a "universal right" of all citizens and the best means of assuring good government.[63] Relating the need for education to the specific goals of the New South crusade, he wrote on another occasion that "ignorance is the parent of poverty, waste, and crime" and maintained that "an ignorant people can never work out a noble civilization." Education, he insisted, "is the fundamental basis of general and permanent prosperity. Poverty is the inevitable result of ignorance. Capital follows the schoolhouse. Thrift accompanies government action in behalf of schools."[64] No stronger plea could have been made for the utility of education in the New South movement, but Curry had one final—and important—touch to add. Negroes, he argued, needed proper schooling quite as much as whites. Acknowledging a selfish reason for his advocacy of Negro education, he wrote that "we are bound, hand and foot, to the lowest stratum of society. If the negroes remain as co-occupants of the land and co-citizens of the States, and *we* do not lift them up, they will drag us down to industrial bankruptcy, social degradation, and political corruption."[65]

Curry was not alone in adding public education to the list of New South demands. In occasional editorials Grady commended Curry for his work and urged the Georgia legislature to authorize units of local government to levy special school taxes and to extend the school term.[66] Edmonds likewise mentioned the importance of education and by the end of the century was demanding that the South pay as much heed to the need of poor Southern white boys as it did to Negroes. He wanted a "white Booker T. Washington" and asked for the emergence of someone who would "do for the poor white boys of his section the effective work which has already been accomplished at Tuskegee."[67] From time to time, too, the meetings of the National Educational Association would ring with pleas for an attack on the problem of Southern ignorance. In 1884, for example, Robert Bingham, a North Carolina educator, said in his address that "the clash of arms ceased nineteen years ago; but the war will not be really ended till the leprosy of illiteracy is removed from the white people whom the war impoverished, and from the blacks whom it enfranchised."[68]

For the most part, however, education remained a relatively minor part of the New South creed, and it was not until the turn of the century that the "education crusade" began to take hold of the Southern imagination. Walter Hines Page was the only one of the prominent New South spokesmen who eventually provided a link between the ideology of the 'eighties and the public school campaign of the early twentieth century. Speaking in Greensboro, North Carolina, in 1897 on "The Forgotten Man," Page denounced the backwardness of the Southern

educational system, castigated the leaders who refused
to appropriate tax funds for schools, and declared that
the inevitable consequence of Southern policy was a large
mass of people who were not only illiterate, but forgotten
as well. This "forgotten man" was the prey of all the
reactionaries in the region. Duped by the politician and
the preacher, he supported the "mummies," the very
people whose position in society depended upon preservation of the status quo. Ignorance trapped the "forgotten
man" in a vicious circle. He voted into office the very men
who quashed the public-education bills that might lift him
out of oblivion. The only way to break this syndrome,
Page said, was to launch a sustained effort of common
people everywhere in the South.[69]

Within a short time the "forgotten man" had become
part of the "indelible imagery" of the Southern people,
and Page's address "created a sensation" from Virginia
to Texas.[70] In the next decade significant improvements
were made in the field of public education and a galaxy
of leaders earned national reputations as spokesmen for
the new enlightenment. But all of this came after the
heyday of the New South movement and was only indi-
rectly related to its creed. Most of the spokesmen of the
'eighties, while they paid lip service to the notion of public
education, preferred to save the region with what seemed
to them to be the less complicated and more speedy method
of industrialization and agricultural reorganization. According to their faith, these reforms would produce the
necessary wealth that one day would finance a desirable,
but not immediately crucial, system of public education.

IV

One of the most venerable of American faiths is the belief that education is everyman's passport to success in a competitive, free enterprise society. In a limited and ambivalent way the New South prophets shared this belief, but one of the reasons why public education received short shrift in their program was that they believed personal success was but incidentally related to formal education. More important, they argued, were the attitudes and moral character that each individual applied to his struggle in life. As they wrote about the New South, they devoted as much energy to defining the value system and qualities of manhood required by the new regime as they did to drafting their blueprint for economic regeneration, sectional reconciliation, and racial harmony. Indeed, their creed held that the new order of affairs could come into existence only if the scale of values which they believed had existed in the Old South were drastically altered. In short, they preached a new set of values as a primary requisite to both collective and individual success.

To begin with, the New South spokesmen believed that the antebellum ideal of the leisured gentleman who scorned manual labor was a relic that had no place in the new age. In the stead of the Old South patriarch, the New South spokesmen would substitute as their ideal the hardworking, busy, acquisitive individual. The new men would be like those Mark Twain had observed on a Southern tour in the 1880's: "Brisk men, energetic of movement and speech; the dollar their god, how to get it their religion."[71] Edmonds explained why when he wrote that "the easy-going days of the South have passed away, never to return. . . . The South has learned that 'time is money.' "[72] This was a lesson that even the aristocrats of the old regime might learn, he wrote on another occasion. "Take the easy-going Southern planter," he predicted, and "turn him loose in a community like that of Birmingham, and the leopard changes his spots in the twinkling of a corner lot!"[73] Kelley made it clear that money was indeed the first goal when he wrote that the man was "a slave or a fool who toils without hope of profit."[74] In an era in which "fruit, not foliage and flowers,"[75] was demanded, the New South prophets proclaimed a "gospel of work as the South's great need" and sure means of bringing praise and position to the very kind of man who lacked status in the old regime.[76] A Scarlett O'Hara would have earned their respect; an Ashley Wilkes their scorn, for, as Watterson declared, the master of the old era, to succeed, must become "the toiler of today."[77] Agreeing with Grady that "the genteel loafer has little place or position in the new system," and with Charles Brantley Aycock that the "most pitiable object in creation is a man who is always idle," Edmonds laid it down as a law of nature that since "the day when it was decreed that in the sweat of his brow man should earn his daily bread, man's greatest blessing has been work."[78] Finally, Edward Atkinson, the friend from the North, rounded out the doctrine with his pronouncement that no society could hope for success when the man who "earns his daily bread by the work of his own hands is not honored."[79]

Closely linked to the "gospel of work" was the doctrine that nonproductive enterprises must assume secondary positions in society. No longer was there either need or excuse for great statesmen who dissipated their time in finely spun constitutional arguments. "Business above

politics," the Grady slogan that was most frequently used
to express this idea, meant that statecraft was another
relic of bygone days. In 1880 Grady wrote of John H.
Inman, a Tennesseean who had made a fortune in New
York as a cotton broker: "I should be charged with irreverence if I wrote down how many politicians . . . this
one young merchant is worth."[80] Apparently worrying
little about the charge of irreverence, he wrote in 1882 that
politicians appeared "cheap" when compared to successful
men of enterprise; in his speech at Delmonico's he announced that the New South men had "sowed towns and
cities in the place of theories, and put business above
politics"; and in an editorial the next year he wrote that
"the man that gives us a new railroad or a new industry
will readily be pardoned if he is a little backward in the
history of parties and such matters."[81] Politics, the New
South advocates agreed, was essentially irrelevant to their
movement and its lure had to be abolished. Edmonds put
it succinctly when he wrote that:

> Politics won't increase the number of factories in a
> town. Politics won't build stores and houses. Politics won't
> attract investors; on the contrary, it often creates such
> oppressive laws for the benefit of its adherents that capital
> is kept away. Politics seldom increases a man's business
> in a legitimate way. In short, in a section which is only
> in the early stages of its development, like the South, the
> professional politician can do untold injury, and is seldom
> or never a power for good.[82]

The attempt to revise society's concept of the successful and honorable man was early linked to the notion of
the "self-made" man. The truly admirable person, Grady
wrote in 1880, was a man who rose to the top "by no
accident of inheritance, nor by capricious turn of luck,

but by patient, earnest, heroic work." He was a man who
had "wrought much out of nothing" and had "compelled
success out of failure."[83] Ideas such as these became the
stock-in-trade of a raft of "success writers" whose literature swept the Northern states in the last quarter of the
nineteenth century and found a congenial home in the
ideological baggage of the New South school. W. H.
Wallace, for example, told the members of the Eutonian
Literary Society of Clinton Academy, South Carolina,
what qualities a young man should cultivate in the New
South: above all the age called for active, energetic, positive men. In a practical age certain things were especially
demanded. "For one thing," he announced, "there is the
assurance that we are in no danger of becoming a dawdling
or effeminate people. A practical people are a sturdy
people—full of life and vigor—energetic and enterprising
—not necessarily intellectual or cultivated in a bookish
sense, but sensible and shrewd and self-reliant." The society of the Old South was "easy going and oligarchical";
it lacked all sense of the practical.[84] In the new, practical
age, success should be man's greatest ambition and three
things were required to achieve it:

> A competence in money, a good reputation and a good
> character are essentials of true success in life, and no
> man having these need have any fear of failure. And all
> these elements are within the reach of every young man
> of even ordinary ability and under whatsoever circum-
> stances his lot may be cast. It is, therefore, possible for
> every man to make his life a success.[85]

William S. Speer, another of the success writers,
published *The Law of Success* (significantly under the

imprint of the Southern Methodist Publishing House) to provide a comprehensive list of maxims for successful living. Basing his advice on the lives of "self-made" men, Speer told one everything from how to select a wife to how to succeed in business; nor did he overlook the "commercial value" of the Ten Commandments. Pointing to the future training of the youth, Speer prophesied:

> The educator of the future will teach his pupils what will pay best. He will teach them the art of thinking, which, for the purposes in hand, I may define to be the art of turning one's brains into money. He will not teach dead languages, obsolete formulas, and bric-a-brac sciences . . . which are never used in the ordinary transactions of the forum, the office, the shop, or the farm.[86]

Wallace and Speer were but two of the many popularizers of the new doctrine of success in the South and their writings accurately reflected the basic beliefs of the New South spokesmen. Grady, for example, was critical of the University of Georgia because it laid too much stress on such subjects as rhetoric and classics, and he urged that additional instruction be given in practical subjects so that graduates would turn more frequently to business careers rather than to the traditional professions.[87] And Edmonds, responding to the plea of a young Southerner who could not find work, assured his correspondent that "we are all cogs in the great machine" and that one could be sure that, sooner or later, "the right spot is found."[88]

The gospel of work and the success formulas found full expression and pseudo-scientific justification in the doctrine of social Darwinism that captivated American thought in the last part of the century.[89] The Southern exponents embraced it warmly and stoutly defended laissez-faire (so long as that doctrine did not preclude government aid to business), scorned labor unions (which they said were not desired or needed by Southern labor anyway), and made a fetish of the theory of free competition. Tompkins expressed the common New South view when he declared that "the survival of the fittest is, has been, and will always be the law of progress."[90] An "apostle of privilege for capital invested in business," he saw the state as the protector of "natural rights" and not as an instrument of "human welfare."[91]

There was in the Southern version of social Darwinism virtually no appreciation of the enigma noted by concerned social critics of the period: the association of poverty with material progress. Rather, the New South spokesmen ascribed failure to personal shortcomings in the belief that the opportunity created by their program made it possible for anyone who applied himself to succeed. For those who should somehow fall by the wayside, men like the Reverend John C. Calhoun Newton would have "wealthy capitalists, and prince merchants, and lordly bankers" come to the rescue, acting as "stewards of God."[92] Nor was there in the New South literature more than a modicum of awareness of the dangers of monopoly capitalism. Even Page, more sensitive than most to social injustice, largely ignored the danger signals until the twentieth century. Like the others, he felt that industrial development held the answer to the region's economic problems, and during the 'eighties and 'nineties he wrote little about child labor, poor working conditions, marginal wages, and the concentration of economic power.[93] Grady did speak on one occasion of the "shame of the robber barons of the Rhine" and he warned against a repetition of this shame in the

South,[94] but his actions and his writings were overwhelmingly and consistently sympathetic to the railroads, the industrial promoters, and the bankers. He never wrote a serious critique of the dangers in the New South program as he contented himself with promises of the blessings to be ushered in by the industrial, urban era.

Finally, the New South spokesmen showed little patience with those who opposed their program because of its alleged materialism. To those who argued that "mammonism" and "money-mania" were threatening to destroy Southern values, the New South prophets replied sternly. Edmonds found it impossible to understand why people were "prone to sermonize against the spirit of 'commercialism.' " They forgot, or perhaps did not know, that it was "the unceasing, untiring commercial energy of the American people which has put this country to the forefront not only in finance, trade and manufactures, but in almost everything which looks to the betterment of mankind."[95] From the North came Mayo's equally outspoken rebuttal. "It is a simple stupidity," he insisted, to "exclaim over this inevitable trend of Anglo-Saxon society, and to denounce it as materialistic or in any way a symptom of social degeneracy."[96] But it was the irrepressible Edmonds who had the last word: material prosperity, which could come only by adopting the New South program, "if not the foundation, is at least an essential factor in ethical advancement." Every noble aspect of civilization—religion, art, education, intellectual activity—depended upon it. Thus, far from threatening moral values, the New South spokesmen were "really preaching the gospel of education. Yea, they are really messengers preparing the way for religious advancement itself."[97]

V

Holland Thompson was the first academic historian to write a general history of the postbellum South. In 1919 he published a slim volume, appropriately entitled *The New South*, and he set the tone of the work by stating at the outset that "somehow, somewhere, sometime, a new hopefulness was born and this new spirit—evidence of new life—became embodied in 'the New South.' "[98] Writing like a latter-day New South prophet, he joyously proclaimed the "new spirit" and the "new life" and designated them as the South's greatest blessings. Perceiving the essence of the New South creed, he saw that its totality was more than the sum of the individual parts and that its great appeal derived from its philosophy of progress, brash confidence, and sense of boundless optimism—qualities that had been strikingly wanting in the Southern mentality of the early postbellum years. The creed, in short, furnished young Southerners with an ideology that could rationalize the failure of their fathers and point the way to a future of unlimited glory.

Few things appealed to the New South spokesmen more than describing the nature of that future. Commonly drawing their pictures against the background of the postwar chaos and dislocation, they stressed the contrast of rapid accomplishment and divine assistance. Grady would dwell lengthily on the utter hopelessness that seemed to cover the South in 1865 and then would proclaim that from "defeat and utter poverty were to be wrought victory and plenty."[99] Edmonds declared that the phenomenal strides made by the South, "notable in themselves," were of "unparalleled significance when viewed against the appalling background of a generation ago."[100] Underscoring the missionary nature of the movement, Grady called upon an audience of Texans to "consecrate" themselves to the cause of both the South and the Union and, with such "consecrated service," he asked rhetorically, "what could we not accomplish?"[101] What, indeed! One had only to sample the titles of articles in the *Manufacturers' Record:* "The South's Brilliant Future," "The Wonderful South," "South's Prosperity; Past, Present and Future," "Forward," and "Why Optimism Should Reign Through the South."[102]

Why optimism should reign was explained by everyone. Joseph G. Brown wrote that "there is a law of nature that out of death comes life," and "out of the dead Confederacy came the new life, the new energy, the new spirit" that was the New South.[103] Kelley discovered the secret of the South of the 'eighties in its "animation" and its hopefulness.[104] The Reverend Mr. Newton said that, to him, the transcendent meaning of the New South creed was that the "time is fully come when our people look, not backward *only*, but also forward; that the South is to have a future."[105] And Broadus Mitchell—himself caught up in the spirit of progress—looked back on the movement from the vantage point of 1921 to declare that the South, by 1880, "was ready to be no longer negative, but affirmative; not just the passive resultant of its past, but the conscious builder of its future. From a consequence, the South was to become a cause."[106]

The contrast between "consequence" and "cause" is precisely what Commager suggests, in the passage quoted at the beginning of this chapter, as the distinguishing characteristic of the American as compared with other people. The American of the nineteenth century was purely "cause" and knew nothing of "consequence," according to this view. And so, in the last analysis, this is what the Southerner of the New South movement wished to become, too. He wished to become independent of the North, as Grady remarked in New York, but he wished more than that, for he had the testimony of Edmonds that it was in his power to make the South "hold a dominating position in this, the dominant power of the world."[107] Thus did he dream of a South that would rise again; not an Old South of political leadership but a New South of industrial might. Entering the struggle on the terms of the other contestants, he would win back for his region its confidence and its right to an equal—perhaps dominant—partnership in the Union he was eager to re-enter.

4

The Innocent South

The condition of the Southern Negro is one
of progressive evolution from the darkness
of slavery into the fullness of freedom.
He is not only a man by the law of the land,
but he is rising toward true manhood by
the exercise of his physical and moral
powers. In all history there has been no
similar instance in which a ruling race has
so nobly and unremittingly aided its former
bondsmen to rise to the highest levels of
which they were naturally capable.

—RICHARD H. EDMONDS[1]

And with the South the . . . [Negro
question] may be left—must be left. There
it can be left with the fullest confidence
that the honor of the Republic will be
maintained, the rights of humanity guarded,
and the problem worked out in such
exact justice as the finite mind can measure
or finite agencies administer.

—HENRY W. GRADY[2]

But the supremacy of the white race of the
South must be maintained forever, and the
domination of the negro race resisted at
all points and at all hazards—because the
white race is the superior race. This is the
declaration of no new truth. It has
abided forever in the marrow of our bones,
and shall run forever with the blood that
feeds Anglo-Saxon hearts.

—HENRY W. GRADY[3]

Taking stock of the New South movement in the mid-'eighties, the liberal Southern clergyman Thomas U. Dudley related its significance to the future of race relations. A successful analysis of the subject, he felt, must begin with the hard fact "that the conditions of our life are all changed; that old things are passed away."[4] That much had "passed away," there could be no denying. The abolition of slavery removed the one unmistakable institutional expression of white supremacy and the Reconstruction amendments proclaimed the former slaves to be the civic and political equals of their erstwhile masters. But Dudley implied too much when he wrote "that the conditions of our life are all changed," for the persistence of old problems and old attitudes bequeathed to the New South spokesmen a dilemma that had beset their predecessors. The dilemma sprang from the contrast between a national legend of moral innocence, in which Southerners always claimed to share, and the reality of Southern determination to maintain a white master class. Although the conditions of life were different, the race problem would continue to cause Southern leaders to reconcile incompatible allegiances with ingenious rationalizations and paradoxical beliefs.

The legend of innocence has been one of the most

tenacious and influential features of American history. Frederick Jackson Turner recognized this when he wrote long ago that "other nations have been rich and prosperous and powerful," but added that the peculiar genius of the American democracy arose from the nation's determination to root out the obstacles to liberty and equality that had plagued other countries.[5] More recently, Reinhold Niebuhr has noted how Americans looked upon themselves from the beginning as a people who "came into existence with the sense of being a 'separated' nation, which God was using to make a new beginning for mankind. . . . We were God's 'American Israel.' "[6] C. Vann Woodward, to cite one final example, writes that "American opulence and American success have combined to foster and encourage . . . the legend of American innocence." Skipping the feudal stage of development, Americans left behind in Europe the "tyranny, monarchism, aristocracy, and privilege" which they thought accounted for most of the world's evils. In time they created the image of a morally innocent nation and came to regard themselves as "a chosen people and their land a Utopia on the make."[7]

Americans, of course, have not been alone in fostering the notion of their unique innocence. Many foreign observers, often in different ways, have been fascinated by the theme. Crèvecoeur, the most famous of the eighteenth-century commentators, was followed by de Tocqueville in the antebellum period and Lord Bryce after the Civil War.[8] But it was a twentieth-century Swede who gave the most complete and influential account of the legend. Gunnar Myrdal, in his massive study of American race relations, called it the "American Creed" and wrote that it was the "cement in the structure" of the American nation. According to Myrdal, Americans had the most explicitly stated "system of general ideas in reference to human interrelations" of any western nation, and he found "the unanimity around, and the explicitness of, this Creed" to be "the great wonder of America." Born of the colonists' dream of escape from Old World oppression, refined by the philosophy of the Enlightenment, codified in the Declaration of Independence, the Creed sustained Americans in their fight for separation from Britain and in every subsequent war. Its core ideas, Myrdal wrote, consisted of the "essential dignity of the individual human being, of the fundamental equality of all men, and of certain inalienable rights to freedom, justice, and a fair opportunity." Its "main norms . . . are centered in the belief in equality and in the rights to liberty."[9]

I

Myrdal's overarching purpose was to document and dramatize the dilemma besetting a people who righteously celebrated freedom and equality but who practiced a virulent form of racism. The dilemma, of course, was deeply rooted in the nation's history. In fact, the American ideal which Myrdal used as his yardstick was most eloquently expressed by Southern slaveholders of the Revolutionary era. Led by Thomas Jefferson, the enlightened men of that generation were clearly pained by the trap which ensnared them. Articulate and passionate spokesmen for a new freedom in their own land, they vigorously condemned slavery as a repudiation of the foundation upon which they made their claim to universal liberty.

Their actions, however, reflected their ideals only modestly, and as they failed to find what they considered to be a practical way to end the institution they called it a "necessary evil" and cherished the hope that one day it would be abolished so that the ideal and the real might be harmonized.[10]

Quite the opposite result followed, however. With the spread of cotton culture into the southwest, the apparently rising profitability of slavery, and the appearance of a militant abolitionist movement that helped to isolate the South from the mainstream of American thought, Southerners abandoned the Jeffersonian rationale and came to look upon slavery as a "positive good," the essential foundation of their way of life. The antebellum pro-slavery theorists, however, did not fully escape the disquiet that had troubled the Jeffersonians. Many of them spoke harshly of Jefferson's idealism and most perverted the basic structure of the Enlightenment rationale upon which the American Creed rested. Nonetheless, the pro-slavery argument emphasized the same generalized democratic values that held the allegiance of other Americans. The difference was that Southerners believed in the necessity of slavery to guarantee constitutional liberty, equality of opportunity, and class harmony. This was a convenient way to eliminate the inherited dilemma, but the copious literature of justification, full of obeisance to liberty and equality, betrays their awareness of its existence and their need to confront it.[11]

The Civil War and Reconstruction drastically altered the material basis of Southern social relations, as Bishop Dudley implied and as the New South spokesmen incessantly announced, but the Southern faith in white supremacy heartily endured. To seize the leadership of their region, the New South prophets saw clearly that they must give full support to their faith. At the same time, however, they recognized that their plans for abundance, reconciliation, and success—so heavily dependent upon Northern approval—could not flagrantly repudiate the American image of itself as a just and humane society; nor, it must be added, did the New South spokesmen wish to think of themselves as anything but enlightened, progressive men pointing to a future in which happiness might confidently be expected by black as well as by white Southerners.

To make credible their position as both friend of the Negro and defenders of white supremacy, the New South spokesmen were inadvertently assisted by men whose impassioned arguments on both the right and the left vacated for them the happy middle ground of moderation. Not surprisingly, there were many more persons occupying the reactionary than the radical position. With pseudo-scientific notions of racial differences, some of the reactionaries declared that the Negro could not withstand the strains of civilized life and would retrogress to a savage state and ultimately to extinction.[12] After the census returns of 1880 indicated an increase in Negro population, less was said about the trend toward numerical retrogression, but the belief in cultural retrogression received greater emphasis. Philip Alexander Bruce, a prolific amateur historian from Virginia, wrote a book about the emancipated Negro in 1889 in which he stated that "every circumstance surrounding the Negro in the present age seems to point directly to his future decadence." He was certain that the blacks would, in time, reach "a state of nature"—whatever that might be. Favoring deportation as the best solution to the problem, but despairing of its practicability, Bruce advocated stern repression "to ward off political ruin and to save society from destruction."[13]

The reactionaries' fear of "destruction" was rooted in their unshakable conviction that God had created the Negro to be a slave and nothing else. Charles Colcock Jones, Jr., president of the Confederate Survivors' Association, believed that the natural harmony which had been destroyed by emancipation could not conceivably be restored with Negroes as free men.[14] Thomas Nelson Page, with the authority of a Virginia patrician, dismissed the notion that the Negro was handicapped in the era of freedom because of the heritage of slavery. On the contrary, he wrote, the Negro had come to America as a "savage" and slavery had been his "salvation," for he did "not possess the faculties to raise himself above slavery" and the whites had assumed the responsibility for his welfare.[15] Expanding on these views a few years later in a book on the Negro as "The Southerner's Problem," Page recorded the universal belief of all Southern reactionary thinkers when he declared that through all history the Negro had "exhibited the absence of the essential qualities of a progressive race."[16]

Reacting to the frustrations of the Reconstruction era and unable to discover or implement a suitable substitute for slavery immediately after the winning of home rule, outspoken Southern racists found outlet in a rhetoric of hate and repression and in increasing acts of both individual and group violence. To the New South spokesmen, excessive vituperation and unleashed violence were objectionable retreats from the challenges of the present and future and therefore promised the South more of the same ills from which she had long suffered. The Reverend John C. Calhoun Newton, for example, wrote in 1887 that

the race question could be settled in one of two ways,
either through repression or through a progressive policy
designed to lift up the inferior race.[17] Bishop Atticus G.
Haygood, whom Newton praised as the guiding spirit in
the New South program of racial progress, agreed that
the policy of repression could solve no problems. It had
been tried many times, from the days of Pharaoh to the
Russia of his own day, and it had met with universal
failure. Recognition of the interdependent needs of white
and black and a plan to elevate the status of both was the
only answer to the South's problems, he declared.[18] Grady
tried to state the nature of the task when he said "it is
to carry in peace and honor and prosperity two dissimilar
races with equal civil and political rights and nearly equal
in number, on the same soil."[19]

The New South spokesmen's critique of the reactionary attitude toward race relations was carefully constructed to concede most of the fundamental assumptions
about the inherent inferiority of the Negroes, and it similarly included abundant reassurance of the need for white
supremacy. Its vaunted realism held, however, that the
future prosperity and success of the region depended upon
cooperation between the races based on a mutual appreciation of the rewards that lay ahead. In an editorial
on the subject, Grady stated his view that it was "impossible for the people of the south, either now or hereafter,
to get along without the negro." The black man was
necessary to Southern progress, he wrote, "and against
this necessity mere prejudice will break in vain."[20] On
another occasion he stated the commonly expressed New
South doctrine that the race question and economic
progress were inseparably bound together; the "glory
and prosperity of the South," he declared, depended upon

an intelligent understanding of their interconnection.[21] Watterson insisted in one of his editorials that the inter-dependence of the races meant that backwardness in the Negro would inevitably retard the white man's progress and must therefore be combated. Kelley argued similarly that a large, trained labor force was indispensable to economic growth, that the plentiful supply of Negro labor should be tapped, and that "the expertness and productive power of labor do not depend on the race, color, or previous condition of servitude of the laborer or artisan."[22]

Edmonds, who was less sanguine about the equality of capacity implied in his friend Kelley's argument, placed a different emphasis on the importance of Negro labor when he wrote that it was a key element in Southern development "because what white men plan is executed by the strong muscles of industrious negroes."[23] And, like the other New South spokesmen, Edmonds frequently expressed the faith that a new birth of Southern pros-perity would cause the race problem to vanish. Blasting Northern policies during the Reconstruction, and warning against further interference in the racial affairs of the South, he promised that "if the South is left to itself, if no inimical legislation interferes with the existing status, economic 'development' will solve all difficulties, and even the troublesome race question will be consigned to oblivion."[24] Thus grounding their argument in apparent realism, the New South prophets gave assurances that their program would preserve white supremacy, insure prosperity, and "solve" the race question.

If the reactionaries provided a useful foil for the New South program, a tiny band of radicals set it off to even greater advantage with a plea for racial equality that could be attacked in order to prove loyalty to the heritage of white supremacy. George Washington Cable, of New Orleans, was the only nationally prominent radical spokesman in the South of the 1880's. Already recognized as a distinguished author—some compared him favorably to Mark Twain and Henry James—Cable moved cautiously but firmly into the controversial debate over Negro rights. In 1885 he achieved national prominence with an essay on "The Freedman's Case in Equity," which appeared in the widely read *Century Magazine*. Cable's essay, which will be considered in more detail later, vigorously condemned the South's denial of constitutional rights to the Negro and issued a moving plea and a tightly reasoned argument for equal justice.[25] The *Century* editor invited Grady to publish a rebuttal and thus gave the leading New South spokesmen the opportunity to declare that Cable's equalitarian arguments, if heeded, would lead to racial amalgamation, the end of white supremacy, and the destruction of society. At the same time, he was given the opportunity to announce opposition to the reactionaries' desire for ruthless repression and praise the New South program of moderation as one that would guarantee liberty and equality to the Negro without sacrificing white supremacy.[26]

II

In rejecting both the reactionary and the radical assessment of the nature of the race problem, the New South spokesmen hoped to present their own program in such a way that it would satisfy the abstract demands of the

American creed of freedom and equality as well as the specific requirements of the Civil War and Reconstruction amendments to the Constitution. Their solution to the problem of freedom, which will be analyzed first, was in several ways a simpler task for their ingenuity than the problem of equality.

The antebellum philosophy of race relations was built on the concept of permanent slavery and it was on the unyielding conviction that the destruction of slavery had been a catastrophic error that the reactionaries took their stand. In contrast, the New South spokesmen boasted that emancipation was a blessing to both races, and many of them argued that slavery had been an error in the first place. Grady spoke for the entire group when he declared that a "higher and fuller wisdom" than that of the South had judged slavery to be wrong, and he expressed his pleasure "that the omniscient God held the balance of battle in His Almighty hand and that human slavery was swept forever from American soil."[27] Similarly, Haygood praised God for freeing the slaves and explained his own conversion from a pro-slavery apologist to an ardent defender of freedom as the result of an intrusion of "new and purer light."[28] Not all agreed with Watterson that slavery had "precipitated an unwilling people" into civil war, but most conceded that it had been a cancer eating at the national fabric; and the nationalism of the New South crusade, like the quest for economic regeneration, led logically to a condemnation of the institution which separated the sections and retarded Southern progress.[29]

The condemnation of slavery and the warm endorsement of Negro freedom thus formed the starting point of the New South departure in race relations. From this

position the New South men had to come to terms with
the most fundamental expression of the citizen's freedom
in a democratic republic: the right to vote. At the birth
of the nation the "American Creed" postulated that
right in general terms, but it was not until the reforms
of the Jacksonian era that white manhood suffrage became
the common practice. With the Reconstruction acts and
the Fifteenth Amendment racial restrictions were removed
and the constitutional requirement of Negro suffrage,
unaltered by the restoration of home rule, presented to
the New South advocates a specific test of their general
endorsement of Negro freedom. Constantly making a great
point of their realism—of dealing in facts, not theories—
they were nowhere confronted more solidly with a set of
facts than in the case of black suffrage. Writing in 1881,
Haygood brushed aside arguments over the wisdom or
constitutionality of the amendment with the declaration
that "the time is past for such arguments; facts and not
theories must be considered now." The fact, he believed,
was unmistakably clear: the Negro "will never be re-
enslaved; he will never be disfranchised."[30]

Haygood's optimistic assessment was typical of the
spirit of his influential book, *Our Brother in Black*, which
appeared just as the New South movement was becoming
fairly launched by its young advocates and formed a link
between them and the older-generation conservatives. In
a symposium in 1879, L. Q. C. Lamar claimed to know of
"no Southern man of influence or consideration" who believed in the possibility of disfranchisement. "Universal
suffrage being given as the condition of our political life,"
he wrote, "the negro once made a citizen cannot be placed
under any other condition."[31] In the same discussion,
Wade Hampton wrote that "it would be almost impossible

to disfranchise the negro."[32] Moreover, both Hampton and Lamar seemed to have no serious regrets. Hampton claimed to have championed limited Negro suffrage during the Reconstruction and Lamar stated that neither he nor his fellow Mississippians would disfranchise the Negro if the option were open to them.[33]

The views of men like Lamar and Hampton became doctrine with the New South spokesmen. An Atlanta *Constitution* editorial in 1880 announced categorically that "the people of the South as a whole . . . recognize the negro as a citizen and acknowledge his right to vote where he pleases and for whom he pleases."[34] Five years later Grady wrote his most serious and responsible essay on the Negro problem in reply to Cable's *Century* article. Scolding Cable for most of his views, Grady expressed displeasure over the manner in which the Negro had received the vote, but pledged himself and his movement to the continued defense of Negro suffrage.[35] Grady's view, like that of all the other New South spokesmen, was rooted in the belief that nothing could be done to alter the situation and that the wise and progressive leader would therefore react positively and creatively to the world as it was. A contributor to the *Century Magazine* accurately caught the mood when he damned the racial views of Southern reactionaries and announced that "opposed to these errors is the spirit of the New South. . . . The negro must be educated in the responsibilities of citizenship, and this training must be made practical by the use of the ballot."[36]

The New South prophets' endorsement of Negro suffrage as an inalienable right of free men was accompanied by a practical limitation of major significance that drew a distinction between participation in the political process and domination of it. The Reconstruction image of "Negro domination" formed the bedrock and justification for the distinction. Like nearly all other Southerners, the New South spokesmen cultivated the myth of Negro rule after the war and chorused their condemnation of the way in which the Negro was thrust into the political life of the region. This view was expressed by the most sincere and articulate spokesmen such as Haygood and Page;[37] it was canonized by the popular Grady, who decried the "great error" of suddenly thrusting an illiterate and inferior people into political responsibility and keeping them there with "the Federal drum-beat" and the glimmer of Union bayonets.[38] In Grady's mind the problem before the New South spokesmen was a staggering one. Inheriting an almost impossible situation, they would stand by past decisions; but, at the same time, they must prevent the recurrence of the previous catastrophe. Never had "such a task been given to mortal stewardship," he wrote.[39] Their assignment was "to carry in peace and honor and prosperity two dissimilar races with equal . . . political rights."[40] To do this, they must discover a formula that would permit the Negro, as a free man, to exercise a free ballot, but to exercise it in such a way that white men would never again be deprived of the control of the region.

The formula was readily discovered in the conviction that political control should rest with men of superior wealth, character, and intelligence—three words that permeate the literature of the Negro question. No one appeared to doubt that Negroes as a group were inferior in all three categories and none felt that a society ruled by what might be regarded as a Jeffersonian "aristocracy of talent" could legitimately be accused of compromising the "American Creed." The formula was especially justified, the New South advocates felt, because it carried with it an attractive quid pro quo. In return for acquiescence in white domination, Negroes could expect to exercise the ballot as a means of developing their sense of responsibility. Page urged upon them the kind of attitude and training made famous by Booker T. Washington at Tuskegee Institute. This approach, he believed, would prepare them for increasing participation in the affairs of government as responsible and intelligent citizens. The road ahead was a hard one, Page warned, but at least it led to the possibility of rich rewards. Reconstruction, with its deceptively charming doctrine of immediate power and authority, had only proved the necessity of a longer training period. Preparing for responsibility under Southern white tutelage (or under Negroes who agreed with the New South creed) was the only realistic course to be followed. In the end, Page promised, whites would come to recognize and reward merit wherever it showed itself, in whatever skin color.[41] The formula which Page spelled out, and which was generally accepted by other New South spokesmen, concluded with the argument that political freedom was not political license and that to be meaningful it must be earned. This, they believed, did no violence to the American commitment to freedom and was the only way to make the Fifteenth Amendment a working reality.

Most of the New South spokesmen were less optimistic about the potential of the Negro than Page, and although they frequently endorsed the advancementthrough-training philosophy their fundamental reason for supporting Negro suffrage was rooted in considerations of practical politics. The Redeemer state governments— the groups that engineered the fights for home rule and dominated the region until the Populist uprising of the 1890's—were overwhelmingly oriented toward commercial and industrial interests. Representatives of a new kind of capitalistic class in the South, they created the ideal political environment for the flourishing of the New South creed. Recurrent assaults against Redeemer control were customarily led by men who either distrusted or openly condemned the New South doctrine. The success with which these dissident elements were defeated frequently depended upon the Redeemers' ability to court or coerce, as the case required, the Negro vote. With dependable regularity, that vote came down heavily on their side and thereby helped to keep in power the regimes most likely to forward the New South program.[42] Thus, despite the rhetoric which denigrated the importance of politics, the New South prophets understood that their fate was linked to Redeemed regimes supported by Negro votes.

Candid confessions of their opportunistic reason for support of Negro suffrage do not appear in the speeches and writings of the New South spokesmen, but the literature of the movement disguises them only thinly. Writing in 1879, Watterson declared that "he is a poor judge of human nature, or else very ignorant of the Southern character, who does not know that the well-being of the negro must originate at home."[43] The implications of this statement, made more specific by New South writers in the 'eighties, were twofold: first, Negro political rights could be adequately protected only if Southerners were not coerced by outside forces and, second, with Negroes free to make their own political decisions they would support the Democratic Party—which was a euphemism for the dominant Redeemer wing of that party. Grady expressed the two related arguments well and frequently. In his New York address he promised justice for the Negro when determination of his fate was left "to those among whom his lot is cast, with whom he is indissolubly connected, and whose prosperity depends upon their possessing his intelligent sympathy and confidence."[44] He frequently insisted that the Negro's natural inclination was to support conservative whites, and he believed it unquestionable that "the negro will find that his best friend is the southern democrat."[45]

Throughout the 'eighties there was a latent division in the thinking of the New South spokesmen that portended the bitter clashes of the 'nineties over disfranchisement. A few of the spokesmen, most notably Page and Haygood, sincerely advocated the Tuskegee philosophy of advancement-through-training that promised eventual recognition and influence to Negroes of merit. In this spirit, they appeared to think in terms of temporary political subservience and could imagine a different kind of racial pattern existing at some time in the future. A larger group, however, followed Grady through a maze of ambivalence, paying homage when the occasion demanded to the theory of reward through merit, but more frequently asserting permanent political subservience as the *raison d'être* of Southern politics. Writing for the New York *Ledger* in 1889, Grady justified white domination in the first instance on the basis of the wealth-intelligence-character formula. Next, however, he compromised this rationale by asserting a purely racial justification: the white race was the superior race and would never "submit to the domination of the inferior race."[46] In one of his most outspoken statements, at the Dallas State Fair in 1887, he proclaimed categorically that white domination must be maintained forever; that infallible decree ordained the political subservience of the Negro race and that any attempt to alter or reverse the relationship between the races must be "resisted at all points and at all hazards—because the white race is the superior race."[47]

It is not likely that Grady and his followers ever seriously examined the intellectual contradiction of their arguments. Cable tried to raise the issue, in his rejoinder to Grady's *Century* essay, when he approved the character-intelligence-property formula but revealed its incompatibility with a rigid racial criterion for rulership. "Which are you really for," he asked Grady, "the color line, or the line of character, intelligence, and property that divides between those who have and those who have not 'the right to rule'? You dare not declare for an inflexible color line; such an answer would shame the political intelligence of a Russian."[48] But Cable's effort was largely wasted, and the Grady wing of the New South movement continued happily declaring belief in both the character-intelligence-property formula and the color line. They were aware of the more superficial aspects of Darwinian theory, as Guion Johnson has pointed out, and they sometimes appealed to it to explain that the Negro was on a lower scale in the process of evolution. In this manner they believed they found justification for the doctrine of permanent inferiority by insisting that the Negro could not "jump stages," so to speak, and must therefore remain subservient to the white man.[49] With this added to their other arguments they maintained that freedom, universal manhood suffrage, and white supremacy not only were not incompatible but were mutually bound together.

III

Satisfied that they had resolved the problem of freedom, the New South spokesmen faced the complex issue of equality. Deeply rooted in the American ideology, the concept of equality was made concrete for Negroes by the first section of the Fourteenth Amendment, which draped over them the cloak of federal protection against discriminatory action by state governments. The union of the abstract idea with the mandate of the Constitution raised one more dilemma for the New South men. Anxious to justify their racial policies in a way that would offend neither the spirit of equality nor the requirement to make and enforce state laws in a nondiscriminatory fashion, they were committed by their racial beliefs to prevent what they called "fusion" or "amalgamation" and they believed that racial separation was essential to that purpose. This "duality," Robert Bingham asserted, "is an absolute necessity. The load of the country in the South must continue to be pulled by a double horse team, so to speak, with the white horse 'in the lead' and the black horse on the 'off side,' to use the farmer's phrase."[50]

Cable had agreed with Grady in opposing fusion, which he called "the maxim of barbarous times and peoples," but beyond that the two men found little common ground in their debate.[51] As Cable viewed it, the New South program, clearly "predicated on white supremacy," meant a catastrophic abridgment of human rights.[52] Its proponents regarded the Negro as an alien, a menial, and a reprobate, and allegations to the contrary were but poor attempts to disguise their true objectives. He believed that the New South prophets really intended to establish a caste system, almost as rigid in its denial of Negro rights as slavery had been. Already, he wrote, there was evidence to support his view, for there was "scarcely one public relation of life in the South" where the Negro was "not arbitrarily and unlawfully compelled to hold toward the white man the attitude of an alien, a menial, and a probable reprobate, by reason of his race and color."[53]

Vigorously challenging Cable's charge that they intended to abridge anyone's rights, the New South spokesmen made no attempt to deny their belief that inherent racial differences had to be recognized and accounted for in public policy. The Negro was an inferior being and no realistic program could ignore that fact. At the Dallas State Fair, Grady declared that God, not man, was responsible for the differences between the races. "Behind the laws of man . . . stands the law of God," he announced, and "what God hath separated let no man join together." The special characteristics of each race were divinely ordained and stood as "markers of God's will." No man, then, should "tinker with the work of the Almighty."[54] Of all God's races, Grady continued, the "Anglo-Saxon" had been designated to play the role of superior. Thus, the question before the South was "a race issue. Let us come to this point and stand here."[55]

Carried away by the enthusiastic response of his Dallas audience (they were in tears by the end of the address[56]), Grady lingered on the subject of Anglo-Saxon superiority. The quaintness of his logic was surpassed only by the eloquence of his delivery. The Chinese Exclusion Act, recently passed by Congress, was universally approved, he felt, not because the Chinese were ignorant or corrupt but because their admission in large numbers would establish an "inferior" race in a "homoge-nous" country of Anglo-Saxons. At decisive points in history, he continued, Anglo-Saxon blood had proved its superiority. It "fed Alfred when he wrote the charter of English liberty" and it had "humbled Napoleon at Water-loo." The last boast had interesting implications for the South which Grady did not pursue: the inference would seem to be that the French, non-Anglo-Saxons, were members of an "inferior," and therefore an "alien," race. Presumably, he did not mean to cast aspersions on those who traced their ancestry to William the Conqueror, nor does it appear reasonable to believe that he would deny "social equality" to the Legares and Hugers of Charles-ton; but he was certain that America had been "conse-crated . . . forever as the home of the Anglo-Saxon, and the theater of his transcending achievement," and that challenges from an alien and inferior Negro race must be understood and defeated.[57]

Anglo-Saxonism was a favorite subject of the New South spokesmen, just as it was with other Southerners. What the comments lacked in sophistication they made up for in fervor. Tompkins declared that as long as there was "any question as to race supremacy, our duty lies first in saving for each State Anglo-Saxon control."[58] Bingham wrote that the "Anglo-Saxon man, God's king of men, will be and must be ahead of the African man . . . and any forced change of the relations will be fatal to the weaker race."[59] Throughout his long editorship of the *Manufacturers' Record*, Edmonds repeatedly declared his faith in the "superiority of the Southern people." He believed the South to be "largely a homogenous popula-tion; Anglo-Saxon to a greater extent than any other large center of the world," and Anglo-Saxonism, he

thought, was "a tremendous factor in the development of
. . . [the South's] interests and in safeguarding its political
affairs."[60]

Basing their justification of separate societies on the
assumed superiority of the Anglo-Saxon "race," the New
South spokesmen added a second argument designed to
prove that Negroes, no less than whites, preferred segregation. This was the contention that both races had inbred
instincts toward separation. Bishop Haygood explained
that the Negroes created their own churches after the
Civil War not out of fear or coercion, but in response to
an inherent instinctive wish. "People who build theories
out of facts," he wrote, "will study such a case as this."[61]
Following Haygood's admonition, the New South spokesmen pictured a harmonious bi-racial society in which
white and black mingled and cooperated in mutual tasks
but separated otherwise. The "intelligent and self-respect-
ing negroes," Grady wrote on one occasion, had not "the
slightest symptom of a desire to push themselves forward
into places where their presence would cause embarrassment or irritation, and the absence of such a desire is perfectly natural. It is the manifestation of the race instinct
. . . and it is attended with not the slightest feeling of
humiliation."[62] Putting the matter succinctly in a later
editorial, he wrote that "the tendency of each race—white
and black—is to gather about its own center. The force
is centripetal, not centrifugal."[63]

The instinct argument was doubly useful to the New
South spokesmen. On the one hand, it helped them to
create their desired image of a rational and humane system that rested on consent, not force. It thus served to
disguise the unilateral way in which Southern racial
policies were determined and, at the same time, reassured

suspicious Northerners that the New South's voluntary program of reconstruction looked to the Negro's interests. On the other hand, it made it easier for the whites to justify their desire to limit the areas of movement of Negroes and restrict contacts between the races. According to Grady, instinct performed the most essential function required in race relations: it was "the pledge of the integrity of each race, and of peace between the races. Without it, there might be a breaking down of all lines of division and a thorough intermingling of whites and blacks." Intermingling, he concluded, would lead to amalgamation and amalgamation to internecine warfare.[64]

As Grady defined the New South doctrine of race relations he wrote loosely of the relationship between racial "integrity," on the one hand, and "social equality," on the other. Neither term was ever clearly explained, but the Cable-Grady exchange in the *Century Magazine* and Grady's editorial comments on Cable make it evident that Grady saw no need to distinguish between constitutionally guaranteed civil rights and personal social privileges, lumping both together under the emotionally explosive rubric "social equality." Thus he reacted editorially to Cable's first *Century* article with vehemence, declaring that "we have for a long time feared that Mr. Geo. W. Cable would come to be a mischievous element in the negro problem. He has exhibited a growing wrong-headedness on this subject, that, starting from a rather sentimental admiration for the idealized quadroon, has developed into a confirmed negromania."[65] With only slightly less restraint, Grady wrote in his formal rebuttal that Cable's advocacy of equal civil rights was a demand that "white and black shall intermingle everywhere," a doctrine that Grady called "impossible," "mischievous," and "monstrous."[66]

Cable and a small group of other liberal writers, both white and black, strove energetically to disentangle the confused concepts of social privileges and civil rights and to dismantle the racist assumptions that underlay Grady's case for segregation. They believed that Southern actions, based on a faulty understanding of the real issues, increasingly tended to blunt the Negro's development and would therefore make impossible the realization of the New South dream. To begin with, they dismissed as irrelevant the issues of social equality and amalgamation. J. C. Price, a Negro educator, believed that history disproved the notion "that to grant a man his civil rights is to make him necessarily a social equal and companion." The poor whites of the South, Price observed, enjoyed their civil rights, but despite their "Anglo-Saxon" blood they were not accepted as social equals by the dominant class of whites. To assume that a similar enjoyment of civil rights by Negroes would lead to social equality, Price concluded, "implies too great a compliment to the Negro."[67] Cable called social equality the "huge bugbear" of Southern fears and continued with the argument that "amalgamation" of the races could most effectively be avoided by rigorous protection of civil rights.[68] He believed that there was little or no racial mixture in communities where Negroes were treated as first-class citizens but that in caste societies the opposite was true. In the South, he wrote, amalgamation took place "in proportion to the rigor, the fierceness, and the injustice with which . . . excommunication from the common rights of man has fallen upon the darker race."[69] Social equality and amalgamation, he concluded, were quite beside the point. "We are debating," he insisted, "the Freedman's title to a totally impersonal freedom in the enjoyment of all impersonal rights."[70]

Conceding that Negroes were, by nearly every accepted standard of measurement, inferior to the whites, Grady's opponents rejected the racial explanation of the inferiority. Lewis H. Blair, a white Virginian, dismissed as nonsense the notion of the divine ordination of segregation and argued that the Negro's lowly state was due to imposed circumstances that had "always been adverse to improvement."[71] Amory Dwight Mayo, whose general sympathy for the New South movement was keen, urged Southerners to view the plight of the Negro in the light of world history. He believed that such a perspective would show that the "defects" of the Negro were not "special race qualities." They could, in fact, be "paralleled by the immorality, ignorance, superstition, and helplessness" of oppressed groups of other races.[72] Cable claimed that Southern policy, based on faulty notions of race, tended increasingly toward compulsory segregation—at the "steamer landing, railway platform, theater, concert hall, art display, public library, public school, courthouse, church"—and thereby perpetuated the shortcomings allegedly the products of racial characteristics. It was like prohibiting a man from entering the water until he could swim; and the South, fearing that the Negro might learn, "hangs millstones about his neck."[73] Finally, George Henry White, the last Negro to represent North Carolina in Congress, told the House of Representatives that Southern racist views created a vicious circle out of which there appeared to be no escape:

> It is easy for these gentlemen to taunt us with our inferiority, at the same time not mentioning the causes of this inferiority. It is rather hard to be accused of shiftlessness and idleness when the accuser of his own motion

closes the avenues for labor and industrial pursuits to us. It is hardly fair to accuse us of ignorance when it was made a crime under the former order of things to learn enough about letters even to read the Word of God.

While I offer no extenuation for any immorality that may exist among my people, it comes with rather poor grace from those who forced it upon us for two hundred and fifty years to taunt us with that shortcoming.[74]

Except for the Northerner Mayo, none of the criticisms above came from New South spokesmen. But there were some members of the movement, notably Haygood, Page, and Watterson, whose views were more liberal than Grady's. For the most part, they regarded social equality as an unreal issue and they were less likely to confuse civil rights with social privileges. Watterson stated his support of equal civil rights on several occasions. He was doubtful about finding a way to "argue away or force down . . . the caste of color," but he wrote that "none more earnestly than the Courier-Journal desires to see this question happily settled."[75] In much stronger language, Page disagreed with the belief that the Negroes were a threat to the whites. "Our civilization menaced by the Negro?" Page asked. "That's a lie and you know it. The only way in which the Negro can be a menace to our civilization is by his ignorance."[76] Haygood wrote that he would not "entangle" his discussion "with the question of the relative capacity of the white and black races" and he found the debate over social equality quite pointless.[77] "There never was in this world, in any nation or community, such a thing as social equality, and there never will be," he wrote in 1889. "The social spheres arrange themselves to suit themselves, and no laws . . .

will change the social affinities and natural selections of men."[78] Both Haygood and Page emphasized the importance of character and training, in contrast to race. "If the negro be a bad man," Haygood wrote, "he is a constant menace to peace and good order. Neither more nor less a menace on account of his color, but a menace on account of his character." On the question of civil rights he was equally outspoken, stating bluntly that "the law does not know color or condition in its definitions; the administrators of the law should not know color."[79]

These qualifications of the Grady doctrine of permanent inferiority—and the recognition of "social equality" as an empty shibboleth—highlight an important aspect of the liberal, minority wing of the New South movement. However, these men agreed with Grady and the majority that the New South would be a dual society with the whites in the role of superiors. Whatever measure of equality the Negro might enjoy—and men like Haygood and Page foresaw more than Grady did— would derive in part from the fact that he was a free man but more significantly from the largesse and judgment of the more fortunate white rulers. Basing their judgments on practical considerations rather than on pseudo-scientific racial theories, the liberal wing, like the larger and louder Grady wing, assigned the Negro to an inferior status which would inevitably compromise his civil rights.

IV

Cable concluded his discussion of "The Freedman's Case in Equity" with the warning that "the South stands on her honor before the clean equities of the [race] issue." The moral issue—the question of honor—which Cable believed lay at the heart of the debate was "no longer whether constitutional amendments, but whether the eternal principles of justice, are violated."[80] He despaired for the future when he could no longer doubt that the moral issue was being buried under layers of empty platitudes. With a summary judgment of Grady's racial views, he asked rhetorically: "Could any one more distinctly or unconsciously waive the whole question of right and wrong?"[81] The question drove to a sensitive nerve, for the New South literature was permeated with pronouncements on right and wrong, justice and injustice. From a variety of sources—dedication to the abstract ideas of liberty and equality; a strong commitment to nationalism; and a need to allay Northern suspicion—the New South spokesmen developed an obvious concern to formulate a critique of their racial program that would satisfy every reasonable demand of justice and honor.

One aspect of their method derived from the growing national dedication to pragmatism, a mode of thought that came naturally to the New South prophets. The pragmatist's stress upon the practical results of experience, as opposed to abstract theoretical considerations, provided a method of analysis that was admirably suited to the complex moral situation which the race question created. Haygood, for example, revealed this clearly when he conceded that segregation in public schools engendered a "spirit of caste" among the whites and, in a strict sense, compromised the full rights of Negroes. But these "theoretical" considerations could not stand alone as guides to action and, in fact, they were offset by experiential knowledge which taught that separate schools were "best" for both races. The "facts" were, Haygood wrote, that

"1. Southern white children, as a class, won't sit at the same desks with negro children; 2. Southern black children, as a class, don't want to sit at the same desks with white children." This mutual desire for unmixed schools, based on a sound knowledge of reality, should be honored, Haygood wrote, and should give "trouble to no soul of man, except to a small class of fanatics, who feel that all things human must yield to their fancies."[82] The lesson of the school house, as Haygood taught it, was applied by the New South spokesmen to other areas and it became their general guide to peace and prosperity. Negroes would recognize that they could not repeat the proven errors of the Reconstruction period and would cultivate a sense of patience rooted in the understanding that full citizenship could come to them only in a slow, evolutionary process built on tangible accomplishments.

Rising from the bottom—a hackneyed idea before Booker T. Washington immortalized it in 1895—was an essential concept in the New South doctrine, and what it implied fitted well into the pragmatic conception of justice that pictured the New South program as a realistic attempt to provide opportunity for Negro advancement after an era of misguidance. Men like Page could become rapturous when writing of the possibilities:

> To teach the Negro to read, whether English or Greek, or Hebrew, butters no parsnips. To make the Negro work, that is what his master did in one way and hunger has done in another; yet both of these left Southern life where they found it. But to teach the Negro to do skilful work, as men of all races that have risen have worked,— responsible work, which *is* education and character; and most of all when Negroes so teach Negroes to do this that they will teach others with a missionary zeal that puts all ordinary philanthropic efforts to shame,—this is to change

the whole economic basis of life and the whole character of a people.[83]

To "change the whole economic basis of life and the whole character of a people" was a tall order, but the New South spokesmen insisted that their realistic integration of the Negro into the new economic life of the region would do just that. Watterson expressed the faith in a pithy epigram. "Under the old system," he wrote, "we paid our debts and walloped our niggers. Under the new we pay our niggers and wallop our debts."[84] In the columns of the *Manufacturers' Record* Edmonds wrote frequently and optimistically about the reliability of Negro labor, its importance to Southern economic development, and the happiness the Negro found in his new opportunities. Negroes were not the "half-paid, half-starved people that some who have never been South have claimed," he wrote; and if the "cranky sentimentalists and the rascally politicians, both North and South, would let him alone to enjoy the fruits of his labor, he would continue happy and contented, and be what he is, the most important working factor in the development of the great and varied resources of our country."[85] Like Edmonds, Grady derided the "purely sentimental" friendship which Northerners expressed for Negroes and contrasted it with the realistic economic opportunities provided by the New South program.[86] He believed that the Negroes of Georgia, typical of all Southern Negroes, "are prospering and are contented," and argued that the material improvement in the life of the Negro honored the black man's ambitions and vindicated the good intentions of the Southern white.[87] A pragmatic evaluation, then, persuaded the New South spokesmen that the larger demands of racial justice were fulfilled by their program, and they dismissed with injured indignation Cable's allegation that the New South creed waived the issue of right and wrong.

To the more specific demands of the Fourteenth Amendment, the New South spokesmen had a response that satisfied their consciences and, after 1896, met the test of the Constitution as well. Grady marked out the lines of approach in an 1883 editorial, applauding the Supreme Court's decision in the *Civil Rights Cases*. Entitled "Where to Draw the Line," the editorial declared:

> The line has been drawn just where it should be. Just where nature drew it, and where justice commends. The negro is entitled to his freedom, his franchise, to full and equal legal rights, to his share in the privileges of government and to such share in its administration as his integrity and intelligence will justify. This he ought to have and he must have. Social equality he can never have. He does not have it in the north, or in the east, or in the west. On one pretext or another he is kept out of hotels, theaters, schools and restaurants, north as well as south.
>
> The truth is, the negro does not want social equality. He prefers his own schools, his own churches, his own hotels, his own societies, his own military companies, his own place in the theater. He is uncomfortable and ill at ease when he is forced anywhere else. Even on the railroads he prefers his own car, if he can be secure from the intrusion of disorderly persons. It is best, for his sake, as well as for general peace and harmony, that he should in all these things have separate accommodation.[88]

The formula that emerged from this editorial was expanded by Grady in subsequent writings and by 1885 it had an attractive name: equal but separate. Commenting editorially on Cable's first *Century* essay, Grady wrote that "the *Constitution* holds that there should be equal accommodation for the two races, but separate. . . . In every theater . . . there should be a space set apart for the colored people, with precisely the same accommodations that are given to the white people for the same price. . . . The same rule should be observed in railroads, schools, and elsewhere."[89] The distinction Cable made between social privileges and civil rights was ignored by Grady, who placed public schools and restaurants as well as street cars and literary clubs in the same category, recommending segregation in all of them and, in one of his last articles on the subject, "separate accommodation everywhere."[90]

In 1896 the United States Supreme Court formally announced its approval of the equal but separate doctrine in the case of *Plessy v. Ferguson*. The decision was restricted to legislation requiring separate facilities on the railroads, but its implications and its subsequent application to other types of segregation were a powerful vindication of the New South doctrine of racial equality within a framework of separate societies. Hammering out the logic of the decision for more than a decade before it was proclaimed by the Court, the New South spokesmen repeatedly emphasized their commitment to the "equal" part of the formula. As Grady put it in 1883, on the occasion of the *Civil Rights Cases* decision, the South would demonstrate that "while she could never have been driven by duress into doing what was clearly wrong . . . she will not be tempted by the removal of all restraint into doing anything that is less than right."[91] Separation, he declared later, would never mean unequal treatment or

that the Negro was "outlawed" in the South.[92] Nor would
it engender among Negroes a sense of debasement, for it
resulted from the ineluctable force of "natural instinct,"
which the Negroes obeyed "without the slightest ill-nature
or without any sense of disgrace."[93]

The racial creed of the New South spokesmen received
a full hearing in the newspapers, national journals, and
books of the time, and it was advanced with all the moral
righteousness necessary to obliterate the vanishing tradition of abolitionism and radicalism and to implant in the
national mind the image of a South that would guarantee
to the Negro a lasting era of freedom, equality, justice,
respect, and opportunity. With sympathy and understanding from the rest of the nation, Grady wrote, the South
would bring its program to fruition. Then the race problem, which once threatened to destroy the South, would
be seen as a blessing. Accusing fingers could no longer
be pointed at the region. It would "stand upright among
the nations and challenge the judgment of man and the
approval of God, in having worked out . . . this last and
surpassing miracle of human government."[94]

5
The Vital Nexus

Furl that Banner, softly, slowly!
Treat it gently—it is holy—
    For it droops above the dead.
Touch it not—unfold it never,
Let it droop there, furled forever,
    For its people's hopes are dead!

—FATHER ABRAM RYAN[1]

Those who use the word [New South] do
not thereby proclaim the history of the
South discarded; do not confess themselves
"unhung rebels," and that they are very
sorry—nothing of the kind do they admit.

—JOHN C. CALHOUN NEWTON[2]

And no history is a matter of record; it is
a matter of faith.

—JAMES BRANCH CABELL[3]

The New South spokesmen directed their program to the present and to the future; their purpose was to rectify the errors of the past. At the same time, they understood the attachment which bound Southerners to their historic memories and were aware of the swollen meaning that now inflated the Southern past as a result of defeat. The bitter quarrels that had divided Southern society during the war were stored in the attic of memory during the chastening aftermath of Appomattox, and a new unity of spirit emerged, expressing itself in a deep reverence for the old regime. At the very moment of its death, as Robert Penn Warren writes, "the Confederacy entered upon its immortality."[4] In this situation the New South spokesmen understood instinctively that no program of reform could do violence to a universally cherished past and hope to succeed.

With the death of an old way of life there came naturally to Southerners the conviction that the history of their region would forever be divided into two eras, separated by the war. Walter Hines Page grew up with this sense of the passage from one way of life to another. Dissecting his native North Carolina through the device of an autobiographical novel, he wrote that the death of his grandfather, who for him represented the Old South, made it appear that "the history of the world fell into two periods—one that had gone before, and the other that now began." When the old man was buried, Page recalled, "we seemed to be burying a standard of judgment, a social order, an epoch."⁵ This burial theme, combined with the sense of an unmistakable divide between the two eras, raised difficult problems for the New South spokesmen. How would they inter the past reverently, yet build a civilization drastically different from the old regime? How would they lead their people out of the ashes of one era into the glory of a new one without repudiating those very qualities which had caused the collapse of the Confederacy in the first place? How, in short, could they relate the New South creed to the values and aspirations of the past?

I

John Randolph Tucker, a proud, self-styled son of the Old Order, doubted that it could be done. Sharing his fears with the 1887 graduating class of South Carolina College, he declared: "You look to a future—a new future; I to the past—the old past. Have they no nexus? Is the New South cut off from the Old South? Is the past of our Southern land to be buried, and the new era to forget and wholly discard its memories, its ideas, and its principles?"⁶ Pleading for a remembrance of the old by the new, Tucker nonetheless appeared to fear the worst, and the subsequent notes of lament that he struck in his address were sounded again and again in the last two decades of the nineteenth century. Charles Colcock Jones, Jr., the colorful Georgian and bombastic president of the

Confederate Survivors' Association, assailed every annual gathering of veterans with copious illustrations of the undermining of Southern civilization put in process by the New South movement. "I call you to witness," he exhorted in his Memorial Day address of 1889, "that by false impressions and improper laudations of the new order of affairs, men in our midst have sought to minimize the capabilities of the past, and unduly to magnify the development of the present."[7] Under what he characterized as the "absurd guise of a New South," Jones alleged that the principles of the old regime were being swiftly discarded in favor of the mammonism of the New Order.[8] He pleaded for resistance to the onslaught; he would "covet a remembrance and an observation of the patriotism, the purity, the manhood, the moderation, and the honesty of the days that are gone."[9]

Writing at the end of the 'eighties, Tucker and Jones expressed no novel ideas but gave force and colorful imagery to a theme of doubt and despair that was already two decades old. Indeed, a dominant ingredient in the pattern of Old South idolatry which they expanded with such conviction had been forecast as early as 1866 by Edward A. Pollard, the Virginian whose Richmond *Examiner* achieved fame as a bitter critic of the Davis administration during the war. To a long, tedious, often opinionated history of the war, published in the year after Appomattox, Pollard gave the title *The Lost Cause*. Besides furnishing the name for what would become in time an obsessive Southern cult, Pollard concluded his history with a jeremiad that would echo through the next generation. "It is to be feared," he wrote, "that in the present condition of the Southern states, losses will be experienced greater than the immediate inflictions of fire and sword."[10] The greater losses were not, Pollard made clear, necessarily to be inflicted upon the South by a vengeful and victorious North. Rather, the danger was within. Speaking of his fellow Southerners, he warned:

> The danger is that they will lose their literature, their former habits of thought, their intellectual self-assertion, while they are too intent upon recovering the mere *material* prosperity, ravaged and impaired by the war. There are certain coarse advisers who tell the Southern people that the great ends of their lives now are to repair their stock of national wealth; to bring in Northern capital and labour; to build mills and factories and hotels and gilded caravansaries; and to make themselves rivals in the clattering and garish enterprise of the North. This advice has its proper place. But there are higher objects than the Yankee *magna bona* of money and display, and loftier aspirations than the civilization of material things. In the life of nations, as in that of the individual, there is something better than pelf, and the coarse prosperity of dollars and cents.[11]

Warning against those "time-servers" in the cause of material progress who would "fill their bellies with husks" while the traditions of the region were subverted, Pollard called for a "war of ideas" to recover and perpetuate the ideals of the old regime.[12]

The "war of ideas" for which Pollard called was devotedly waged by a small band of other champions of the Lost Cause in the years after Appomattox. Like Pollard, they found it impossible to conceive of a vital nexus between the ideals of the antebellum era and the emerging New South creed. Albert Taylor Bledsoe, the former University of Virginia professor whose writings on slavery had earned him a prominent place in the ranks of pro-slavery theoreticians, took up the editorship of the *Southern Review* after the war to damn Yankee civilization.[13] A doctrinaire latter-day agrarian, he declared that virtue and innocence sprang from close connection with the soil. Industrialization, urbanization, and "materiality" —which he designated as the "great defect of Northern civilization"—undermined the spiritual character of the people. The "whole spirit of Christianity," he felt, opposed Northern civilization; and for the South to enter upon a fierce competition for industry would surely invite the sacrifice of the "fine sense of honor which formed the beautiful enamel of Southern character."[14]

Another Virginian, Robert L. Dabney, much respected for his achievements and views as a religious leader, was similarly depressed by a course of events which seemed to him to repudiate the principles of the old regime. Summing up the views he had held since the war, he warned the students of Hampden-Sydney College in 1882 that a now-decadent country seemed to regard the principles of the Old South as "too elevated" to be of relevance any longer. He would have the youth of the South think otherwise. The most pernicious doctrine they could accept, he warned, was the notion that "the surest way to retrieve your prosperity will be to BECOME LIKE THE CONQUERORS." The people who "make selfish, material good its god," he declared, "is doomed."[15]

Bledsoe and Dabney and others who found the new age uncongenial thus heaped abuse on what they considered to be the brutal materialism of Northern civilization and, ineluctably, they came to interpret the New South movement as a new and sinister form of scalawaggery: a profoundly misguided attempt to install the god of Yankee civilization in the shaken temples of the land of purity. Thus, by the time Tucker and Jones and others were hurling their epithets at Grady and Edmonds and their allies, the notion of a bitter conflict between the principles of the Old and the New South was well established. According to this view, the progressive triumph of the ideals of the New South was premised upon the repudiation and annihilation of the values of the Old South.

The response which Pollard's somber augury of 1866 found in the years of the New South crusade created a historical tradition that survives in the works of twentieth-century scholars. In 1952, for example, the editors of an anthology of Southern literature declared that between 1870 and 1900 "there arose in the South two conflicting ideological groups" whose views were diametrically opposed.[16] These rival groups engaged in a contest whose essential nature two distinguished historians described as a difference "between those who looked to the past and those who looked to the future."[17] To many historians and especially to those who were part of the Vanderbilt Agrarian movement in the 1930's, those who looked to the future—the New South prophets—cast only glances of derision at a past which they condemned. Frank L. Owsley declared that the New South creed involved the "repudiation, more or less complete, of the Old South";[18] and Herman C. Nixon was persuaded that the " 'New South' came to imply that there had been an 'Old South' deserving of repudiation . . . and that a Southern economic revolution, entirely beneficent, had occurred without any evolutionary background."[19] Writing of the cotton mill development of the 'eighties, Robert S. Cotterill, the 1948 president of the Southern Historical Association, insisted that contemporaries, in their enthusiasm, "all agreed that it was new; it was a revolution, unrelated to the past, barren of ancestry, destitute of inheritance."[20] In a more recent and comprehensive judgment, William B. Hesseltine characterized the New South movement as one that would "abandon its past, forsake its rural folkways, and discard the romantic notions and constitutional theories which led to disastrous defeat—to build a new society on a Northern model."[21]

Two related themes appear in this thesis of a New South–Old South conflict. On the one hand, the New South spokesmen are depicted as realistic, hardheaded men of affairs who, wedded uncritically to nationalism and economic progress, abandoned romanticism, denied the existence of a treasured heritage, and determined to repudiate their past in order to clear the way for an industrial utopia of the future. On the other hand, they are described, with apparent logic, as men who saw neither nationalism nor industrial development in the Old South and therefore advertised their program as "barren of ancestry, destitute of inheritance." The two themes, united in an attractive thesis of total hostility between the old and the new, leave no room for interconnecting values and traditions.

The thesis misleads more than it enlightens. To be sure, it is true that the New South movement was vigorously opposed and that the Lost Cause mystique generally served as the rationale for the opposition. It is also possible to argue, depending upon what one considers to be central to the Southern experience, that the New South program, in its essence, implied the abandonment of critical Old South values. It is not true, however, that the New South spokesmen were, or considered themselves to be, detractors of the old regime. Neither evidence nor common sense will support such a view. On the contrary, one of the major and inescapable concerns of the New South advocates was to emphasize the "Southernness" of their movement and to romanticize the past out of which it came, to which it was related, and whose essential aspirations it was to fulfill.

The literature of the New South movement is permeated with a sense of the organic relationship between the old and the new. Out of this literature two complementary patterns emerge. First, the New South spokesmen fashioned an interpretation of the region's past that was congenial to the New South mentality; that is, they discovered in their history a heritage of nationalism and industrialism which, when properly understood, linked past, present, and future inseparably and harmoniously. Second, they almost invariably committed themselves to the romantic, idealized legend of the Old South—the same legend that was used by Tucker and Jones to excoriate them. Despite mutually exclusive aspects of the two views, most New South spokesmen found no difficulty in subscribing to both and, as will be seen, their double allegiance was crucial to their program.[22]

II

The hold of the Southern past on its sons, whether Old South idolaters or New South crusaders, is strikingly illustrated by a comparison of attitudes toward the old regime held by Northern and Southern advocates of a New South. Daniel A. Tompkins and William D. Kelley, two prominent spokesmen in the movement, shared identical views of the needs of the postbellum South. Both served the cause zealously, and when discussions were limited to the problems of the present one would find it difficult to determine which was the Southerner and which the Northerner. There was, however, a vital and illuminating difference between the two in their attitudes toward the old regime. Kelley, a Northerner whose sympathies had once been with the abolitionists, owed no emotional commitments to the region he proposed to save. He felt no pang of conscience, no reservations, no crisis of identity while developing a devastating critique of the old regime and broadcasting it throughout the South.[23] Tompkins, on the other hand, had roots in the plantation tradition and his emotional ties, whatever his economic theories, were with the land of his birth. A distant cousin of John C. Calhoun, Tompkins found much to admire in the early nationalism of the South Carolinian and often reminded his fellow Southerners that Calhoun, too, had once subscribed to the New South goals of industrialization and nationalism. Thus, while Tompkins happily shared Kelley's critique of the economic aspects of the Old South, he would not follow the Pennsylvanian into a condemnation of the moral values and intellectual qualities of his forebears.[24]

Like Kelley, the Northerner Alexander K. McClure, who made modest contributions to the New South movement, declared that "the Old South is dead. It has passed away; it is buried; it is forgotten."[25] But the Methodist bishop from Georgia, Atticus G. Haygood, ever reverent toward the past, could scarcely agree that "it is forgotten." To ask any Southerner, no matter how committed to change, to repudiate his past would be like asking New Englanders to prove their "intolerance of persecution by declaring Cotton Mather to have been a hypocrite and a villain."[26]

What the Southern leaders in the movement searched for, and quickly found, was a reading of the past which would prove conclusively that, in the words of the clergyman John C. Calhoun Newton, those who stood for a New South "do not thereby proclaim the history of the South discarded; do not confess themselves 'unhung rebels,' and that they are very sorry—nothing of the kind do they admit."[27] Such a historical formula would be of little interest to men like Kelley and McClure; indeed, they would probably consider it a little subversive. But, to the Southerners, it was both an emotional and a strategic necessity.

The formula was found readily enough in the economic history of the institution of slavery. The spread and solidification of slavery in the early nineteenth century, according to the New South view, had bottled up capital in land and slaves, and had precluded the development of manufacturing on a significant scale. Before the perfection of Whitney's cotton gin and the opening up of the lands of the southwest, Tompkins argued, the South was well on the way to a bright industrial future. The natural course of Southern development was disrupted by the "peculiar institution" which was, in Tompkins's opinion, responsible "for the frightful calamity that the South has suffered."[28] Manufactures, he argued, had no chance in the contest with slavery, for "apace with all the growth of the South the institution of slavery was also growing, and the falling off of the development of Southern resources may be observed to have kept pace with the growth of slavery." Once the incubus was removed, "the former spirit of enterprise" began to show itself.²⁹ By the turn of the century, when manufactures and commerce had once again been established as an integral part of the Southern economy, Tompkins declared that the South had simply returned to its true and ancient ways.³⁰ Repeatedly, in pamphlets and in the pages of its own journals as well as in Edmonds's *Manufacturers' Record*, Tompkins outlined his method of joining the past with the present: the antebellum years, the years of the spread and dominance of slavery, had been but an interregnum, an interruption of the true course of Southern history. Therefore, those who espoused the cause of industry in the South need feel no sense of repudiation; rather, they were the keepers of the older, authentic tradition.

Edmonds reiterated Tompkins's comments on the state of manufacturing in the early nineteenth century and he likewise stressed the limiting effects that slavery had on industrial development. On one occasion he characterized the role of slavery in the Old South in an analogy to a steam engine. Southerners had wished to utilize the steam engine, he explained, but the Negro slave was forever sitting on the safety valve. Ultimately, an explosion came, in the form of the Civil War and Reconstruction. The New South had not been satisfied with a patched-up engine; a new one was built, and "this engine is now running on a good track, no longer obstructed by the rocks of debt, a disorganized labor system, and all the unmasked problems, political and business, against which the old engine so often bumped."³¹

Unlike Tompkins, however, Edmonds was not inclined to regard the antebellum period as an interregnum, despite the pernicious effects of slavery. Rather, he found in the industrial crusade of the 1840's and 1850's a continuation of the earlier trend as well as the genesis of the postbellum New South movement. Striking off one of his numerous pamphlets, he complained that people of his generation were "too prone to believe that the Old South was a non-progressive, pastoral country." Such beliefs were responsible for the wickedly unfair characterization of the New South as a bastard offspring.[32] Actually, Edmonds wrote on another occasion, a true reading of history would show that the New South was simply "taking up the unfinished work of the Old South so rudely interrupted by the shock of war";[33] it was but seeking, through "vigorous" effort, "to regain the relative position held in 1860."[34]

Tompkins and Edmonds, each in slightly different ways, thus found the nexus between the Old and the New South and both men penned many lines contesting the allegations of repudiation hurled at them by disciples of the Old South. Addressing a pamphlet to the youth of the region, Edmonds warned them against falling in with the "sentiment so industriously cultivated" about the relationship between the Old and the New South. "We are told that the New South is a new creation altogether different from the Old South," he wrote; and, sounding the note of distress, he complained that "verily, we almost believe [it] . . . ourselves." Such teachings, Edmonds averred, were completely false—false alike to the past, "to the present and to the future."[35] "The South of today is no novel creation," he asserted in another pamphlet. "It is an evolution."[36]

One of Edmonds's favorite themes in the pages of the *Manufacturers' Record* was the doctrine of a "revived South." Insisting that the antebellum period had produced "the greatest business leaders of that generation," he could not understand why many men of his day saw in the New South movement a repudiation of the past.[37] In viewing the New South as an "evolution," or as "revival of the Old South,"[38] Edmonds helped to weave a pattern industriously worked by the other New South spokesmen. Grady found that the New South was "simply the Old South under new conditions."[39] Less well-known advocates agreed. One explained that the New South was "the old South asserting herself under a new dispensation," while a second spoke simply of the "Renewed South."[40] Whether renewed, rejuvenated, reborn, or the paradoxical "new," it was always the South; and allegations of alien influence and paternity were bitterly resented.

Walter Hines Page was one of the anomalies in the New South movement. His credentials as a New South spokesman were validated by the Vanderbilt Agrarians in the 1930's, who regarded him as an enemy of the Southern tradition more formidable than Grady. Certainly he was the most intellectually sensitive of the New South prophets. No one reading his bitter "Mummy Letters" would accuse him of dropping a veil of fancy over the Old South, and, as the disillusioned pages of his autobiographical novel show, he regarded the cult of the Lost Cause as a liability of the first order.[41] Yet, in his own special way, Page performed an intellectual operation on the Old South which, in its ultimate significance, served the same purpose as the Edmonds-Tompkins formula.

To Page, the South had abandoned the course of wisdom and justice when it jettisoned the philosophy of Jefferson and substituted the narrow views of Calhoun, Yancey, and Davis. The South of the Age of Jefferson,

Page believed, had been innocent of militant sectionalism and sensitive to the problems of all its people, including the slaves. It had also, of course, played a dominant role in directing the fortunes of the nation. Disaster awaited at the end of the road from Monticello, which the South traveled from the 1820's onward. The Jeffersonian dream was abandoned on the journey. Page's biographer recounts the tragic contrasts which impressed themselves on Page's sensitive mind:

> Instead of a system of free white labour, the extension of slavery; instead of public schools supported at State expense, a system of privately managed instruction, shabby and inadequate, usually in the control of religious sects; instead of a great body of intelligent citizens, more than a third of the white population unable to read and write. Thus had the South turned its back on its democratic leader![42]

The about-face which Page now urged on Southerners did not, according to his view of history, constitute a repudiation of the Southern past. Like Tompkins, Page could look upon the prewar years as an interregnum and proclaim that the New South movement would vindicate the authentic Southern tradition—the tradition of Jefferson. Moreover, like the other New South spokesmen, Page did not urge, as some have alleged, that Northern civilization serve as the South's exclusive guide. There was plenty in the Southern past, he felt, to give sustenance to his movement. He made this clear in an article published early in his career. "The New South cannot build up its possible civilization merely by looking backward and sighing, nor yet by simply passing blindly forward

in the new paths that are now open." To achieve greatness the South needed to fuse reverence for the noble
qualities of the past with "vigorous work for the future."[43]

The attempt of the New South spokesmen to link
their movement with the Southern past thus involved the
development of historical formulas to underscore the
degree to which the South had once been both broadly
nationalistic and economically progressive. Advanced on
the eminently sensible grounds that internal opposition
to the movement would diminish in proportion to the
degree of "Southernness" that infused it, the argument
muted the revolutionary aspects of the New South program. The South, its aspiring leaders realized, had had
enough of revolutions; and no sane advocate of change
wished to be cast in the role of a revolutionary.

III

One of the ironies of Southern history lies in the simul-
taneous rise during the 1880's of both the New South
creed and the mythic image of the Old South. Sweet
"syrup of romanticism," to use Professor Woodward's
term, flowed over the Old South in the same decade that
the New South spokesmen's ideal of a bustling, rich, and
reconstructed South captured the American imagination.[44]
Joel Chandler Harris introduced Uncle Remus to the
general public in 1880 and Thomas Nelson Page's idyllic
old Virginia became a national treasure after the publication of "Marse Chan" in 1884.[45] Grady's landmark address before the New England Society of New York was

only two years later. To compound the irony, most of the New South spokesmen accepted the mythic view of the past, rarely failing to preface a New South pronouncement with warm praise and nostalgic sighs for the golden age that had passed. While Old South idolaters such as Charles Colcock Jones, Jr., shuddered with horror at the mention of the New South, its spokesmen showed no such single-mindedness, and the warm reception they gave the emerging legend further emphasizes the attempt to relate their movement to the values and aspirations of the past.

The legend of an Old South whose character was shaped by a noble plantation regime did not, of course, emerge unheralded in the 1880's. Its origins are in the antebellum period itself. In his illuminating study, *Cavalier and Yankee*, William R. Taylor shows that the myth-making first appeared shortly after the War of 1812. William Wirt's biography of Patrick Henry, published in 1818, was the most notable precursor of the later tradition. "It was a utopia set in the past," Taylor writes.[46] Wirt "constructed for himself exactly the kind of legendary Southern past into which successive generations of Southerners were to retreat in full flight from the problems of the present."[47] Wirt's preliminary work was overshadowed in importance in the thirty years before the war by polemics and novels, reflecting the increasing alienation of Southern thought from dominant American values and ideals. From Thomas Roderick Dew in the early 'thirties to George Fitzhugh in the mid-'fifties, Southern pro-slavery theorists lauded a stratified agrarian society in terms which they thought the ancient Greeks might have understood.[48] In fiction, John Pendleton Kennedy inaugurated the plantation tradition in 1832 by idealizing his own times and by presenting much of plan-

tation life at its best.[49] "Doing so," remarks one historian
of the plantation in literature, "he gave matter and method
for a literary tradition."[50] The tradition was amply exploited by a host of other writers in the next thirty years.

The intensity of the abolition controversy led both
defenders and opponents of slavery to enlarge and perpetuate the myth. The defenders, for obvious reasons,
exaggerated the grandeur of their civilization, while the
abolitionist assault had the ironic outcome of adding credibility to the myth. In drawing pictures of the horror of
Southern society, abolitionists invariably had their dramas
of exploitation played on enormous estates presided over
by wealthy planters who lived life on the grand scale.
The contrast between the opulence of the planter and
the misery of the slave no doubt served the abolitionist
purpose, but it also contributed to one of the rare points
of agreement between Southerners and Northerners. As
Francis Pendleton Gaines observes, the opponents in the
slavery controversy "agreed concerning certain pictur-
esque elements of plantation life and joined hands to set
the conception unforgettably in public consciousness."[51]
A half-century after Harriet Beecher Stowe outraged the
South with *Uncle Tom's Cabin*, Joel Chandler Harris
took puckish delight in telling a Northern audience that
"all the worthy and beautiful characters in her book . . .
are the products" of a slave society, while the "cruelest
and most brutal character . . . is a Northerner."[52]

When the war came, both sides entered it with rival
myths which succored them during the four years. The
North's "Armageddonlike vision," Edmund Wilson
writes, directed a "holy crusade which was to liberate
the slaves and to punish their unrighteous masters."
While Northerners saw themselves as acting out the

"Will of God," Wilson continues, Southerners undertook the equally noble cause of "rescuing a hallowed ideal of gallantry, aristocratic freedom, fine manners and luxurious living from the materialism and vulgarity of the mercantile Northern society."[53]

Neither myth, of course, died with the conclusion of the war. During the Reconstruction era, the rhetoric of the Northern press and the "bloody shirt" campaigns of victorious Republican politicians kept the vision of a holy crusade alive, although it became hopelessly tarnished as time passed. Curiously, however, Northern novelists began in 1865 to develop a theme of reconciliation that dominated fictional treatments of the war and paved the way for the later emergence of Southern writers on the national scene. Examining the works of fifty-five novelists who produced sixty-four civil war books between 1865 and 1880, Joyce Appleby writes that "for the Northerner who wrote a novel simply to entertain, forgiveness was the order of the day." The plantation romance, as it would appear in the 'eighties, was undeveloped in these works, but all of the later themes of honest misunderstanding, purity of motive, and the integrity of Southern civilization are present.[54]

The sympathetic mood cultivated by the Northern novelists was expanded by the Southern writers of the late 'seventies and 'eighties into a national love feast for the Old South. Southern authors began appearing regularly in the pages of the national periodicals in the mid-'seventies, in the wake of the enthusiasm created by *Scribner's* "Great South" series, a detailed and sympathetic description of the region by Edward King.[55] By 1881, the editor of *Scribner's* was noting that a recent number of the magazine had contained seven contributions by Southerners. Hailing the new contributors, he confidently announced that "a new literary era is dawning upon the South."[56] A decade later the same editor would report to Joel Chandler Harris the petulant query of a Northern author, "When are you going to give the North a chance!"[57]

The new development came as no surprise to Albion W. Tourgee, the carpetbag judge of North Carolina whose own fiction had a considerable following in the period. As early as 1865 he had predicted that, within thirty years, "popular sympathy will be with those who upheld the Confederate cause . . . our popular heroes will be Confederate leaders; our fiction will be Southern in its prevailing types and distinctively Southern in its character." Writing in 1888, Tourgee felt that his prediction had been more than borne out, seven years in advance of the deadline. "Our literature has become not only Southern in type," he declared, "but distinctly Confederate in sympathy." Poring over all the popular monthlies of recent issue, Tourgee could not find a single one without a "Southern story" as one of its most "prominent features."[58]

Thus it was that the romantic view of the Southern past achieved what Gaines calls a "complete conquest" in the 'eighties. An enormous number of authors, the most prominent of whom were Harris and Page, "fed to the public fancy some variety of the plantation material."[59] At the same time, the mythic view of the past was achieving the status of an inviolable shibboleth through other means as well. Schoolbooks and educational curricula carefully guarded the old memories. Religious imagery and political rhetoric were built on appeals to former glory. And numerous organizations devoted their full time to perpetuating the correct view of the past. To Jones' Confederate Survivors' Association there were soon added the United Daughters of the Confederacy, for women, and the United Confederate Veterans for men. All basked in the admiration shown them by *The Confederate Veteran*, a reverent journal established in Nashville in 1893 to represent the various memorial groups. One contributor to the *Veteran* stated simply what had now become the orthodox Southern view of the past:

> In the eyes of Southern people all Confederate veterans are heroes. It is you [the Confederate veterans] who preserve the traditions and memories of the old-time South— the sunny South, with its beautiful lands and its happy people; the South of chivalrous men and gentle women; the South that will go down in history as the land of plenty and the home of heroes. This beautiful, plentiful, happy South engendered a spirit of chivalry and gallantry for which its men were noted far and near.[60]

In the mythic image of a chivalric and gallant South there remained no traces of the corrupting influences once imputed by the abolitionists. The descendants of Garrison were ambushed after the war, and by 1880 nothing remained of the abolitionist tradition except the exaggerated accounts of plantation splendor. "Abolitionism was swept from the field," according to Gaines; "it was more than routed, it was tortured, scalped, 'mopped up.' "[61] Remaining was only the enchanting picture of a near-perfect society in which, as Thomas Nelson Page believed, "even the moonlight was richer and mellower . . . than it is now."[62] This rich and mellow moonlight beamed on a country studded with magnolias that offered sweet scents and a becoming background for beautiful maidens. The fathers of the maidens, invariably courtly, noble, and generous, presided over enormous plantations and thousands of lovable, amusing, and devoted slaves. Work was apparently infrequent and leisure was put to constructive and cultivating uses. During the numerous holiday seasons—and especially at Christmastime—the regal splendor of the regime was particularly brilliant, enriching the lives of both white and black. Patriarchal in the extreme—yet underneath wholesomely democratic— the stratified society provided precisely the right niche for each member: each fulfilled his true nature; none was dissatisfied.

The New South prophets had no objection to the beautiful maidens, but their program would amend or replace many other aspects of the civilization cherished in the myth. Whirring cotton mills and crimson blast furnaces were preferred to magnolias and moonlight; the factory with its hired hands was superior to the inefficient plantation; bustle and energy and the ability to "get ahead," rather than a penchant for leisure, should characterize the leadership of the New South. Grady made the difference clear when he told his New York audience: "We have sowed towns and cities in the place of theories, and put business above politics."[63]

Unmindful of paradoxes, the New South spokesmen subscribed with ardor to the mythical conception of the Old South. Grady expressed reverence for the "imperishable knighthood" of the old regime; he admired the leisure and wealth which gave to the Old South an "exquisite culture"; he praised the civilization that produced gentle women, honest and devout citizens—all in that dreamlike time when "money counted least in making the social status." On another occasion, he referred to the sea-island plantations of Georgia as "royal homes: . . . principalities in area, dukedoms in revenue." The man who promised an industrial utopia to his own generation could say of the past that "the civilization of the old slave *regime* in the South has not been surpassed, and perhaps will not be equaled, among men."[64] The reciprocal love between master and slave, a basic foundation on which the society rested, was a thing of beauty which came into glorious blossom during the South's great testing time. Speaking before a group of Boston merchants, Grady related a "vision" of the war:

> The crisis of battle—a soldier struck, staggering, fallen. I see a slave, scuffling through the smoke, winding his black arms about the fallen form, reckless of the hurtling death—bending his trusty face to catch the words that tremble on the stricken lips, so wrestling meantime with agony that he would lay down his life in his master's stead.[65]

Edmonds, among the most versatile of the New South leaders, crusaded tirelessly for the industrial order of his day, traced a continuity of development from the Old to the New South, and urged upon his fellows the romantic view of the old regime. He would never want Southerners to forget, he wrote, "to hold in tenderest reverence the memory of this Southern land; never forget to give all honor to the men and women of ante-bellum days; remember . . . that the Old South produced a race of men and women whose virtues and whose attainments are worthy to be enshrined not only in every Southern, but in every American heart."[66] Moreover, in the midst of the South's industrial development, he warned Southerners never to let it be said "that in the struggle for industrial advance-

ment the South has lost aught of the virtues, domestic
and public, aught of the manliness and self-reliance,
aught of the charms of her women and the honor of her
men which hallow the memory of the Old South."[67]

By the turn of the century, as these examples suggest,
it caused no embarrassment for New South prophets to
espouse the creeds of both the Old and the New South.
A North Carolina bank president was typical of the New
South accommodation of both creeds when he began an
address before the American Bankers' Association by paying reverential homage to the Old South before praising
the New. "Prior to the civil war," the talk began, "our
Southern land . . . was the home of culture and refinement.
With thousands of slaves to cultivate their broad acres,
our people lived in ease and plenty."[68]

The allegiance given to the myth of the Old South by
the propagandists for the New Order is in itself evidence
of the extent to which the romantic view prevailed in
the South. Further evidence is found in unsuspected
places, the most notable of which is in the writings of
Booker T. Washington. Normally, one would not expect
the most influential champion of Negro freedom of his
generation to contribute to a romanticized view of the
slave regime into which he had been born. And, of course,
there are many aspects of Washington's picture of the
Old South which do not harmonize with the Thomas
Nelson Page version. Washington's picture differed from
the stereotype in his emphasis on the miserable living
conditions of the slaves, the torturous flax shirt, the
unpalatable rations, and the absence of the kind of
"civilized" living that he was later to champion. Important, too, is his contention that the slaves he knew understood and desired freedom, receiving it first with great

jubilation and later with a sobering sense of responsibility.[69]

However, much of Washington's picture resembles
the stereotyped version. He stresses the loyalty of the
slaves to their masters and insists that it was based on a
genuine love. When young "Mars' Billy" died there was
great sorrow in the quarters and it "was no sham sorrow
but real." There is no sense of resentment, and when
emancipation brought hard times to a former master the
slaves rallied and stood by him in his adversity. Washington explained that "nothing that the coloured people possess is too good for the son of 'old Mars' Tom.' "[70] One
is reminded of Irwin Russell's famous lines which began
by extolling the virtues of "Mahsr John" and conclude:

> *Well, times is changed. De war it come an' sot de niggers
> free,*
> *An' now ol' Mahsr John ain't hardly wuf as much as me;*
> *He had to pay his debts, an' so his lan' is mos'ly gone—*
> *An' I declar' I's sorry for my pore ol' Mahsr John.*[71]

Washington's account of Reconstruction is equally
congenial to the romantic version. In his autobiography
he includes the standard comic view of the newly freed
Negro, stating that the principal crazes were for Greek
and Latin and public office. He is critical of the precipitous
way in which the Negro was pulled up from the bottom
rung of society, and he has harsh words to say about
Negro preachers, teachers, and politicians. Most important of all is what is not said: nowhere in *Up from
Slavery* does one find an indictment of the native white
Southerners' behavior during Reconstruction. The Negro
suffered in the end, Washington felt, in large part be-

cause "there was an element in the North which wanted to punish the Southern white men by forcing the Negro into positions over the heads of Southern whites."[72]

IV

The commitment of both black and white New South prophets to the romantic view of the past was not made without purpose. To some extent, to be sure, there was no alternative for many of them, for their own emotional requirements as well as the need for public acceptance dictated that they operate within the intellectual framework of the time and place in which they lived. But however compelling the emotional and strategic considerations may have been, they were matched in appeal to the New South spokesmen by several concrete, useful functions which the myth of the Old South could perform in the cause of the New South movement. Washington, as will appear in the next chapter, had special reasons for mythmaking. The white leaders in the movement quickly perceived and ably exploited the benefits that the myth offered them. For one thing, they would not have agreed with those later historians who saw the romantic legend exclusively as a source of fruitless ancestor worship and rancorous sectionalism. On the contrary, a close examination shows that it was nationalism rather than sectionalism, an identification rather than a separation, of interests that emerged as benefactors of the myth.

The triumph of the romantic legend in the North in the 'eighties was essential to this result. Once before, in the antebellum period, the Southern mythmakers had found allies in the North, although the Yankee authors of the Southern myth were a distinct and largely uninfluential minority in their society. Several Northern writers, disturbed by a rapid social mobility and an accelerating materialism which produced, in Taylor's words, "glowing optimism and expectations of a secular millennium," consciously cultivated the plantation theme to bare the disquieting developments in their own region. To them, the culture of the South had "many of the things which they felt the North lacked: the vestiges of an old-world aristocracy, a promise of stability and an assurance that gentility—a high sense of honor, a belief in public service and a maintenance of domestic decorum—could be preserved under republican institutions."[73] In the New South era similar doubts caused some of the North's finest writers to use the Southern romance to damn the excesses of the Gilded Age. Woodward has recently called attention to the fact that Herman Melville, Henry Adams, and Henry James each wrote works which included a Confederate veteran who "serves as the mouthpiece of the severest stricture upon American society or, by his actions or character, exposes the worst faults of that society." These three authors, Woodward writes, detested the "mediocrity, the crassness, and the venality they saw around them," and they found the Southerner "a useful foil for the unlovely present or the symbol of some irreparable loss."[74]

To most Northern writers and readers of the 'eighties and 'nineties, however, the commitment to the romantic legend masked few disturbing social thoughts and stemmed from simple needs. According to Gaines, the Northerner had a romantic, innate "love of feudalism" and a yearning to identify vicariously with aristocratic societies. The plantation, "alone among native institutions," he continues, satisfied "this craving for a system of caste."[75] Both the craving and the myth that satisfied it continued long beyond the years of the New South movement. Gunnar Myrdal, noting the enduring fascination of the American with the romantic legend, wrote in 1944:

> The North has so few vestiges of feudalism and aristocracy of its own that, even though it dislikes them fundamentally and is happy not to have them, Yankees are thrilled by them. Northerners apparently cherish the idea of having had an aristocracy and of still having a real class society—in the South. So it manufactures the myth of the "Old South" or has it manufactured by Southern writers working for the Northern market.[76]

The complex strands that wove together the myth of the Old South—alienation of the Southerner from national values and ideals in the antebellum period; alienation of a few Northerners, both before and after the war, from the strident pace of material progress; innocent love for another, grander civilization on the part of most—did not obscure for the New South spokesmen the incalculably valuable service it could perform in the cause of sectional reconciliation, a basic tenet of the New South creed. If the myth in antebellum days had bespoken alienation on the part of Southerners from national ways, in the postbellum period it worked in precisely the opposite direction, uniting the two sections. To the South it gave a vitally necessary sense of greatness to assuage the bitter wounds of defeat; to the North it offered a way in which to apologize without sacrificing the fruits of victory.

Henry Grady has always been regarded as the chief peacemaker among the New South spokesmen, but Joel Chandler Harris, his friend and colleague on the Atlanta *Constitution*, served the reconciliation cause in a more subtle and perhaps more effective manner. Many of Harris's stories are unmistakable attempts to heal sectional wounds and unite former enemies. While Grady was serving the cause as the ever-available orator, the shy Harris worked quietly in the background through Uncle Remus.

How Harris served the cause of reconciliation—and, in a larger sense, how the plantation literature promoted national identification of interests—is tellingly illustrated in the comparison of two versions of one of Harris's early stories. The original version appeared in the *Constitution* in 1877 under the title "Uncle Remus as a Rebel: How He Saved His Young Master's Life."[77] The second version, entitled "A Story of the War," appeared in the first of Harris's books, *Uncle Remus: His Songs and His Savings*, published late in 1880.[78] The plot is similar in both stories. Uncle Remus saves his young master from certain death by shooting a Yankee sniper. In both stories Remus thinks only of his love for his master and mistress. He knew the Yankee was there to free him, but when he saw what was going to happen he "des disremembered all 'bout freedom" and pulled the trigger.[79] In the first version, that intended for relatively local consumption, the Yankee is killed. In the second telling, however, Harris is aware of his national audience. Here the sniper loses an arm, but not his life. He is nursed by Remus and Miss Sally, the plantation belle, regains his health, and wins the hand of his lovely nurse. Clearly, the second version reveals Harris consciously courting the North, as John

Stafford points out, by demonstrating that "a Yankee is good enough to join the Southern aristocracy." Moreover, "the North and the South are symbolically wed; and the North accepts the paternalistic pattern. Thus is the patron flattered and at the same time the self-respect of the South retained."[80]

The intersectional marriage, symbol of reconciliation, was a standard device used by Southern writers of the period. Harris used it to good effect again in "Aunt Fountain's Prisoner." Aunt Fountain, the plantation mammy, says of the Yankee bridegroom: "He ain' b'long ter we-all folks, no furder dan he my young mistiss ole man, but dee ain' no finer w'ite man dan him. No, suh; dee ain'." Cheered by this judgment, New South readers both North and South must have been pleased also to read that this Yankee revived the sagging fortunes of the old plantation by a stern application of "vim and vigor," New South qualities *par excellence.*[81] Thus, as Harris would have it, the marriage of a Yankee to a Southern belle, lovely flower of the old regime, excited Northern sympathy and admiration for the honorable qualities of Southern life and, at the same time, showed Southerners that their future would be prosperous if new concepts of work and organization were accepted.

The role of the Negro and of race relations was of special importance in the romantic legend and, in persuading the North to view the "quaint darky" through Southern eyes, the mythmakers accomplished at least two important results. First, by convincing Northern readers that relations between the races were kindly and mutually beneficial a principal obstacle in the way of sectional harmony was removed. The North had doubted this point, but on the authority of Harris and others it

came to accept the Southern point of view.[82] Second, the
acquiescence by the North in the Southern scheme of
race relations permitted the South to deal with (or to fail
to deal with) its race problems unmolested.

Humor was a standard and effective device used by
Southern writers to mollify the Northern conscience, for,
as Sterling Brown caustically observes, "if the Negro
could be shown as perpetually mirthful, his state could
not be so wretched."[83] In a more sophisticated vein,
Stafford comments that Harris's use of ironic comedy
invariably produced the "understanding laugh" which
gave emotional release from doubts and guilt feelings and
induced whites to tolerate what otherwise would appear
to be an evil situation. The "pure humor" of Uncle Remus,
then, won "acceptance for the existing class harmony."[84]
To humor there was added the element of the essential
difference between white and black, the image of the
Negro as an exotic primitive, as

> *Original in act and thought,*
> *Because unlearned and untaught.*[85]

To make the ideal of blissful race relations a convincing one, the humorous and primitive Negro is, in
hundreds of contemporary stories, the guardian of the
old memories and traditions. Far from resenting his life
under slavery he finds freedom uncongenial—"I wants
ter git shet er dis heah freedom," exclaims a Negro who
was freed by his master before the war[86]—or at least not
as satisfactory as the "old days," and to every passerby
he recounts the glories of yesteryear. Tourgee designated
this stereotype the "poor 'nigger' to whom liberty has
brought only misfortune, and who is relieved by the dis-

interested friendship of some white man whose property he once was."[87] In Page's "Marse Chan" and "Unc' Edinbrug's Drowndin'," two of the Virginian's most famous tales, it is the former slave who tells the story, glorifies the past, and laments its passing.[88] In one of Harry Stillwell Edwards's stories the old mammy lives out her years in sight of the grave of her mistress, where she may better preserve the memory of happier days.[89] The longing for the past is everywhere expressed. Old Sam, the faithful body servant in "Marse Chan," declares "Dem was good ole times, marster—de bes' Sam ever see."[90] Chad, the loyal servant in Francis Hopkinson Smith's novel of the Virginia gentleman, feels likewise: "Dem was high times. We ain't neber seed no time like dat since de war."[91] And, in one of the poems of Miss Howard Weeden, the old Negro feels that

> *I ought to think 'bout Canaan, but*
> *It's Ole Times crowds my mind,*
> *An' maybe when I gits to Heaben*
> *It's Ole Times dat I'll find!*[92]

Behind the façade of this pleasant fable of Negro happiness and devotion in the regime of slavery there were, of course, harsh realities. Tourgee admitted that there were some real examples upon which the stereotype was built, "but they are not so numerous as to destroy the charm of novelty." About the Negro "as a man, with hopes, fears, and aspirations like other men," he wrote, "our literature is very nearly silent." Moreover, as John M. Webb observes, "the fable applies only to the house slaves who had intimate contact with the whites."[94] But, as the legend would have it, the pleasant state of affairs was a general, not a particular or isolated, characteristic of antebellum life.

The generality of the situation, of course, was meant to apply to the postwar years as well as to the slavery regime. In addition to promoting sectional reconciliation and, in further removing the North from agitation of the race question, the image of the happy Negro helped to destroy one of the burdensome obstacles in the way of Northern investments in the South. Northern capitalists constantly complained of the unsettling conditions in the South stemming from racial friction. To the New South spokesmen it seemed clear that friction would disappear and capital come rolling in once the race question were left entirely up to Southern determination. This is what Tompkins meant when he wrote that "an excess of zeal in the cause of freedom" on the part of Northerners could serve no useful purpose and was, in the long run, to the disadvantage of the Northern capitalists themselves.[95] The myth of the Old South, with its charming picture of the lovable and loving Negro, served well to jettison the zeal which Tompkins felt was rocking the boat.

Finally, in the South itself the romance of the past was used to underwrite the materialism of the present. The names and signatures of Confederate generals were everywhere in demand by railroad companies and corporations, for the New South prophets were well aware that the blessing of a "colonel" (if there were no generals handy) would do as much to float bonds and raise subscriptions as a dozen columns of optimistic statistics in the *Manufacturers' Record*. In *Colonel Carter of Cartersville*, a successful third-rate novel of the period, one of the characters observes wisely that "in a sagging market the colonel would be better than a war boom."[96] The marriage of the gentle life of the past and the bustling era of the present was perhaps nowhere better symbolized than in the advertising columns of that journal of worship, *The Confederate Veteran.* There one learned that Confederate flags could be purchased from a New York firm and the aspiring capitalist found notices of potentially prosperous factories up for sale.[97]

V

The several specific uses to which the mythic conception of the Old South were put to serve the needs of the New South movement help to make intelligible the paradoxical commitment of the New South prophets to the legendary romance. Professor Woodward, in his skeptical assessment of the movement, feels that the "bitter mixture of recantation and heresy" which infused the New South creed "could never have been swallowed so readily had it not been dissolved in the syrup of romanticism."[98] But the sugar coating of the pill of the New Departure, important though it was, does not fully account for the phenomenon of mythmaking. More profound, more universal and less tangible forces were at work as well. Henry James suggested some of these when he wrote:

> The collapse of the old order, the humiliation of defeat, the bereavement and bankruptcy involved, represented, with its obscure miseries and tragedies, the social revolution the most unrecorded and undepicted, in proportion to its magnitude, that ever was; so that this reversion of the starved spirit to the things of the heroic age, the four epic years, is a definite soothing salve.[99]

That there were deep wounds whose treatment required a soothing salve is abundantly clear. The South had so irrevocably committed its soul to the war that when defeat came it was more than a surrender of ambitions for independence; it was a crippling blow to the most basic assumptions upon which life in the region was lived. Pride and hope were destroyed by defeat, and humiliation was added by the Reconstruction. Under the circumstances, the search for self-confidence and a return of pride quite naturally involved more than a program of building on the ashes. Somehow the ashes themselves had to be ennobled. The myth worked powerfully to achieve this purpose: it gave back those very things which the Yankee had tried to take away—the knowledge of a proud past and a noble heritage. Without that knowledge, Grady once remarked, "the New South would be dumb and motionless."[100]

The search for a noble past, like the attempt to discover a heritage of nationalism and industrialism, engaged Southerners in an emotional and intellectual quest common to other people in other times. Nations that have been either victimized or blessed by profound social upheaval have commonly undergone, in one way or another, the experience of replanting the bared roots to the past; of developing the mythmaking process to satisfy collective needs. And for Southerners of the New South era, should they be charged with distortion of the past, their reply might be, with the Virginia novelist James Branch Cabell, that "no history is a matter of record; it is a matter of faith."[101]

6
The Emperor's New Clothes

What a pull it has been! Through the ashes
and desolation of war—up the hill, a step
at a time, nothing certain—not even the
way! Hindered, misled, and yet always
moving up a little until—shall we say it?—
the top has been reached, and the rest is
easy! . . . The ground has been prepared—
the seed put in—the tiny shoots tended
past the danger-point—and the day of the
mighty harvest is here!

—HENRY W. GRADY, 1889[1]

Twenty-odd years ago . . . I fondly
imagined a great era of prosperity for the
South. . . . I saw in anticipation all her
tribulations ended, all her scars healed, and
all the ravages of war forgotten, and I
beheld the South greater, richer and mightier
than when she moulded the political policy
of the whole country. But year by year
these hopes, chastened by experience, have
waned and faded, until now, instead of
beholding the glorious South of my
imagination, I see her sons poorer than

when war ceased his ravages, weaker than
when rehabilitated with her original
rights, and with the bitter memories of the
past smouldering, if not rankling, in the
bosoms of many.

—LEWIS H. BLAIR, 1889[2]

The Emperor took off all his clothes, and the
impostors pretended to give him one
article of dress after the other of the new
ones which they had pretended to make.
They pretended to fasten something around
his waist and to tie on something. This
was the train, and the Emperor turned
round and round in front of the mirror.

"How well His Majesty looks in the new
clothes! How becoming they are!" cried
all the people round. "What a design, and
what colors! They are most
gorgeous robes."

"The canopy is waiting outside which
is to be carried over Your Majesty in the
procession," said the master of the
ceremonies.

"Well, I am quite ready," said the
Emperor. "Don't the clothes fit well?" Then
he turned round again in front of the
mirror, so that he should seem to be looking
at his grand things.

—from ANDERSEN's *Fairy Tales*[3]

Allegiance to both the myth of the Old South and the dream of a New South was but one of several contradictions imbedded in the New South creed. There were many others: an institutional explanation of industrial backwardness in the Old South coupled with the faith that natural resources could not help but assure industrialization in the New; an elaborate propaganda campaign to attract immigrants into the region negated by hostility to the immigration pool easiest to tap; a gospel of economic interdependence and reconciliation with the North as part of a campaign for independence and domination; a lauding of freedom for the Negro in a politics of white supremacy; dreams of equal treatment of allegedly unequal races in separate societies devoted to mutual progress—these are among the most obvious.

Rich in paradoxes, the New South creed also had an ironic outcome. Designed to lead the region out of poverty, it made converts by the thousands in all parts of the country of men who looked forward confidently to a South of abundance. Instead, the expectations were unrealized and the South remained the poorest and economically least progressive section of the nation. The plans for regional and personal success, the restoration of self-confidence, and a position of influence and respect in the nation likewise fired the imagination and gained legions of adherents, but they too were largely unfulfilled and at the end of the New South crusade the region found itself in the uncomfortable, if familiar, role of a colonial dependent. Rid of many of the humiliating frustrations of the early postwar years, it was saddled with new ones that had greater staying power. Finally, the dream of a just and practical solution to the race question appealed to former abolitionists and radicals as well as to long-time racists because it promised that justice and practicality could be balanced, that Southerners themselves could do what Yankee reformers had failed to do, and that a harmonious biracial society would emerge and permit Americans to forget about injustice to the black man. Instead, violence increased in the 'eighties, and disfranchisement and rigid segregation followed later as the Negro reached the nadir of his history as a free man.

Unable to bequeath to the next generation of Southerners a legacy of solid achievement, the New South spokesmen gave them instead a solidly propounded and widely spread image of its success, a mythic view of their own times that was as removed from objective reality as the myth of the Old South. In creating the myth of the New South, they compounded all of the contradictions originally built into their creed, added others, and crowned their professions of realism with a flight of fantasy.

I

In the early stages of its development, the New South idea was essentially a program of action. It promised the future but was candid in its discouraging evaluation of the present. In fact, one of the most important arguments of the New South advocates in the early years was based on a frank and distressing contrast between the South and other parts of America. The contrast gave birth both to the method and the purpose of the program. Never doubting the vitality of the human resources, and convinced of the superiority of natural ones, the New South spokesmen believed that by adopting the ways of the industrial age in the same way other Americans had done their dream would be realized. That dream was essentially a promise of American life for the South. It proffered all the glitter and glory and freedom from guilt that inhered in the American ideal. Sloughing off those characteristics which had marked him as poor, quarrelsome, unprogressive, guilt-ridden, and unsuccessful, the Southerner would—if he heeded the New South prophets—become the American he was entitled to be: prosperous, successful, respected and admired, confident of the future.

In 1880 Atticus G. Haygood declared that the New South meant, above all, that a time would come when "the words 'the South' will have only a geographical significance."[4] He foresaw the end of sectionalism and the integration of the South into the mainstream of American progress. Much remained to be done, Haygood felt, and he predicted that it would take at least twenty years for the New South program to succeed. By 1886, however, Grady was rapturous and confident in declaring to his New York audience that the South had "wiped out the place where Mason and Dixon's line used to be."[5] Elsewhere in the same address, and increasingly in the statements of Grady and other New South prophets, their program began to assume the solidity of accomplished fact. Almost imperceptibly at first the promotional strategy changed from the original emphasis on the gap separating accomplishment from ambition to a parade of "facts" that proved the rapidity with which the gap was being closed. As the strategy changed, a bewildering mixture of fact and fancy, wish and reality, emerged. Writing early in 1887, Wilbur Fisk Tillett, a theologian from Vanderbilt, declared "that such a marvelous advance has been made in the South in the last ten years as has rarely been made in any country or in any part of any country in an equally limited period in the history of the world." The New South, which had first "showed itself in 1880," had by 1886 "proved its name by evidences so powerful and convincing that only the blindest can fail to see them."[6]

As if to prove their clear vision to Tillett, an astonishing number of writers testified to Southern advance; and if proclaiming it to be could make it so, the South after the mid-'eighties was no longer the poverty-stricken, despondent region of old. Charles Dudley Warner reported in 1886 that the South was in the throes of a mighty "economical and political revolution" whose story would be "one of the most marvellous the historian has to deal with."[7] A year later he wrote that in the "New Industrial South the change is marvellous, and so vast and various that I scarcely know where to begin in a short paper." The region as he saw it was "wide-awake to business, excited and even astonished at the development of its own immense resources."[8] Pronouncements from Northern friends like Warner were always especially welcomed and frequently quoted by the New South spokesmen. Kelley was aware of this when he added to his own glowing descriptions of the region the remarks of James M. Swank, general manager of the American Iron and Steel Association. According to Swank the South had "experienced in 1886 a new birth." Proof of this signal event, he wrote, could be seen in any set of industrial statistics as well as in the fact that "even its own journals and public men now speak of it as the New South." The New South child, Swank concluded, was on the verge of achieving "those beneficent industrial results which have made the North so rich, so prosperous, and so aggressive."[9]

Like the Northerners, Grady's friend Marion J. Verdery wrote in 1887 of the "blessed dawn" that brought "new strength, new hope, new energy, and new life, all of which combined in sacred pledge to make the New South."[10] But it was Grady himself who played the most important part in creating the image of a dynamic and successful movement, and in his editorials one can trace the evolution of the process. A few selections will illustrate the transition from a mood of optimism in 1881 to a declaration of triumph in 1886. Reviewing business failures over the previous two years, Grady wrote in the summer of 1881 that, despite the rise in failures that year, "the business of the southern states is now considered sound and promising." The next summer he was happier with his review of recent developments. The agricultural outlook had never been as good and "never before has the material development of Georgia made such rapid progress as during the last twelve months." The mood continued unabated, and at the end of the summer of 1883 he wrote that "very few of us know how rapidly the south is progressing in a material sense. We know that we are getting on well, but we have not taken time to set down and measure the pace or the extent of the recuperative process." Without such measuring, however, it was clear that "the situation is altogether hopeful."[11]

By the end of 1884 it was clear to him that the optimism of the previous years was well founded and that an even more confident position was warranted. "This section is rapidly filling up with manufactories," he wrote, "and industry and enterprise in all forms and shapes are making the south their headquarters, and they have come to stay." In the summer of 1885 he took note of a recession but declared that hard times were not "enough to stop southern enterprise." He then reviewed a set of optimistic reports in the *Manufacturers' Record* and concluded that they showed "a remarkable degree of industrial activity in the south." A year later he was again relying on Edmonds, whose survey of the region led him to remark that "if the most enthusiastic southerner is not satisfied with this bird's-eye view of the progress of his section, he must be one of the impracticables. It seems to us that we are entering upon an almost ideal era of progress." By the end of the year, on the eve of his journey to Delmonico's, he was certain that he had been right: "a tidal wave of prosperity is rushing over this region," he announced, "and we must prepare to size it up and utilize it."[12]

From the time he spoke to the New England Society of New York, in December 1886, until his death three years later, Grady's typical comments, in both editorials and speeches, emphasized the marvel of Southern achievement. To one audience he explained that "the Eldorado of which I have told you" sprang inevitably from the South's monopoly of "the three essential items of all industry—cotton, iron and wool." From this "assured and permanent advantage" there had developed "an amazing system of industries."[13] After reciting the funeral tale to the Boston Bay State Club, he noted that great changes had occurred since his fellow Georgian had been dispatched to his grave so unceremoniously attended by the fruits of Southern industry. Twenty years after the burial

Georgia could boast the biggest marble-cutting establishment in the world in addition to a half-dozen woolen
mills in the immediate vicinity of the grove in which the
man was put to rest. In the same speech, Grady told of
a friend who had returned from the war without a pair of
pants to his name. His wife sewed trousers out of an old
dress, and with five dollars the man bought old timber
with which he built a shack. Now, twenty years later,
the same man had a large wardrobe and a good home.
He was typical of the whole of Georgia, Grady concluded,
for "we have prospered down there."[14] Finally, in one of
his last speeches, he reviewed the South's struggle against
poverty, the carefully laid plans for a society of abundance, and finished with the good news that "the day
of the mighty harvest is here!"[15]

The only New South spokesman whose superlatives
were even more extravagant than Grady's was the in-
domitable Edmonds. Devoting his journal almost exclusively to the promotion of the economic development of
the South, Edmonds ground out endless statistics em-
bellished with hortatory comments to support his claim
that the region was "throbbing with industrial and railroad activity" and that capitalists "in Europe and America
are looking to the South as the field for investment."
In 1890 he published a pamphlet called *The South's
Redemption.* Revealingly subtitled "From Poverty to
Prosperity," it furnished other New South writers with
highly quotable copy and summed up the theme of a
feverish period of propagandistic activity of the *Manufacturers' Record.*[16]

Between 1886 and 1890 Edmonds never veered from
his mission of substantiating the double claim that the
South's future was brilliant and that its present was
unrivaled. In the same month that Grady spoke in New

York, Edmonds wrote that "never before probably in the history of this country has there been such an era of industrial development as we now see in the South." Every "click of the telegraph" announced a new factory. In a later column he declared that "prosperity seems to reign everywhere," and rejoiced in his belief that industrial growth "extends over the whole section." Another article welcomed the "veritable invasion of the South" by eager Northern and Western investors who came to enrich themselves but, unlike the Union invaders of the 'sixties, came to enrich the South as well. On another occasion he wrote that the "marvelous industrial development" of the South was having extraordinarily good effects on agriculture so that the dream of a balanced economy was in fact coming true. Finally, in 1890 he made it unmistakably clear that the New South was a great and present reality. With allusions to his friend Kelley's statement that the South was the "field of American adventure" and the "coming El Dorado of American adventure," he wrote:

> There is no diminution, no falling off in the South. In all lines of industry the advance is steady and continuous. . . . The old agricultural South has ceased to be. . . . From henceforth the South stands in the front rank as the "field of American adventure" and the exponent of American progress. . . . It is in truth not "the coming," but the existing "El Dorado of American Adventure."[17]

Declarations of the reality of the opulent South made it logical for the New South spokesmen to proclaim the achievement of their other goals of reconciliation with the North and the acquisition of a new sense of power and faith in the future, for the creation of a triumphant

South was premised upon the successful conversion to the industrial age. All of the New South advocates, and countless contributors to the national periodicals, remarked on the vanishing sectional animosities, and the favorite explanation for this happy state of affairs was the economic interdependence which bound North and South together. Watterson thanked God that it was at last possible to say of the South "it is simply a geographic expression" and Tompkins rejoiced in the fact that "the institutions and interests of the American people are identical and common."[18] Telling his New York audience that the South had torn down sectional barriers, Grady made it plain that the new era of harmony emanated from his part of the country. After Sherman had left Atlanta in ashes, he said, the city was rebuilt, and "we have caught the sunshine in the bricks and mortar of our homes, and have builded therein not one ignoble prejudice or memory."[19] It may have been Grady's words, rather than the bricks, that caught the sunshine, but certainly the theme of reunion was a dominant one of the 'eighties.[20] Warner was typical of the Northern observers when he wrote that "Southern society and Northern society are becoming every day more and more alike."[21]

With the end of prejudice and discord and with the advent of industrial might came the sense of power and achievement that was the ultimate goal of the New South movement. "Above all," Grady said in New York, "we know that we have achieved in these 'piping times of peace' a fuller independence for the South than that which our fathers sought to win in the forum by their eloquence or compel in the field by their swords."[22] In response to a critic's suggestion that Northern financial and industrial interests were decisive in the movement and that perhaps the South was not quite as independent as he believed,

Grady replied confidently that such charges were completely erroneous. Citing Fulton County, Georgia—the "capital" of the New South—as typical of the region, he stated that only 774 Northerners were numbered in a total population of 47,588.[23] More to the point, Grady would believe, was the analysis of Kelley, who wrote in 1888 that the magnificent progress taking place in the South could "justly be regarded as the work of Titans."[24] And as others looked on the scene later they declared that these titans had brought into existence a South that was everywhere blessed with "plenty and prosperity"; that the South, at last, had risen "victorious in peace from the desolation of war."[25] The metamorphosis was now complete. During the years of conception—the 'seventies—"New South" meant an idea, a program, a goal; by the end of the 'eighties it denoted a whole region that had acted upon the idea, followed the program, and achieved the goal.

II

Walter Hines Page was the only one of the notable New South spokesmen who believed that failures outnumbered the successes of the movement. A persistent critic of the defects in Southern society, Page participated in one crusade after another to save his native region; in the 'eighties he was at one with Grady and Edmonds in looking to industrialization for the answer to the region's problems; in the later 'nineties he joined the education crusade, hoping that a new enlightenment would bring salvation; still later he put his hopes in elimination of the hookworm and for a while appeared to think that the South could be saved only when the ill health which plagued so many of her people disappeared. More cosmopolitan and sensitive than the other New South spokesmen, Page was always suspicious of the extravagant claims made by Southerners. In his autobiographical novel, for example, he recalled his experiences as a schoolboy and wrote that "nobody tells the whole truth about institutions. They prefer to accept traditions and to repeat respectful formulas."[26] By the 'nineties the New South claims had become "respectful formulas" and Page was losing faith with them.[27] Touring the region in 1899, he had hoped to see a South that would justify the optimistic statistics he read in the *Manufacturers' Record*, a journal of which he was the second largest stockholder.[28] Instead, he saw a land that appeared to him to be "listless, discouraged, poverty-stricken, and backward-looking," and he returned from his journey "infinitely sad."[29]

Ten years earlier, Lewis H. Blair, a native Virginian and former Confederate soldier, had been similarly disillusioned by the contrast between what he called the "real South" and what he read in the New South propaganda sheets.[30] "Judging by the glowing reports in the newspapers for the past three years," Blair wrote, "we must conclude that the South is enjoying a veritable deluge of prosperity." According to the propaganda, the South was "surpassing even the Eastern States," and had become a place "where poverty is unknown and where everybody is industriously and successfully laying up wealth."[31] The irate Virginian traced the source of this "mischievous and misleading" information to the "so-called Manufacturers' Records" that had become so popular in the 'eighties. Commenting on their objectivity, he wrote:

Such journals proceed on the same plan as would the Superintendent of the Census in 1890, should he, instead of actually enumerating the people, start with the population of 1880, and add thereto not only all the births, but also all the stillbirths, all the miscarriages, and all the abortions since that year, and deduct nothing for deaths in the meanwhile.[32]

It was the habit of these journals, Blair claimed, to arrive at figures of total aggregate manufacturing capital in the South by including in their estimates not only established firms but those that were merely in the planning stage as well. Failures and bankruptcies were seldom recorded; the inevitable trend had to be upwards.[33]

Edmonds was a natural target of such criticisms and, though not named, it was probably he in particular whom Blair had in mind. Edmonds was accustomed to such charges and occasionally reprinted them in the *Record* to provide a springboard from which to launch an optimistic picture of Southern achievements. In 1887 the Newberry, South Carolina, *Observer* commented that the statistics in Edmonds's journal "make a fine showing." But the ordinary Southerner "feels something like the penniless boy who stands out on the sidewalk and gazes wistfully through plate-glass windows at the beautiful display of toys and candies within!" Edmonds replied that the boy was penniless because he spent too much time gazing; wealth was there for those who wished to work.[34] On another occasion the Baltimore *Sun* described what it considered to be "The Real Condition of the South" in gloomy terms. Edmonds countered with a long statistical table which he believed proved that "none can question" the industrial advance of the region.[35] Even more pointed was an editorial comment in the Chattanooga *Times* that passed off one of Edmonds's statistical surveys as "about three-fourths moonshine and wind." Edmonds characterized this attack on his veracity as "the insolent snarls of envious curs," the product of an editor who was a "disreputable falsifier . . . moved by enmity and spite."[36] With this background, Blair did not exaggerate when he declared that "to doubt the current charming presentations of Southern growth and prosperity is to bring down anathemas upon one's head. What! the South not prosperous. Impossible, they cry; and the individual who questions is an idiot."[37]

Risking the anathemas, Blair wrote a penetrating analysis of the economic and racial problems of the South. His thesis was that the prosperity of the region depended upon the elevation, not the degradation, of the Negro; and because Negroes were not being elevated and Southern economic advance not planned intelligently, the region sustained one setback after another. "We are," he feared, "making an Ireland of the South, and are digging broad and deep graves in which to bury prosperity and all its untold advantages."[38] To support this view he attacked not only the statistics but the integrity of the New South spokesmen. He also pointedly began his analysis with Georgia—"as she has been held up as a model to all the other States"—and, with what he called reliable statistics, he concluded that "the people of Georgia had not added materially to their wealth during the twenty years preceding 1886."[39] Clearly, this was not Henry Grady's doctrine.

Blair and Page had perhaps let their disappointment cause them to underestimate the material advances that were evident in the South, for it is obvious that impressive forward strides had been taken since the end of the war. Factories had been built where there were none before, boom towns dotted the region, railroad mileage increased substantially, and investors, both foreign and domestic, were genuinely impressed by the future prospects of Southern development. Moreover, there was a romantic quality to the New South quest for riches and power that stirred the souls of observers in all parts of the country. Recognizing all of these factors, however, nothing can gainsay the fact that Blair and Page came closer to describing actuality than Grady and Edmonds did or that the New South writings were that fuzzy medley of strong belief and personal experience out of which social myth emerges.

In his general history of the post-Reconstruction South, C. Vann Woodward shows the gap that separated South from North by using per capita wealth figures. In 1880, when the New South movement was just taking hold, the per capita wealth of the Southern states was $376 and the national average was $870. By 1900 the figure for the South had increased to $509 while the national average had risen to $1,165. Expressed in percentages, the per capita wealth of the Southern states in 1880 was 56.8 per cent below the national average. In 1900 it was 56.3 per cent below. The very slight gain on the North which is reflected in these data is misleading, however, because the figures include valuations of Southern railroads, mines, mortgages, and other properties owned by "outside interests."[40] Estimates of per capita income show a similar pattern. In 1880 the per capita income in the South was $88; the national average was $175. By 1900 the South's per capita income had risen to $102 while the national average had moved to $203. Expressed in percentages, the per capita income of the South in 1880 was 49.7 per cent below the national average; in 1900 it was 49.8 per cent below.[41]

These figures show that the per capita wealth of the South increased by 13.5 per cent between 1880 and 1900 and that per capita income increased by 15.9 per cent in the same period. The gains are significant, of course, and they provided just enough substance to make the myth of the New South credible to many persons. But in truth the industrial evolution of the postwar years was neither extensive enough nor revolutionary enough to make much impact on the standard of living of the great mass of Southerners. In the first place, the movement was extremely limited. In 1900, as in 1880, the overwhelming majority of the population was engaged in the extractive industries of agriculture, forestry, fisheries, and mining. With 67.3 per cent of its labor force employed in these occupations in 1900 the South was a unique section of the country. The comparable figure for New England, the New South spokesmen's primary model, was 17.6 per cent. Only 6.3 per cent of the Southern labor force was employed in manufacturing in 1900, which reflects but a modest rise from the 4.6 per cent that was claimed by manufacturing twenty years earlier.[42] Remaining an essentially raw-material economy, the South suffered "the attendant penalties of low wages, lack of opportunity, and poverty."[43]

In addition to the limited extent of industrial development, the industries that did emerge and expand were largely of the low-wage variety. This was particularly true in the case of the cotton-textile industry, which became to many New South spokesmen the symbol of their movement. The low wages paid by Southern factories were further entrenched by the exploitative nature of the early industrial movement. Dependence on child labor and, for a good period of time, on convict labor as well, scarcely validated the happy images woven into the picture of the New South. William H. Nicholls, an economist who has brooded over the Southern past, sums up the failures of the period by writing that "the rate of industrialization in the South during the post-bellum years of the nineteenth century, while no inconsiderable achievement, was hardly sufficient to make more than a small dent in the low-income problems of its overwhelmingly rural-agricultural population."[44]

As reality failed to bear out the New South dream of opulence so, too, did it fail to record success in the campaign for power and independence. With a few notable exceptions, the New South program produced no real Southern Rockefellers and Carnegies, but only a large number of their liveried servants. It was by adopting the ways of Northern industry—by putting business above politics and sowing towns and cities in the place of theories—that the new power and independence were meant to have been gained. But as the industrial pattern deviated from the Northern model the achievement of these goals became impossible. Instead, as of old, the South remained saddled with the burdens of a colonial economy.

Her railway system fell under the control of Northern financial tycoons like J. P. Morgan and her iron and steel industries, during and after the depression of 1893, succumbed to the control of outsiders, culminating in 1907 when United States Steel achieved effective domination of the Tennessee Coal and Iron Company. Even the proud mills, so many of which were built with local money raised in patriotic subscription campaigns, fell into the colonial pattern. Their chief products were often sent North for final processing and their dependence on Northern capital and Northern commission houses belied the claims of self-determination.[45] Finally, many of the South's natural resources—the most celebrated guarantee of industrial progress and power—came to be controlled by men from outside the region. As Woodward writes, the South's "rich mineral deposits . . . were 'Southern' monopolies only in the sense that the sulphur of Sicily, owned by a British syndicate, was once a 'Sicilian' monopoly. Protected by patent laws, franchises, options, or outright possession of mineral lands, the Melons, Rockefellers, Du Ponts, and other capitalists monopolized 'Southern monopolies.' "[46]

To explain why the New South movement failed to produce the blessings it promised is a task well beyond the scope of this study, but a few observations on the nature of the problem may help to cast light on other questions which are of primary concern. To begin with, the persistent optimism of the New South spokesmen was grounded in an unrealistic conception of the industrial process. Repeatedly they claimed that the region's rich endowment of natural resources was a sure guarantee of industrialization. The falsity of this assumption requires no elaboration. As David M. Potter has observed, "a vital distinction separates mere abundance—the copious supply of natural resources—and actual abundance—the availability to society of a generous quota of goods ready for use."[47] The two are related, of course, but the history of the modern world—including the history of the Old South—shows that the potential does not automatically lead to the actual and that "environmental riches" in fact occupy "a relatively small place in the explanation of economic growth." Much more important are institutional and human factors which increase the capacity of society to produce.[48]

It is probably true that the New South dream of rapid industrialization and urbanization, with the attendant benefits of power and prestige for the region, was an unrealistic one to begin with because of the plethora of both economic and non-economic obstacles which had to be surmounted. Among economic factors which militated against success was the relative lateness of the Southern industrial movement. Beginning after industrialism was well advanced in other parts of the country, the South had a critical shortage of entrepreneurial talent, skilled workers, "and other external economies whose presence in the already industrially established North tended to make industrialization there self-generating." The lack of these advantages in the South, as Nicholls observes, meant that "it was the old agrarian pattern— only slightly modified by the development of such low-skill manufactures as textiles—which tended to be self-generating."[49] In addition to these economic problems, cultural, intellectual, and social patterns in the region also militated against rapid industrialization on the Northern model. Loyalty to an agrarian past and determination to preserve the value system produced by it as well as an essentially romantic and static conception of history, class, and race were not compatible with swift industrialization and urbanization.

The New South spokesmen were aware of some of these problems and it would be unfair to say that they did not try to face up to some of those that they saw. One is especially impressed by their attempt to revise attitudes toward the industrial society and its principal ideological appurtenances. But more striking are their several failures: they straddled fences, arguing that the peculiar sense of honor and personal identification of the slave regime could be maintained and fulfilled in an industrial age; they rejoiced in the wealth of natural resources, but were prevented by race and class biases from developing a program to utilize adequately the human resources; they knew they lacked capital, but their plan for getting it encouraged a colonial relationship that tended to drain the region of its wealth; and, finally, their retreat into mythmaking—the most pervasive feature of the New South movement after the mid-'eighties—betrays the absence of the kind of single-minded realism which they correctly said the situation required but so signally failed to embody in their leadership.

III

The final element in the myth of a New South was the image of a region free from the legacy of racial injustice, and the reality of an innocent South was proclaimed quite as fervently as the existence of an opulent and triumphant South. As early as 1885, Grady outlined all of the principal beliefs that became woven into this part of the New South creed:

> Ten years ago, nothing was settled. There were frequent collisions and constant apprehensions. The whites were suspicious and the blacks were restless. So simple a thing as a negro taking an hour's ride on the cars, or going to see a play, was fraught with possible danger. The larger affairs—school, church, and court—were held in abeyance. Now all this is changed. The era of doubt and mistrust is succeeded by the era of confidence and goodwill. The races meet in the exchange of labor in perfect amity and understanding. Together they carry on the concerns of the day, knowing little or nothing of the fierce hostility that divides labor and capital in other

sections. When they turn to social life they separate. Each race obeys its instinct and congregates about its own centers. At the theater they sit in opposite sections of the same gallery. On the trains they ride each in his own car. Each worships in his own church, and educates his children in his schools. Each has his place and fills it, and is satisfied. Each gets the same accommodation for the same money. There is no collision. There is no irritation or suspicion. Nowhere on earth is there kindlier feeling, closer sympathy, or less friction between two classes of society than between the whites and the blacks of the South to-day.[50]

Other New South writers added illustrative detail to this picture of a harmonious biracial society in order to buttress its credibility, but only one dimension remained to be added to foreclose dispute of Grady's joyful conclusion. Throughout the 'eighties the question of Negro endorsement of the New South creed was debated, but without the commanding authority of a recognized Southern Negro leader to offer his stamp of approval. With the rise of Booker T. Washington all of this changed, and after Washington announced his famous "Atlanta Compromise" in 1895 lingering doubts vanished, consciences everywhere were eased, and the New South program was accepted as an honest, biracial attempt to resolve the race question logically and justly.

Washington's rise to fame and power is part of the folklore of America, but it is also an essential part of the mythology of the New South movement. James Creelman of the New York *World* testified to this when he filed his story on Washington's 1895 address. Nothing since Grady's "immortal speech" before the New England Society of New York, Creelman wrote, had shown "so profoundly the spirit of the New South."[51] That Washington should have been heralded as a new prophet of the New South is hardly surprising. Quite apart from his racial views, the ideas he expressed and the life he lived were wonderful examples of New South precepts put into action. It was not simply that he had risen out of slavery and by industry, frugality, and perseverance had achieved eminence, or that he minimized the importance of politics and stressed economic advance. Equally important in identifying him as a New South man were his views on labor unions, which he distrusted, and his generally conservative position on political, economic, and religious questions. Like the white New South spokesmen and the Northern businessmen they befriended, Washington accepted the social Darwinism of his age and subscribed with conviction to Andrew Carnegie's gospel of wealth.[52]

When Washington came to the Atlanta Exposition in 1895 he found a setting ideally suited to his message. Designed to advertise the material and intellectual progress of the South, the Exposition included displays from the Negro population, attesting to the advance of the race. Washington's invitation to speak, considered by many to have been a bold experiment, seemed fitting testimony to the opportunity which the dominant race provided for the Negro. Washington himself regarded his presence on the speaker's platform as proof of his belief that men of merit, whatever their skin color, would not be denied opportunity in the South.[53]

"One-third of the population of the South is of the Negro race," Washington began his momentous address. "No enterprise seeking the material, civil, or moral welfare of this section can disregard this element of our population and reach the highest success."[54] From this opening assertion of the interdependence of the races, Washington developed a masterly presentation of the New South philosophy of race relations. All of the major concessions demanded of the Negroes were there: admission of the false start of the race during Reconstruction; recognition of the fact that "it is at the bottom of life we must begin"; unabashed faith that the Southern white man was the Negro's best friend; and conviction that it was in the South "that the Negro is given a man's chance in the commercial world."

With disarming concessions to the white man's view of things, Washington spoke with apparent candor on the basic issues of freedom and equality. Freedom should not be confused with irresponsibility, he declared, noting that it was out of ignorance and misdirection that Negroes, in the first years of freedom, wrongly preferred political eminence to industrial pursuits. The great danger to the race, Washington felt, was that "we may overlook the fact that the masses of us are to live by the production of our hands, and fail to keep in mind that we shall prosper in proportion as we learn to dignify and glorify common labour." He issued no threat to the political domination of the white race, promising instead that a continuation of the liberal white views which had brought about the Exposition would lead to the abolition of racial friction in a society in which Negroes "will buy your surplus land, make blossom the waste places in your fields, and run your factories." By continuing to offer economic and educational opportunities to the Negroes, the whites "can be sure in the future, as in the past, that you and your families will be surrounded by the most patient, faithful, law-abiding, and unresentful people that the world has seen."

Washington's comments on equality were likewise

satisfying to his white listeners. He assured them that the Negro wished to have opportunities in education and in industry, but that social equality was beyond the pale. "In all things that are purely social," he said in the passage that was most frequently quoted by the Southern press, "we can be as separate as the fingers, yet one as the hand in all things essential to mutual progress." And to emphasize the point, he added: "the wisest among my race understand that the agitation of questions of social equality is the extremest folly."

Washington's address profoundly strengthened the racial component of the New South myth. Widely reported in the press and the national periodicals, it seemed more than sufficient to vindicate Henry Grady's declarations of the previous decade.[55] Typical of magazine editorial response was the comment in the *Outlook* that no other speech at the Exposition had "so notable an effect" as Washington's, and the editor rejoiced at the "spirit of hearty good fellowship" produced by the affair.[56] More extravagant praise of both Washington and the New South movement came from the *Century Magazine*, long a friend of the South. "No patriotic American could have read the reports of the opening exercises of the Atlanta Exposition," the editor declared, "without feeling a thrill of joy run through his veins." The occasion marked "the jubilee of the new South—a South of industrial development and agricultural progress." Everywhere people were "joyous and confident," and not the least reason for celebration was the fact that the Exposition marked the symbolic "burial forever of the old South and negro slavery," proclaimed by Washington with "impassioned eloquence" and received by his white audience with "a perfect tumult of enthusiasm and delight."[57] Clark Howell, Grady's successor at the *Constitution*, spoke for the New South men: "The whole speech," he declared, "is a platform upon which blacks and whites can stand with full justice to each other."[58]

In the decade before Washington's address, lynchings and other forms of violence directed at the Negro increased sharply; by the time he spoke, the movement to disfranchise all Negroes had succeeded in two states, Mississippi and South Carolina, and was gaining momentum in the others; in the decade after he spoke more Negroes were disfranchised, and the doctrine of segregation espoused by Grady was enacted into law with a vengeance by Southern state and local governments. Humiliated by the Jim Crow system and reduced to a political cipher by the disfranchising conventions, Negroes lacked the economic security which might have permitted them to resist these movements. Industrialism had offered them virtually nothing during the 'eighties and 'nineties, and the great majority of their race continued to find that their lives were "circumscribed by the farm and plantation." Each year there were a few more black men who owned their own land, but in 1900 three out of every four who farmed were croppers or tenants whose livelihood was determined by white men.[59] Despite all this, Washington continued to act the role of a leader who believed that things were getting better. In his autobiography, written at the turn of the century, he declared that "despite superficial and temporary signs which might lead one to entertain a contrary opinion, there was never a time when I felt more hopeful for the race than I do at the present."[60] His faith in progress, as Samuel Spencer writes, "made him continue to insist . . . that race relations were steadily improving."[61]

IV

The figure of Washington on the podium at Atlanta poignantly evokes the inner meaning of the myth which he helped to establish. He both creates it and is himself caught by it. More than any other Southerner, the Negro needed to see progress, prosperity, and racial justice— if not at hand, clearly visible around the corner. But as these goals eluded their pursuers the belief in fulfillment was more fervently stated. This is not to suggest that Washington and Grady and their fellow New South spokesmen believed all they wrote. Much was pure propaganda and they knew it. The white spokesmen were engaged in wooing both Northern capital and Northern approbation and in establishing their own hegemony in the South. And Washington, like them, knew his audience and spoke what it wanted to hear. He, too, was wooing his oppressor and establishing himself as a powerful and exclusive leader of his race. In his testimony is all the strange mixture of wishful thinking and calculated opportunism that gave to the myth of the New South its singular force.

The opportunism is easily understood as a necessary tactic of ambitious men in a difficult situation, but the wishful thinking sprang from more complex sources. In part it derived from the universal need to make experience intelligible and agreeable; and for men deeply committed to a cause, only the most unmistakable jolts of defeat would cause them to abandon the belief in progress. For the New South men there was always enough evidence of advance to escape such a fate: factories were built, some men did accumulate fortunes, the North was more kindly disposed toward and respectful of the South, and life did become better for some Negroes. Perspective, too, is part of the answer. Washington's point of reference was slavery, and he was comforted and encouraged by the fact that at least Negroes had not been re-enslaved. For the white New South spokesmen, the background against which they wrote their accounts heightened the contrasts and exaggerated the images they saw. They saw Southern economic achievements against a scene of grinding poverty, increasing political power and self-determination against an experience of galling powerlessness, attempts at reconciliation against the legacy of hatred and mistrust, and concessions to the Negro against a backdrop of slavery and black codes. It is not surprising that in describing their region's attempt to don the mantle of the American heritage they implored their countrymen to admire the Emperor's new clothes.

Their legacy to the twentieth century was a pattern of belief in which Southerners could see themselves and their section as rich, successful, and just. Uncritically it could be assumed that because their "facts" proved it, opulence and power were at hand; that because men of good will and progressive outlook proclaimed it so, the Negro lived in the best of all possible worlds. It was both comfortable and to one's apparent advantage to accept this picture of society. Just as the fair picture of the antebellum South gave Southerners courage and pride while at the same time offering blandishments to Northern antagonism, so the picture of a New South had the double effect of ameliorating the bleak realities of the present and winning approbation and respect from the world outside.

The Enduring Myth

Seventy-five years after Henry Grady presented his vision of hope and good cheer to the New England Society of New York, a distinguished Texas historian who had spent most of his adult life puzzling over the South's problems launched a modest crusade of his own to fire the ambitions of his people with a vision of unbounded progress and prosperity. "I have turned myself into a propagandist," Walter Prescott Webb announced. His mission, he said, was "to tell my tale to various audiences who would listen, and to give them the evidence I had gathered as to the future prospect."[1] Both the evidence and the prospect sounded familiar to anyone who recalled the rhetoric of the New South men of the nineteenth century. "The story I am going to tell," Webb promised, "differs from much that is said and written about the South." His was to be a story "of cheerfulness, of optimism and hope, a story calculated to lift the spirit, turn the eyes of a Southerner . . . to a future so bright as to be to some all but unbelievable." Lamenting the many wrongs the South had suffered and the unique hardships it had endured, he promised release from the burdens. "As things stand now, as I see the South for the next seventy years," he declared, Southerners should take hope as never before "because it is not only possible but it is also probable that this next century will belong to the South."[2]

Before the decade was out, a United States senator
from South Carolina appeared before a Congressional
committee to present to its members—and to the nation—
a confession that probably came neither easily nor naturally to him. Governor of the state during the early
'sixties, he had embraced Webb's optimistic view of the
South's future; and, like the historian, he did his part to
attract industry to the state and to infuse its people with
a spirit of progress. Now, in 1969, Ernest F. Hollings had
decided to bring to a dramatic end his allegiance to the
tradition of New South boosterism. Having just completed a personal inspection tour of the state, he told the
committee of the widespread hunger, disease, and poverty
he saw. "We should be ashamed of this hunger," he said.
Adding the further confession that his knowledge of its
existence was no recent acquisition, he explained his
previous silence on the subject directly and credibly:
"We didn't want the vice president of the plant in New
York to know the burdens" of locating in South Carolina,
he commented. "We told him only of the opportunities."
Whites had been victimized by the state's backwardness,
but according to Hollings Negroes were the principal
sufferers. Lack of adequate nourishment, and not skin
color, was sufficient to account for the black man's plight.
"He is dumb because we denied him food," the Senator
declared. "Dumb in infancy, he has been blighted for
life."[3]

Walter Webb was no Henry Grady and Senator
Hollings can scarcely be regarded as a modern-day Lewis
Harvie Blair or George Washington Cable, but the juxta-
position of their responses to some of the problems of the
South in the 1960's is a fair reminder that the legacy of
the New South movement has been an enduring one and

that efforts to cope with its mythology persist seventy years after the original movement reached its climax.

I

In response to the South's crisis of defeat and despair, the New South spokesmen had designed for their beleaguered region a homegrown plan of reconstruction. To industrialize the South, revive its agricultural prosperity, inject its people with a spirit of confidence and zest, harmonize relations between former enemies, and honor the demands of the war and Reconstruction amendments— all of these were noble and ambitious goals. They were also goals that flattered the nation's image of itself as a land of opportunity, success, and justice and therefore had the special appeal of making the South appear to be ready to undertake on its own, free of outside pressure, the process of dismantling its heritage of dissidence and sectionalism. Used in this manner as a compelling justification for Northern abandonment of the Reconstruction, the New South doctrine also defined for Southerners an attractive substitute. Finally, the new creed of progress was tied from the outset to a relatively small group of merchants, industrialists, and planters. This new ruling class, supported by the New South creed, forged what it supposed was a mutually advantageous partnership with Northern capitalists and fastened its control over the region's destiny in the 1880's.

As the regime tightened its hegemony in the 'eighties, the ideology which had contributed to its acceptance evolved into a powerful social myth, further strengthening the existing order and impressing upon Southerners a pattern of belief that would be increasingly difficult to throw off. In the next decade these beliefs survived their first severe test and emerged stronger and more intimately related to the order they sustained. Throughout the 'eighties discontent with the Redeemer regimes had been apparent, but it was not until the Populist uprising of the 'nineties that a formidable assault was mounted. A potentially erosive force for the New South beliefs, the agrarian revolt instead proved to be crucial in assuring their longevity. Persuaded that the economic and political system established by the Redeemers restricted opportunity and deprived the Southern masses of hope for the future, the desperate agrarians who joined in the Populist movement naturally fixed on the New South doctrine of progress, prosperity, sectional reconciliation, and racial harmony as their principal target. But the frenzy of their attack, far from discrediting the mythology, worked rather to strengthen it. Respectable and conservative Americans reacted with unbridled disdain to what they regarded as the wild schemes and subversive tactics of the agrarian radicals so that the New South view of the world seemed, by contrast, to represent sanity, moderation, and security.

The turbulence of the 'nineties, heightened and brought into focus by the Populist revolt, accelerated the movement of the 'eighties toward racial subordination and resulted in the perfection of a far-reaching program of disfranchisement and segregation. To many it seemed that the Jim Crow system was a natural addition and reassuring guarantee of the safety of those standards celebrated in the New South myth, an institutionalization

of ideas already approved as right. Thus, at the opening
of the new century several fundamental patterns had been
established: the incipient New South creed rationalized
the abandonment of Reconstruction and the inauguration
of the Redeemer regimes in the 1870's; the mature doctrine undermined the first menacing reform movement
designed to overhaul that order in the 1890's; the Jim
Crow system was added as an insurance measure; and
the New South myth, fully articulated, offered a harmonizing and reassuring world view to conserve the
essential features of the status quo. The New South
movement itself was simultaneously ended. During the
next seven decades Southerners would celebrate the
achievements of Grady and his fellow prophets and with
the regularity of an inherited ritual they would proclaim
the arrival of even newer new Souths; but there never
again appeared a cohesive group that could legitimately
be called the party of the New South. There was no need
for one so long as the mythology created by the first one
endured.

II

The use of the New South myth as a foil to Reconstruction, Populism, and later assaults on the socio-economic
system shaped by the Redeemers suggests that its tenacious influence may be explained simply by regarding it
as essentially an instrument manipulated by interest
groups opposed to change; and examples of the way in
which opportunism of this sort has kept the myth vital

and effective are plentiful. Time and again attempts to expose the poverty and want in the region have been frustrated by appeals to the myth, a fact all the more remarkable because of the continuing failure of the Southern economy—a failure about which there is little argument today. The extensive literature on the breadth and depth of economic want in the South exposes the emptiness of the myth and needs no elaboration here. As Joseph J. Spengler, a Duke University economist, noted recently, "the South has been doing badly for at least a century." Fixing on per capita income as "the best single indicator of the performance of the southern economy," he concedes that the region improved markedly in the period 1929–63, but then explains how "this improvement merely reduced the margin of the South's inferiority; it did not move southern incomes up in the national income structure." As Spengler points out, twelve Southern states fell among the fifteen lowest in per capita income in 1962, and the nine lowest positions were a Southern monopoly.[4]

During the Depression one might have anticipated dissipation of the myth of abundance and opportunity, but the power of the old belief was frequently demonstrated and nowhere more dramatically and characteristically than in the reaction to the President's *Report on Economic Conditions in the South*, published in 1938. Product of a long and searching examination of the region's basic problems, this pamphlet distilled the essence of more than a decade of pioneering research. President Roosevelt, much to the delight of the social scientists on whose work the report was based, supported their analysis and recommendations, and announced in his foreword that he regarded the South as "the Nation's No. 1 economic problem."[5] So frank a remark wounded pride and set off

a violent reaction. But it was the content of the report—
which, if accepted, would totally destroy the bastions of
belief upon which all the comforting ramifications of the
myth could rest—that elicited resistance. In taut language
and authoritative tables it laid bare the economic backwardness and social suffering of the region. "The low
income belt of the South," it declared, "is a belt of sick-
ness, misery, and unnecessary death."[6] As cries of foul
misrepresentation rang out in all parts of the region,
Senator Josiah Bailey of North Carolina declared that the
South had made remarkable progress and argued that
emphasis should properly be placed on the achievements
of "our forefathers who rebuilt the South after the Civil
War." Arkansas Senator John E. Miller said that the
South needed to be left alone, not ridiculed. And the ghost
of Edmonds guided the editorial response of the *Manufacturers' Record*. "This section has been unwisely characterized as the economic problem No. 1 of the nation,"
the journal lamented. "Quite the opposite is true. The
South represents the nation's greatest opportunity for
industrial development."[7]

Important though the myth was as a bulwark against
change, a conscious manipulation cannot fully account for
its vitality and effectiveness. Myths are something more
than advertising slogans and propaganda ploys rationally
connected to a specific purpose. They have a subtle way
of permeating the thought and conditioning the actions
even of those who may be rationally opposed to their
consequences. They arise out of complex circumstances
to create mental sets which do not ordinarily yield to intellectual attacks. The history of their dynamics suggests
that they may be penetrated by rational analysis only as
the consequence of dramatic, or even traumatic, altera-

tions in the society whose essence they exist to portray. Thus, the critique and dissipation of myths becomes possible only when tension between the mythic view and the reality it sustains snaps the viability of their relationship, creates new social patterns and with them new harmonizing myths.

The New South myth has been no exception. In race relations, it formed the intellectual and moral touchstone to which all discussion of the Negro's role in Southern society was ineluctably referred for more than half of the present century. Influential in different ways, it has exerted its power over demagogues and racists as well as liberal reformers and well-meaning paternalists. Negroes and white Northerners have likewise responded to and been shaped by it, and much of foreign opinion has reflected its power. This is not to say that the dominant racial attitudes of the twentieth century all derived from the New South myth or that it was the first universally accepted conceptualization of racial sentiments. The fundamental ambivalences of hate and love, fear and trust, oppression and paternalism, repulsion and attraction underlying race relations have a history as old as the country; and successive institutional arrangements resulting from particular historical circumstances have each rested on their peculiar myths. What is true is that the New South myth perfectly complemented the post-Reconstruction search for a new modus operandi in race relations and came to be the intellectual and moral foundation of the Jim Crow system of the twentieth century.

In the thirty years before the Civil War, the slave regime rested securely on an elaborately structured pro-slavery myth. Emancipation and the subsequent failure of the abolitionist-Reconstruction creed of equality to find expression in a viable social system was followed by a period of uncertainty and flux in which no monolithic pattern of race relations emerged. Disfranchising measures and segregation statutes, beginning in the 1890's, rapidly changed all of this, creating a social system that rivaled the old slave regime in its concreteness and universality. By constitutional mandate and legislative statute Negroes were once again set apart as a distinct group within which individual differences were officially unrecognized as significant considerations of public policy. Accepted widely as the final solution to the conundrum presented by the demands of Negro freedom and the American tradition of equality, this new order was neatly rationalized by the New South myth. Defining each individual's role in life and the expectations placed on him by society, the myth was adopted by the Supreme Court in 1896, attractively encased in the slogan "equal but separate," and began a dominion over the American mind that conditioned and controlled the perception and programs of the most disparate groups so that, in its cumulative effect, it worked as a powerfully conservative force, protecting and maintaining the Jim Crow system to which it was wed.

Providing initially the intellectual and moral basis for the abandonment of sectional quarrels over the Negro's place in American society, the myth enjoyed a remarkably long period of freedom from the kinds of frontal assaults that might have helped to undermine it. The National Association for the Advancement of Colored People, founded in 1909, never accepted the moral ideal on which the myth rested, and its officers, especially W. E. B. DuBois, produced an impressive literature of dissent. But the NAACP attack was blunted by two unyielding obstacles. First, the white North was not to be aroused to any new crusades on the part of the black man and, for the most part, it rested comfortably with the assurance that, after all, equal treatment—even though separate—was more than Yankee reformers had ever been able to institute on a permanent basis. Second, Negro leadership itself was seriously divided. Booker T. Washington had placed his authoritative seal of approval on essential elements of the myth; after his death, in 1915, many Negro leaders who competed for the honor of inheriting his mantle—and especially those who worked in the South in cooperation with white liberals and Northern philanthropists—deemed it wise to give formal approval to the doctrine that separate could be equal and that whatever reforms or modifications of the existing order might be required could be achieved within the framework of separate societies. Such an admission, even if only temporary strategy, inevitably strengthened the hold of the myth.

A potential source of difficulty for the myth was the growing strength and influence of Southern liberalism and the work of one of its chief manifestations, the interracial movement. Liberal Southerners, anxiously addressing themselves realistically to the region's problems and demanding genuine reforms of the status quo had always existed in the South, but their number and influence had been minuscule in the last three quarters of the nineteenth century. During the first two decades of the twentieth century the liberalism of the so-called Progressive Movement in the South had been largely for whites only and, despite a growing concern on the part of a small group of respectable professional men, it concerned itself only incidentally with race relations. After the First World War, however, an enduring interracial reform organization established a foothold, and during the next quarter-century its educational work focused attention on the inequities of the Jim Crow system and its action wing engaged energetically in programs of reform. Directed by the patient and imaginative Will W. Alexander, the Commission on Interracial Cooperation found allies all across the region, enlisted support from most of the professions, and succeeded in making race relations a "problem" suitable for study and an object of regional concern rather than unqualified pride. In these important ways the first steps by which the myth might be eroded were taken with both caution and determination.

But the liberals in the interracial movement, though genuinely distraught by racial injustices, were authentic heirs of the myth and their thought and programs were directed and limited by acceptance of the belief that coercive separation was compatible with genuine equality. The great mass of white Southerners, like complacent and inarticulate Northerners, believed not only in the possibility but in the actuality as well. Liberals were distinguished from conservatives in this regard chiefly by their determined efforts to prove that, in nearly all areas of life, the separate societies were grossly unequal. Devoting most of their thought to long-range programs to ameliorate the situation—Will Alexander once remarked that "this situation will not be very greatly affected by any program or any set of men who do not think about it in terms of twenty-five to fifty years"[8]—the Interracial Commission undertook programs to supply legal aid for intimidated Negroes, agitated for an end to police brutality, urged equal pay for equal work, tried to encourage greater and more accurate reporting of Negro accomplishments, and campaigned vigorously against the most blatant abuses of Negroes, such as lynching. The achievement of these and other objectives of the liberals appeared to pose no threat to the system of segregation—an assumption the reformers themselves apparently shared—and thus by concentrating their energies on making a genuine reality of the ideal of the myth they greatly qualified their potential as forces of its erosion.

The interracial movement was but one manifestation of a general intellectual awakening that occurred during the interwar period, giving birth to a new brand of social criticism and reform agitation. Indigenous in origin, it appeared first in the 1920's as a response to the material stagnancy of the region and the spiritual malaise reflected in such phenomena as fundamentalism, prohibitionism, Ku Kluxery, and other offspring of a backward and depressed society. In the 1930's it assumed new directions and received added momentum and national attention as the New Deal emerged as a sympathetic partner in its endeavors. Journalists and publicists set out on voyages of exploration and came back to produce an impressive literature of discovery that revealed a South quite unlike the region celebrated in the myth. Social scientists in the universities announced the coming of a new critical realism that would free the region of its meretricious images, a first step they believed toward constructive reform. In Chapel Hill, sociologist Howard W. Odum, enjoying the support of reform-minded presidents, directed an academic enterprise that resulted in a staggering number of studies of the region and helped to make the University of North Carolina the intellectual center of the new realism. What Odum and his fellow sociologists did for the Southern present, the historians of the 1930's accomplished for the past. Questioning most of the received

truths, these revisionist scholars began to expose the
sordid aspects of slavery, dismantled the Cavalier myth,
recorded the disaffection and disloyalty that plagued the
Confederacy, found Reconstruction to be full of progressive, democratic reforms, questioned the motives and
achievements of the Redeemers, and wrote sympathetically of the Populist uprising of the 'nineties.

The outburst of reassessment and scholarly activity
during the interwar period was matched, if indeed not
surpassed, by a literary awakening that broke with the
sentimental plantation tradition, furnished painful and
ironic images of the region that shocked and startled those
who had been reared in the comfort of the old tradition,
and brought unprecedented acclaim to Southern writers.
Recalling his own impressions of the early 'thirties, one
historian believed that the "awakening of historical scholarship . . . was only a minor aspect of a wider intellectual
awakening in the South. The most brilliant manifestation
was in the field of letters and literary criticism."[9] James
Branch Cabell and Ellen Glasgow had presaged the new
spirit in novels published before the 'twenties, but the major authors—Faulkner, Warren, Ransom, Tate, and Wolfe,
among others—appeared during the interwar years. Miss
Glasgow voiced the concern that permeated their best
works. What the South needed, she explained, was blood
and irony: blood, "because Southern culture has strained
too far away from its roots in the earth"; irony, as "the
safest antidote to sentimental decay." The South, she
believed, was a region where "a congenial hedonism had
established . . . a confederacy of the spirit," where "pride,
complacency, . . . self-satisfaction, a blind contentment
with things as they are, and a deaf aversion from things
as they might be . . . stifle both the truth of literature and

the truth of life."[10] It was against this kind of South that the Southern writers revolted, and their novels wrestled with the human dilemma of all mankind in a Southern setting that seemed peculiarly appropriate for the revelation of ruthlessness and compassion, deceit and honor, cowardice and courage, the will to endure and the passion to destroy.

A revolt against the literary traditions and intellectual aridity of the region, the revolution in letters affirmed the faith that to probe honestly, even if devastatingly, was a surer means of honoring and strengthening the worthy qualities of the South than to remain mired in the treacly sentimentality of the past. But the term "revolt" suggests perhaps too much. For the most part, its influence was restricted to a small intelligentsia, Northern as well as Southern. Despite its artistic merit and critical acclaim it failed to mirror the fundamental aspirations and beliefs of the population in the way that Thomas Nelson Page had done for his generation. Thus, while the judgment of literary critics will come down strongly on the side of Faulkner, Warren, and Wolfe, the book-reading public preferred *Gone With the Wind* and treasured it as the best fictional treatment of the South to appear in the twentieth century. Margaret Mitchell's portrayal of the myths of the Old South, the Lost Cause, and the Reconstruction were artistically superior to Page's, but her novel was squarely in the plantation tradition of the previous century, and its immense success, coupled with the sensational reception of the movie version, attests both to the continuing vitality of the romantic view and the apparently impossible task of rooting out comfortable myths without profound social upheaval.

The intellectual awakening was closely related to the

Depression and the crisis of faith which affected all parts
of the country. Likewise, just as the New Deal wrought
profound changes in the social, economic, and political
structure of the nation, so the new realism in the South
was accompanied by programs of action that jostled the
established order. But other parallels between national
and regional developments stand out as more significant.
Just as the New Deal failed to disturb the fundamental
props of the capitalist structure of the country, so, too,
the reform literature and agitation in the South failed to
dismantle the main outlines of the Redeemer order established in the post-Reconstruction era. Despite all the enthusiasm for overhauling the Southern system, the
changes that in fact came about were relatively minor.
Economic power, at the end of the 'thirties, continued to
rest where it had been before; impoverished croppers and
mill hands continued to symbolize the region's economic
failures; the Negro, despite modest improvements in his
status, remained ensnared by the ramifying tentacles of
the Jim Crow system; and the original burst of enthusiasm for FDR soon gave way to a renewed spirit of sectionalism and an enduring sense of alienation from the reform-
ist tendencies of the New Deal.

Surveying the South's political structure in the mid-
'forties, in a work that probed deeply into the mental,
social, economic, and racial patterns of the region as well,
V. O. Key, Jr., wrote what is probably the most cogent
and devastating epilogue to the story of the Southern
intellectual awakening that has yet appeared. Viewing
politics broadly as the system of relationships and pro-
cedures whereby society concentrates, orders, and controls
power in such a way that fundamental issues that arise
among classes, sections, and interests may be reconciled

into a program advancing the general welfare, Key rigorously analyzed the Southern performance and recorded the "cold, hard fact that the South as a whole has developed no system or practice of political organization and leadership adequate to cope with its problems."[11] Key's influential study, though not designed for the purpose, was nonetheless a sobering and exhaustive documentation of the fact that neither the New Deal nor the Depression, neither the Southern realists nor the action programs they sponsored or inspired, had succeeded in destroying the viability between the social order and the mythic representation of it, despite all the strains that had been placed on that relationship.

III

With the coming of the Second World War the strains eased and the relationship was fortified. Wars commonly redefine the nature of domestic concerns and cause old issues to be shelved; this one was no exception. The New Deal reform impulse, which had already begun to weaken, was now replaced by the demands of national mobilization for victory. The Depression had produced a national crisis, but not one that brought unity and a common sense of national identity. The stunning attack on Pearl Harbor and the revulsion at the inhumanity of the Nazi onslaught guaranteed near-unanimous support in this national crisis and thereby re-created a sense of national purpose and identity. Under the circumstances, sectional and class quarrels receded. The evil of Hitler's design and the desperate nature of the struggle against it revived the nation's tarnished image of itself as a unique force in human history: once again entrusted with a special mission, it emerged from its isolation to save its gallant but hapless allies—and freedom as the western world knew it —from final destruction. Southern leadership relaxed with the disappearance of the New Deal demands for further reform, and all Southerners shared in the sense of urgency and mission. The war thus worked to affirm the national myth of a powerful Republic devoted to preserving liberty and justice and, simultaneously, to strengthen the image of the South as a fully integrated part of the Republic and its calling.

Accompanying the revival of this sense of national mission was a return of prosperity, induced largely by the demands of war production. Depression conditions vanished in all parts of the country, but in the South the arrival of more jobs and higher incomes was especially remarkable. War plants and shipyards moved into the region to provide employment for thousands of men and women who came home every Friday afternoon to cash checks the likes of which had not been seen before. There were grumblings, as a cumbersome rationing system interfered with the free expenditure of the new income, but on the whole the nation's faith in itself as a land of opulence and opportunity was re-established and the South's share of the new abundance was large enough to absolve the myth of the New South from the insults and doubts it had suffered in the 'thirties. Predictions that the war would be followed by a spiral of inflation and then depression were not borne out, and the South continued on an upward-bound course of economic development. Publicity focused on the growing occupational diversification of the region, and although income analyses of 1950 and 1960 showed that the South was still well below national per capita averages the gains were striking, the gap closing, and the augury reassuring. Few observed that perspectives were clouded by the intense recollections of the Depression, against which the advances were measured, and there were few Jeremiahs about to remind optimists that the New South spokesmen of the 'eighties had also reached favorable interpretations of economic development by comparing their present with the misery of the Civil War and Reconstruction. Walter Webb sympathized with this refusal to let a long view undermine more optimistic contrasts, and remarked sourly, "those who teach [Southern] history and those who study it are likely to be so conditioned that they take a somber view of not only the past but also of the future." The historical viewpoint, Webb appeared to be saying in 1960, was unconstructive; what Southerners needed was to see "that the South today is the most thriving" region in the United States.[12]

But disturbing crosscurrents were at work as early as the war period, and by the mid-'fifties the myth would once again be under severe strain. During the war racial tensions had risen alarmingly, partly as a result of the unevenness of the new prosperity and partly because of the unavoidable contrast between the reality of Jim Crow at home and the war propaganda image of democratic virtue struggling to destroy a racist Behemoth in Europe. Southern liberals, with increasing uncertainty, had maintained their position that separate could be equal; but now they began to question that assumption more frequently. Appropriately, Alexander was among the first and clearest prophets of a new attitude. Writing in *Harper's* late in the war, he confronted the inherently incompatible elements in the Southern—and American—racial credo. Americans believed, Alexander wrote, that the Negro should be educated, but that he should also be segregated. The sticking point in this policy was that segregation "tends to defeat the inspiring work of Negro education." Education of Negroes had not been a mistake, he wrote, for "here we see American faith and American idealism at its best." But education for Negroes had proceeded along self-defeating lines because "segregation . . . is rooted in fear and in doubt as to whether our democratic principles will really work. It remains to be seen whether or not our faith in democracy is strong enough to overcome our fears as to what may become of its consequences." Whatever the outcome, Alexander was sure of the approach that would determine it. "Unless the problem of segregation can be solved," he warned, "there is no hope of any alleviation of the race problem in America."[13]

In the first decade after the war there was little reason to believe that the problem of segregation would be solved, but Alexander's concern accurately reflected changing attitudes toward the race problem that would cause liberals as well as conservatives to confront the equal-but-separate doctrine in ways they had not dreamed of before. The liberals, uncertain of the consequences of dispensing with an assumption that had increased their numbers and guided their constructive reform work for a generation, quarreled among themselves and eventually suffered a rupture when the Southern Regional Council, successor to the old Interracial Commission, declared segregation to be incompatible with the achievement of equality. Former friends of the liberal movement—typified by Richmond editor Virginius Dabney—now parted company, unable to believe that their old ideas could no longer serve as progressive guidelines. Many of the former liberals joined the conservatives and supported their attempts to save the equal-but-separate doctrine from destruction. Since the late 'thirties the Supreme Court had appeared increasingly likely to qualify or perhaps even strike down the doctrine. Faced with this possibility, Southern conservatives adopted a new strategy. Conceding now that Negro schools were inferior to white schools, they started a massive building campaign to make them equal in all tangible respects, hoping that such a demonstrable effort to equalize facilities would deter the Court from making a frontal assault on the doctrine itself. South Carolina Governor James F. Byrnes was candid about it: "To meet this situation we are forced to do now what we should have been doing for the last fifty years."[14]

New schools were built, but the strategy failed and the Supreme Court decision of May 17, 1954, striking down the fifty-eight-year-old Plessy doctrine of equal but separate, ushered the South and the nation into a new era of history whose course is as yet unspent. For the myth of the New South the events of the Second Reconstruction have been more devastating than any previous assault. From the beginning of the South's program of massive resistance to school desegregation to the Selma–Montgomery march a decade later the nation was overwhelmed with the most graphic evidence of racial injustice and brutality. Obsessively caught up with the drama of the South's turmoil, the nation saw more clearly and more eagerly than ever before the protective coloring stripped from the Southern ethos and the stark form of its racial bedrock revealed. Moreover, the dynamics of this reconstruction ran differently from those of the first. The course of change, especially after the beginning of the nonviolent direct action movement in 1960, was heavily influenced by Southern Negroes. Inspired by the young leaders of the Student Nonviolent Coordinating Committee and by Martin Luther King and his Southern Christian Leadership Conference, they proved both their desire for change and their determination and ability to bring it about. With the Negro revolt as the driving force and the excesses of white Southern response as the catalyst, the national government became increasingly active so that by the summer of 1965 virtually every piece of federal legislation desired by civil rights leaders had become law and the nation seemed assured of vigorous executive support and favorable judicial interpretation.

With such legislation and such pressures taking the limelight, a third influence contributing to the erosion of the myth was the subtle shift in thought that began to affect white Southerners. Despite recurrent attempts to picture the Negro revolt as a product of the communist conspiracy or another sinister form of outside agitation, the widening arc and undiminished force of the revolution made these comforting explanations less and less plausible so that, haltingly and reluctantly, more of them began to believe that Negroes, after all, were not happy in the South in their present conditions. And as those conditions were altered by legislation, judicial and executive actions, and concessions wrung by the demonstrators, white Southerners found themselves in situations they had never believed possible. One after another, old customs and institutions were revised or eliminated and situations abounded for which the myth could by no stretch of imagination remain instructive. At each stage of the social revolution Southerners, horrified by new demands placed upon them, found themselves frequently accepting, by contrast, the latest change—not always as reasonable and just, but at least as one the region had found it could live with—so that each year saw more unprecedented racial patterns at variance with "equal but separate" and a widening acceptance of those new patterns.

Exposing the claims of racial justice and harmony as a hollow sham, the events of the Second Reconstruction also put other parts of the New South doctrine in a harsh light. Regional publicists continued to praise the allegedly increasing benefits of a dynamic economy, and typical of scores of journalistic reminders was the boast that "the once-sleeping South has taken off like an inter-planetary missile. . . . The New South has come in with a clap of thunder."[15] But as national faith in the region's claims to racial justice crumbled under bright exposure, so too did the South appear to the nation as a region in which poverty was widespread, incomes shamefully below the national average, and job opportunities—especially for Negroes—severely limited. The situation was in many respects a novel one for Southerners. In the 1880's, when economic advances were modest in comparison with the 'fifties and early 'sixties, the nation welcomed Southern claims and accepted them at face value. During the 1930's, when all parts of the country were in tight straits, analyses of the South's economic backwardness, while arousing sectional hostility later in the decade, did not compare with the way in which the criticism during the Second Reconstruction aroused indignation and rekindled the flames of sectionalism. Now it was the South alone that offended the national dream of opulence and opportunity, and that offense was part of a larger pattern of crimes that everyone appeared to agree was peculiarly Southern.

The myth of national harmony and regional triumph

was another casualty of the Second Reconstruction. More than at any time since the 1860's, disharmony, virulent sectionalism, and an unending series of frustrations and defeats characterized the Southern experience. To some observers it seemed as though a spiritual malaise had seized the region. To others, with an historical bent of mind, it appeared that the South was determined to relive the most disastrous period of her history. Reacting to assaults from columnists and television pundits, clergymen and college professors, black and white demonstrators, and all branches of the federal government, Southerners revived the old rhetoric of interposition, nullification, and secession, issued ringing manifestos of warning and defiance, and in the heat of resistance to the civil rights movement spawned hate groups, a supercharged literature of Negrophobia, and instituted repressive measures to stifle internal dissent. Believing themselves to be under siege from a hostile nation determined to destroy them, they joined to their ritual of oppression stratagems of defense that could scarcely have been better calculated to stiffen the national will, bring on greater displays of federal power—including armed force—and thus assure the collapse, one after the other, of each new measure of defiance and the fateful creation of changes in their society they had sworn could never be made.

The irrationality and violence of the Southern response to the civil rights movement poignantly evoked memories of the calamitous dispute over slavery a century earlier; and in both national crises the South's mythic view of itself powerfully influenced its actions. The myth of the Old South furnished slaveholders with a comprehensive world view in which they could see themselves and their region as guardians of liberty, defenders of republican virtue, protectors of Negroes, and keepers of a gentlemen's code of honor. Accused by the nation of being enemies of liberty, subverters of republican virtue, oppressors of Negroes, and perpetrators of snobbish values, their behavior was hardly surprising. A century later, the myth of the New South expressed the Southerner's view that his was a land of riches, that it accepted and exemplified the American credo of bountiful opportunity, defended the nation's honor, and provided (or was on the point of providing) equally bountiful but harmoniously separate opportunity for the Negro. All of these views were now ridiculed during the Second Reconstruction: the new affluence and success so apparent on the surface hid a class system that exploited the masses of whites and restricted wealth to the few; the South's nationalism was a stranglehold on Congressional committees; and its oppression of the Negro caused it to be a stain on the nation's honor. Incredulity and wounded pride, mixed with a measure of fear, were the inevitable products of these assaults; and incredulity, offended pride, and fear are the handmaidens of irrational thought and violent action.

IV

With bewildering rapidity, however, the perspective of the mid-'sixties was lost in the kaleidoscopic swirl of events that followed in the last half of the decade. As so often before, the race problem made the difference and caused Americans to see both the nation and the South in a new light. After the victories in the spring and summer of 1965, the civil rights movement, partly because of its successes, splintered and lost direction. As it searched for a new focus the South continued the slow process of absorbing the changes that had already taken place. Demands made upon the region became fewer or took less dramatic forms. Integration proceeded in orderly fashion in more schools each year. Negroes were seen in greater numbers in occupations and public places previously barred to them. The tension and fear which had made racial change electric in the previous decade receded and Southern claims of progress toward racial justice assumed a superficial plausibility impossible to imagine in the recent past.

Simultaneously, the dynamic patterns set off by the Negro revolt in the South now spread outside the region—and the tactic of nonviolence was left behind. Starting with the Watts riot in 1965, non-Southern urban centers were hit with racial violence and police overkill on a grand scale. Earlier, the nation's anxious moments had come in the late summer in anticipation of the violence that would attend school openings in the South. Now, anxiety heightened during the spring in expectation of summer turmoil in Northern cities. The country witnessed the irony of Dr. King leading his Southern Christian Leadership Conference workers into Chicago in a vain effort to find solutions. A puzzled and frustrated people began to reorient their research programs and redirect their philanthropy outside the South. The blue-ribbon Kerner Commission, instructed to study the virulence and ubiquity of racial discord, reported in 1968 that "our nation is moving toward two societies, one black, one white—separate and unequal."[16] Incredible though it seemed, bigotry and oppression of blacks almost overnight ceased to be regarded as a Southern monopoly. Public leaders, including Southerners, spoke fervently of their determination to root out the racist cancer and pointed to the remarkable achievements of the past decade as proof of their good intentions. But the cancer spread. In the ghettoes and on the college campuses racial confrontations, charged with the electricity of black power, became almost a way of life in the last half of the 'sixties, and progress toward alleviation of their causes was uneven and unimpressive. In these circumstances the nation's image of itself as a land of moral innocence became a fragile inheritance, in more danger than ever before of being shattered.

The events of the late 'sixties threatened not only to dissipate the idea of racial justice but to dissolve other components of the nation's historic myth as well. Repudiations came from all directions, and for increasing numbers of persons faith in the old ideas was weakened or destroyed. The myth of American abundance and economic opportunity was attacked not only as an inaccurate reflection of reality but also as an unworthy ideal. Critics declared that the ideal rationalized an economic system whose excessively materialistic value premises promoted acquisitiveness and impersonality of the kind that led straight to a grasping, automated society undeserving of pride and loyalty. Lacking in novelty, this argument nonetheless gained added force because of other critiques of the nation's economic system. Wealthier than ever before in history, America was paradoxically afflicted with a more acute awareness of poverty than at any time since the Depression. Worse yet, the new discovery of poverty seemed especially enigmatic—precisely because of the generally high level of productivity—and for that reason doubly noxious. Other ironies abounded: a society of abundance institutionalized anti-poverty programs; a land of opportunity created head-start and upward-bound programs for youngsters deprived of opportunity; and manpower retraining schools were conducted for men and women lacking in skills that a free enterprise society would employ.

Criticism of the American record and ideal of economic progress was met by persuasive counterargument, and could be regarded as but another phase in a creative tradition of dissidence that always before had strengthened the nation. But only the most ingenious twists of imagination could keep alive the old idea of national invincibility. Mightier than ever before, the country was less able to wield its power to achieve its ends than it had been during the presidency of Theodore Roosevelt. This paradoxical and frustrating situation had been in the making for two decades. With Russia as a dedicated and successful antagonist and the atomic bomb a threat of annihilation, foreign policy since the onset of the Cold War was based on acceptance of the fact that single displays of decisive might to produce once-for-all solutions—so long an American characteristic—were no longer tenable. The Korean War, with its limited objectives, institutionalized the new foreign policy and President Truman's dismissal of General MacArthur—a warrior of the old school—was its most pointed symbol. Frustrations stemming from the new situation heightened throughout the 'fifties and early 'sixties, with important repercussions in domestic affairs, but it was not until the escalation of the war in Vietnam, in the last half of the decade, that the meaning of the nation's loss of power was driven home with a kind of terrible finality. Applying to the Vietnamese

conflict the limited-war concepts which had been successful in Korea, the nation met discouragement and failure.
No matter how many men were sent into battle or how
many bombs were dropped, the prospects of military
victory would not brighten. Productive of deep fissures
at home and mounting abuse from friends abroad, the war
dragged on—a disturbing testimony to the ironic outcome
of America's historic conception of itself as master of its
own fate, exemplar of the democratic faith, and beacon
of liberty for the rest of mankind.

V

An ironic history—like the evil of race prejudice—was
once thought to be something from which all Americans
except Southerners were immune. But now that the nation
as a whole was caught up in a maelstrom of contradictions its differences from the South appeared to be less
significant than ever before. Since the Civil War most
Americans had believed that the South would be absorbed
into the mainstream of national development when its
socio-economic system and moral views became standard
"American." Hearteningly, the region made impressive
material progress during the years after the Second World
War, and in the later 'sixties it adjusted its attitudes
toward the Negro remarkably. But the importance of these
developments was undercut by the ironic twist of the
national experience itself. In the final analysis, regional
distinctions receded because of the infiltration into the
total American experience of the elements of pathos, frus-

tration, and imperfection that had long characterized the South.

As America entered a new era of history and as national images were undermined, the myth of the New South appeared to be losing its *raison d'être*. Southerners accepted new racial patterns that gave to the black man more dignity and greater opportunity than he had ever known before—only to see sharply highlighted the inadequacies of integration and the immensity of the problems caused by a heritage of oppression. The region's continuing economic progress, more substantial than ever before, was beset by the same kind of critiques that confounded national advances. Its growing identity with the national viewpoint, made possible initially by the nationalization of the race problem, was unrewarded by a sense of relief and achievement because the nation itself appeared to have lost a sense of destiny. Thus deprived of the larger frame of reference which had always conditioned its character and given it its special appeal, the myth paradoxically pictured a regional way of life in harmony with a mirage.

Admirable in its vision, the New South creed had been manipulated through most of its history by men who served the region poorly, and the hold it gained over the American mind had obstructed more frequently than it had promoted achievement of its ideals. In the end, it was the force of outside pressure combined with the Negro revolt that made a reality of at least part of its ideal. Study of the history of the New South creed should contribute to greater understanding of the special mental and material forces that have shaped the Southern experience—an important end in itself. But reflection on its relationship to the American faith in opulence, triumph,

246 ~ The New South Creed

and innocence may also illuminate the ways in which rigidification of even noble human aspirations can result in powerful myths that shroud and institutionalize abhorrent realities. The dynamics of mythmaking suggest that resolution of the nation's dilemmas cannot be accomplished by clinging doggedly to its old myths—but also that rediscovery of their core of nobility could yet result from the contemporary turbulence caused by pressures from without and revolt from within.

Notes

PROLOGUE: The New South Symbol

1. Joel Chandler Harris, ed., *Life of Henry W. Grady, Including His Writings and Speeches* (New York, 1890), p. 109.
2. *Manufacturers' Record*, March 17, 1888.
3. The industrial journal *The New South* was published in Birmingham in the 1880's. *New South* (titles vary) was an organ of the Communist Party of the U.S.A., published in Chattanooga and Birmingham in the 1930's; it was a successor to *Southern Worker*.
4. George B. Tindall, "Mythology: A New Frontier in Southern History," in Frank E. Vandiver, ed., *The Idea of the South: Pursuit of a Central Theme* (Chicago, 1964), p. 10.
5. David M. Potter, "On Understanding the South: A Review Article," *Journal of Southern History*, XXX (November 1964), 460.
6. Mark Schorer, "The Necessity of Myth," in Henry A. Murray, ed., *Myth and Mythmaking* (New York, 1960), p. 355.
7. C. Vann Woodward, "The Antislavery Myth," *American Scholar*, XXXI (Spring 1962), 325.
8. Quoted in Everett Carter, "The 'Little Myth' of Robert Penn Warren," *Modern Fiction Studies*, VI (Spring 1960), 3.
9. William E. Dodd, *Statesmen of the Old South; or, From Radicalism to Conservative Revolt* (New York, 1911).
10. David M. Potter, "The Enigma of the South," *Yale Review*, LI (Autumn 1961), 144.
11. Twelve Southerners, *I'll Take My Stand: The South and the Agrarian Tradition* (New York, 1930).
12. Potter, "Enigma of the South," 150.

248 ~ The New South Creed

13. Ulrich B. Phillips, "The Central Theme of Southern History," *American Historical Review*, XXXIV (October 1928), 31.
14. C. Vann Woodward, "The Search for Southern Identity," in his *The Burden of Southern History* (Baton Rouge, 1960), pp. 3–25; Harry Ashmore, *An Epitaph for Dixie* (New York, 1958); George B. Tindall, William B. Hesseltine, Cleanth Brooks, and Rupert B. Vance, "The Status and Future of Regionalism—A Symposium," *Journal of Southern History*, XXVI (February 1960), 22–56; John T. Westbrook, "Twilight of Southern Regionalism," *Southwest Review*, XLII (Summer 1957), 234.
15. Edgar T. Thompson, ed., *Perspectives on the South: Agenda for Research* (Durham, 1967), p. xi.
16. W. J. Cash, *The Mind of the South* (New York, 1941), pp. ix–x.
17. The following works are especially helpful: Clement Eaton, *The Mind of the Old South* (Baton Rouge, 1964); Clement Eaton, *The Freedom-of-Thought Struggle in the Old South* (New York, 1964); William Sumner Jenkins, *Pro-Slavery Thought in the Old South* (Chapel Hill, 1935); William R. Taylor, *Cavalier and Yankee: The Old South and American National Character* (New York, 1961); Rollin G. Osterweis, *Romanticism and Nationalism in the Old South* (New Haven, 1949); and Eugene D. Genovese, *The Political Economy of Slavery: Studies in the Economy and Society of the Slave South* (New York, 1965). For a survey of the literature see Herbert J. Doherty, Jr., "The Mind of the Antebellum South," in Arthur S. Link and Rembert W. Patrick, eds., *Writing Southern History: Essays in Historiography in Honor of Fletcher M. Green* (Baton Rouge, 1965), pp. 198–223.
18. There has also been a relative paucity of articles on the postwar period. David Potter's study of articles appearing in the *Journal of Southern History* from 1935 through 1949 shows that, of those that could be classified by period, 48.8 per cent were written on the period 1830–65 while only 16.3 per cent were devoted to the entire period since the Reconstruction; David M. Potter, "An Appraisal of Fifteen Years of the *Journal of Southern History*, 1935–1949," *Journal of Southern History*, XVI (February 1950), 25–32. During the period 1950–63, the proportion on the era since

1877 went up slightly, to 21.9 per cent of the total classi-
fiable by period, but studies in intellectual history are remarkably few; Paul M. Gaston, "The 'New South,'" in
Link and Patrick, eds., *Writing Southern History*, p.
332.
19. Tindall, "Mythology," in Vandiver, ed., *The Idea of the
South*, p. 15.
20. Woodward, *Burden of Southern History*, pp. 16–22.

1   Birth of a Creed

1. Daniel Harvey Hill, "Education," *The Land We Love*,
   I (May 1866), 8.
2. Edwin DeLeon, "The New South: What it is Doing and
   What it Wants," *Putnam's Magazine*, XV (April 1870),
   458.
3. Benjamin H. Hill, Jr., *Senator Benjamin H. Hill of Georgia:
   His Life, Speeches and Writings* (Atlanta, 1893), pp.
   335–6.
4. Joel Chandler Harris, ed., *Life of Henry W. Grady, Includ-
   his Writings and Speeches* (New York, 1890), p. 449;
   Raymond B. Nixon, *Henry W. Grady: Spokesman of the
   New South* (New York, 1943), pp. 243–53.
5. Robert S. Cotterill, "The Old South to the New," *Journal
   of Southern History*, XV (February 1949), 3.
6. Port Royal [S.C.] *The New South*, March 15, 1862. The
   story of the sea-islands is told in Willie Lee Rose, *Rehearsal
   for Reconstruction: The Port Royal Experiment*
   (Indianapolis, 1964).
7. The standard monograph on the pro-slavery philosophy
   is William S. Jenkins, *Pro-Slavery Thought in the Old
   South* (Chapel Hill, 1935). Southern attempts to stifle
   dissent are the subject of Clement Eaton, *The Freedom-of-
   Thought Struggle in the Old South* (New York, 1964).
8. Ben Allston, "Address . . . Before the Winyah Indigo
   Society," *DeBow's Review*, VII (August 1869), 669.
9. J. D. B. DeBow, "The Future of the South," *DeBow's
   Review*, I (January 1866), 8–14.
10. Matthew Fontaine Maury, "The American Colony in Mexi-
    co," *DeBow's Review*, I (June 1866), 623–30.

11. *Ibid.*, p. 623.
12. A. P. Merrill, "Southern Labor," *DeBow's Review*, VI (July 1869), 592.
13. J. D. B. DeBow, "The Future of South Carolina—Her Inviting Resources," *DeBow's Review*, II (July 1866), 38.
14. DeBow, "Future of the South," p. 14.
15. J. D. B. DeBow, "Manufactures, the South's True Remedy," *DeBow's Review*, III (February 1867), 176–7.
16. Robert M. Patton, "The New Era of Southern Manufactures," *DeBow's Review*, III (January 1867), 56–69.
17. Charles J. James, "Cotton Manufactures—Great Field for the South," *DeBow's Review*, I (May 1866), 504–15.
18. "Exodus," *DeBow's Review*, V (November 1868), 983. See also S. H. Gilman, "Cotton Manufacturing in or near the Cotton Fields of Texas Compared with the Same at any Point Distant Therefrom," *DeBow's Review*, V (September 1868), 837–40.
19. John C. Delavique, "Cotton," *DeBow's Review*, IV (December 1867), 571. See also H. T. Moore, "The Industrial Interests of the South," *DeBow's Review*, V (February 1868), 147–55.
20. John A. Wagener, "European Immigration," *DeBow's Review*, IV (July and August 1867), 94–105.
21. E. C. Cabell, "White Emigration to the South," *DeBow's Review*, I (January 1866), 92.
22. William M. Burwell, "To the Patrons of DeBow's Review," *DeBow's Review*, V (March 1868), 332–3.
23. D. H. Hill, "Education," p. 2.
24. *Ibid.*, pp. 8–9.
25. *Ibid.*, p. 9.
26. D. H. Hill, "Industrial Combinations," *The Land We Love*, V (May 1868), 31.
27. D. H. Hill, "The Old South," *Southern Historical Society Papers*, XVI (1888), 425. Hill's magazine is appraised briefly in Ray M. Atchison, "*The Land We Love:* A Southern Post-Bellum Magazine of Agriculture, Literature, and Military History," *North Carolina Historical Review*, XXXVII (October 1960), 506–15.
28. William Lee Trenholm, *The South: An Address on the Third Anniversary of the Charleston Board of Trade* (Charleston, 1869), p. 1 and *passim*.
29. Richmond *Whig*, "The Industrial Policy of the South," in *DeBow's Review*, VI (November 1869), 929.

30. Harry Simonhoff, *Jewish Notables in America, 1776–1865* (New York, 1956), pp. 378–81; *Who Was Who in America: Historical Volume, 1607–1896* (Chicago, 1963), p. 144.
31. DeLeon, "New South," p. 458.
32. *Ibid.*, p. 459.
33. *Ibid.*, pp. 459–60.
34. Edwin DeLeon, "The New South," *Harper's New Monthly Magazine*, XLVIII (1874), 270–80; 406–22; XLIX (1874), 555–68. Edwin DeLeon, "Ruin and Reconstruc-struction of the Southern States," *The Southern Magazine*, XIV (1874), 17–41, 287–309, 453–82, 561–90; Edwin DeLeon, "The Southern States Since the War," *Fraser's Magazine*, XC (1874), 153–63, 346–66, 620–37.
35. B. H. Hill, Jr., *Senator Benjamin H. Hill*, pp. 335–7.
36. On Hill's life see Haywood Pearce, Jr., *Benjamin H. Hill: Secession and Reconstruction* (Chicago, 1928).
37. Nixon, *Grady*, p. 245 *n*.
38. B. H. Hill, Jr., *Senator Benjamin H. Hill*, p. 342.
39. *Ibid.*, pp. 342–3.
40. William D. Trammell, Review of "*Address Delivered Before the Alumni Society of the University of Georgia. By Benjamin H. Hill*," *The Southern Magazine*, X (June 1872), 751–61. William D. Trammell, *Ça Ira, A Novel* (New York, 1874).
41. Trammell, *Ça Ira*, p. 41.
42. Another novelist who turned to the emerging New South point of view as a field for fiction was John Esten Cooke. One of his characters states that "the old Virginia system resulted in immense comfort, but it did not result in profit, which is a good thing, however it may be denounced by some. Profit means prosperity, and prosperity means churches, lyceums, academies, schools, railroads, material advancement and happiness." *The Heir of Gaymount* (New York, 1870), p. 56.
43. Margaret J. Preston, "Gospel of Labor," *The Southern Magazine*, IX (December 1871), 733–4.
44. Harris, ed., *Grady*, p. 6.
45. Nixon, *Grady*, p. 136.
46. Quoted in S. Frank Logan, "Francis W. Dawson, 1840–1889: South Carolina Editor" (unpublished master's thesis, Duke University, 1947), p. 74.
47. *Ibid.*, pp. 67, 214.

48. " 'The Great South' Series of Papers," *Scribner's Monthly*, IX (December 1874), 248.
49. Albion W. Tourgee, *A Fool's Errand, By One of the Fools: The Famous Romance of American History* (New York, 1879), p. 292.
50. *Ibid.*, p. 345.
51. Raleigh *News and Observer*, November 29, 1880, quoted in Broadus Mitchell, *The Rise of the Cotton Mills in the South* (Baltimore, 1921), pp. 89–90.
52. Atlanta *Constitution*, November 7, 1880.

2   The Opulent South

1. Atlanta *Constitution*, August 20, 1884.
2. *Manufacturers' Record*, August 20, 1887. See also William D. Kelley, *The Old South and the New* (New York, 1888), pp. 161–2.
3. *Manufacturers' Record*, June 1, 1889.
4. Charles R. Anderson, ed., *Sidney Lanier*, 10 vols. (Baltimore, 1945), IX, 230.
5. David M. Potter, *People of Plenty: Economic Abundance and the American Character* (Chicago, 1954).
6. C. Vann Woodward, *The Burden of Southern History* (Baton Rouge, 1960), p. 17.
7. Douglas C. North, *The Economic Growth of the United States, 1790–1860* (Englewood Cliffs, N.J., 1961), p. 122.
8. Eugene D. Genovese, *The Political Economy of Slavery: Studies in the Economy and Society of the Slave South* (New York, 1965), pp. 124–53.
9. Thomas Prentice Kettell, *Southern Wealth and Northern Profits, As Exhibited in Statistical Facts and Official Figures: Showing the Necessity of Union to the Future Prosperity and Welfare of the Republic* (New York, 1860).
10. Eric F. Goldman, *Rendezvous With Destiny: A History of Modern American Reform* (New York, 1952), p. 3.
11. The generalization holds true for lesser New South spokesmen as well. Nearly all of them were young men in the 'eighties. The years in which they matured had a sobering effect on them but, unlike the older generation—veterans

of secession and defeat—they were full of youthful optimism about the future.

12. Raymond B. Nixon, *Henry W. Grady: Spokesman of the New South* (New York, 1943), chaps. 2–3.

13. *Ibid.*, chaps. 3–9.

14. Joel Chandler Harris, ed., *Life of Henry W. Grady, Including His Writings and Speeches* (New York, 1890), p. 449.

15. Howard Bunyan Clay, "Daniel Augustus Tompkins: An American Bourbon" (unpublished doctoral dissertation, University of North Carolina, 1950), pp. 1–4.

16. *Ibid.* See also George Tayloe Winston, *A Builder of the New South, Being the Story of the Life Work of Daniel Augustus Tompkins* (Garden City, 1920). "The only thing I wanted the paper for," Tompkins declared, "was to preach the doctrine of industrial development and the reasons for it"; Clay, "Tompkins," p. 60.

17. Yoshimitsu Ide, "The Significance of Richard Hathaway Edmonds and His *Manufacturers' Record* in the New South" (unpublished doctoral dissertation, University of Florida, 1959), p. 34.

18. *Ibid.*, pp. 34–5.

19. *Ibid.*, pp. 43–5, 53–4.

20. Burton J. Hendrick, *The Training of an American: The Earlier Life and Letters of Walter H. Page, 1855–1913* (Boston, 1928), pp. 1–41.

21. *Ibid.*, pp. 42–108.

22. Joseph Frazier Wall, *Henry Watterson: Reconstructed Rebel* (New York, 1956), pp. 3–33.

23. *Ibid.*, pp. 34–50.

24. [E. L. Godkin], "The White Side of the Southern Question," *The Nation*, XXXI (August 19, 1880), 126.

25. Daniel A. Tompkins, *Fourth of July Address at Gastonia, N.C.* (n.p., 1902), p. 10.

26. Ide, "Edmonds," p. 25.

27. Kelley, *Old South and New*, pp. 2, 121.

28. *Ibid.*, pp. 121, 159.

29. Daniel A. Tompkins, *Manufactures* (Charlotte, 1900), p. 5.

30. Harris, ed., *Grady*, pp. 90–1; Atlanta *Constitution*, February 20, 1881.

31. John W. Johnston, "The Emancipation of the Southern Whites," *Manufacturers' Record*, July 9, 1887.

32. Kelley, *Old South and New*, dedication page.

33. Tompkins, *Manufactures*, pp. 4–5.
34. Ide, "Edmonds," pp. 85–6; R. H. Edmonds, *The Old South and the New* (n.p., 1903), pp. 3–5.
35. D. A. Tompkins, "Southern Prosperity," *Manufacturers' Record*, June 4, 1887.
36. W. H. Page, "Study of an Old Southern Borough," *Atlantic Monthly*, XLVII (May 1881), 648–58.
37. Hendrick, *Page, Earlier Life*, p. 161.
38. *Ibid.*, p. 168.
39. Nicholas Worth [pseud., Walter Hines Page], *The Southerner* (New York, 1909), p. 316.
40. Josephus Daniels, *Tar Heel Editor* (Chapel Hill, 1939), p. 256.
41. Hendrick, *Page, Earlier Life*, pp. 176–81.
42. W. H. Page, "The Rebuilding of Old Commonwealths," *Atlantic Monthly*, LXXXIX (May 1902), 654.
43. Atlanta *Constitution*, June 4, 1885.
44. Ide, "Edmonds," pp. 109–17.
45. Anderson, *Lanier*, V, 334–58.
46. *Ibid.*, I, 34–9. Lanier's role as a New South man is an interesting one, deserving a study in its own right. His "New South" essay and his sympathy for the farmer, expressed in such poems as "Corn," have led some students to see him as a forerunner of the Southern Agrarians of the 1930's, certainly no admirers of the New South movement. This view is re-enforced by his poem, "The Symphony," a poetic diatribe against the materialism engendered by the industrial movement (see Anderson, *Lanier*, I, 46–56). The Agrarians, however, were highly critical of Lanier, partly because they scorned his literary talents but also because they felt he had sold his soul by writing promotional literature for Florida and because they regarded him, in essence, as a New South publicist. Edwin Mims, *Sidney Lanier* (Boston, 1905), offered an interpretation of Lanier that pictures him as a New South man. Aubrey Starke's *Sidney Lanier, A Biographical and Critical Study* (Chapel Hill, 1933), appearing at the height of the Agrarian movement, aroused considerable controversy by depicting Lanier as a forerunner of the Agrarians. Robert Penn Warren, one of the Agrarians, attacked this interpretation in a scorching essay in *The American Review*, II (November 1933), 27–45.

47. *Manufacturers' Record*, December 11, 1886; Atlanta *Constitution*, January 11, 1882.
48. Atlanta *Constitution*, August 10, 1884.
49. *Ibid.*
50. *Ibid.*, December 13, 1882. For other editorials on crop diversification, see issues of January 11, 1882, March 4, 1882, September 30, 1882, October 14, 1883, August 10, 1884, and January 19, 1886.
51. *Ibid.*, February 24, 1883.
52. *Ibid.;* Kelley, *Old South and New*, p. 121.
53. Genovese, *Political Economy of Slavery*, pp. 180–220.
54. *Manufacturers' Record*, December 11, 1886.
55. Atlanta *Constitution*, January 19, 1886.
56. *Ibid.*, November 29, 1886.
57. William Peterfield Trent, "Dominant Forces in Southern Life," *Atlantic Monthly*, LXXIX (January 1897), 50.
58. *Manufacturers' Record*, March 9, 1889.
59. Harris, ed., *Grady*, pp. 113–14.
60. *Manufacturers' Record*, February 11, 1888.
61. Kelley, *Old South and New*, p. 75.
62. Richard H. Edmonds, *Tasks of Young Men of the South* (n.p., 1903), p. 9; *Manufacturers' Record*, March 9, 1889.
63. John C. Calhoun Newton, *The New South and the Methodist Episcopal Church, South* (Baltimore, 1887), pp. 9–27.
64. Kelley, *Old South and New*, pp. 12–13.
65. Harris, ed., *Grady*, pp. 204–5. In an editorial column, Grady fairly boiled with indignation because no native Georgia materials were selected in the construction of the Georgia capitol; Atlanta *Constitution*, September 27, 1884. The funeral oration was immensely popular with the New South spokesmen. Tompkins, for example, repeated it from memory on at least one occasion; Tompkins, *Manufactures*, p. 3. Edmonds made the same point, in a rhetorically less effective manner, when he wrote: "We use Northern stoves to cook our food; Northern tableware, from knives and forks to coffee and tea pots; we cover our table with Northern cloth and sit in Northern-made chairs; we furnish our homes with Northern-made carpets and furniture; we lie down at night on Northern-made beds, and cover ourselves with Northern-made blankets; we wash in Northern-made basins, dry our faces on Northern-made towels, brush our teeth with Northern-made brushes, comb our hair with Northern-

made combs, put on clothes made from Northern goods;
we ride in Northern-made wagons and carriages drawn by
Northern-made harness, travel in Northern-made cars running on Northern-made rails and drawn by Northern-made
locomotives. We do all this in spite of the fact that the
South is the best country in the world for manufactures.
Not only ought we to manufacture all these things for
home consumption, but we ought to be pushing out and
supplying the wants of other sections." Ide, "Edmonds,"
pp. 82–3.

66. Quoted in Nixon, *Grady*, p. 182.

67. Atlanta *Constitution*, October 20, 1883, May 15, 1884,
April 23, 1885, and December 5, 1889.

68. *Manufacturers' Record*, September 4, 1886, and April 20,
1889.

69. Edmonds, *The South's Redemption: From Poverty to Prosperity* (Baltimore, 1890), p. 5.

70. *Manufacturers' Record*, November 6, 1886; Ide, "Edmonds,"
pp. 195–207.

71. Sample works include William H. Harrison, Jr., *How to
Get Rich in the South. Telling What to Do, How to Do It,
and the Profits to be Realized* (Chicago, 1888), and Eugene
C. Robertson, *Road to Wealth Leads Through the South*
(Cincinnati, 1894). Evidence of the extensiveness of the
promotional campaign is abundant, but for a particularly
impressive source see the seventy volumes of pamphlets in
the Francis W. Dawson collection at the University of North
Carolina. Scarcely a volume of the collection is without
several examples of promotional literature.

72. *Manufacturers' Record*, March 19, 1887. Grady was also
enthusiastic about Hillyard's volume and Edmonds's scheme
for promoting it. He believed that the book would "give
outsiders a better idea of the material greatness of the
new south than anything that has yet appeared in print."
It was a happy omen, and "the signs of the times are all
that we could desire." Atlanta *Constitution*, March 20,
1887.

73. Ide, "Edmonds," pp. 89–91. Annistonians followed up
Kelley's article with a eulogy to "the great Pennsylvania
statesman," and a paid advertisement seconding Kelley's
designation of their community as "The Model City of the
South"; *Manufacturers' Record*, February 25, 1888. Edmonds joined the chorus the next month, citing Anniston

as a wonderful example of the South's progress—progress that had "already astonished the world"; *ibid.*, March 10, 1888.

74. Atlanta *Constitution*, November 16, 1881.
75. Eugene V. Smalley, "The New Orleans Exposition," *Century Magazine*, XXX (May 1885), 4.
76. Atlanta *Constitution*, October 12, 1887.
77. "Studies in the South," *Atlantic Monthly*, LI (January 1883), 95.
78. Rowland T. Berthoff, "Southern Attitudes Toward Immigration, 1865–1914," *Journal of Southern History*, XVII (August 1951), 328–60; C. Vann Woodward, *Origins of the New South, 1877–1913* (Baton Rouge, 1951), pp. 297–9.
79. *Manufacturers' Record*, February 11, 1888.
80. Atlanta *Constitution*, February 17, 1888.
81. W. N. Reeves, "The Unemployed—Send Them South," *Outlook*, XLIX (February 10, 1894), 286.
82. Atlanta *Constitution*, March 30, 1881.
83. *Ibid.*, April 11, 1885.
84. *Manufacturers' Record*, May 19, 1888.
85. Atlanta *Constitution*, March 20, 1885.
86. Robert L. Brandfon, *Cotton Kingdom of the New South: A History of the Yazoo Mississippi Delta From Reconstruction to the Twentieth Century* (Cambridge, Mass., 1967), p. 141.
87. Atlanta *Constitution*, April 23, 1886.
88. *Ibid.*, August 27, 1889.
89. Wilbur Fisk Tillett, "The White Man of the New South," *Century Magazine*, XXIII (March 1887), 776.
90. *Manufacturers' Record*, September 6, 1890.
91. *Ibid.*, July 2, 1887.
92. Harris, ed., *Grady*, p. 109.
93. Kelley, *Old South and New*, pp. 161–2.
94. Edmonds, *South's Redemption*, p. 3.

3 The Triumphant South

1. Henry Watterson, *The Compromises of Life* (New York, 1903), p. 289.

258 ~ The New South Creed

2. Quoted in William Malone Baskervill, *Southern Writers: Biographical and Critical Studies* (Nashville, 1907), p. 134.
3. Richard H. Edmonds, *Tasks of Young Men of the South* (n.p., 1903), p. 9.
4. Amory Dwight Mayo, "Is There a New South?" *Social Economist*, V (October 1893), 208.
5. Paul H. Buck, *The Road to Reunion, 1865–1900* (Boston, 1937), p. 22.
6. Henry Steele Commager, *The American Mind: An Interpretation of American Thought and Character Since the 1880's* (New Haven, 1950), p. 5.
7. C. Vann Woodward, *The Burden of Southern History* (Baton Rouge, 1960), pp. 18–19.
8. Edward Atkinson, *Address Given in Atlanta . . . for the Promotion of an International Cotton Exhibition* (Boston, 1881), p. 8.
9. Benjamin H. Hill, Jr., *Senator Benjamin H. Hill of Georgia: His Life, Speeches and Writings* (Atlanta, 1891), p. 460.
10. Edward Mayes, *Lucius Q. C. Lamar: His Life, Times and Speeches, 1825–1893* (Nashville, 1896), p. 187.
11. Quoted in Raymond B. Nixon, *Henry W. Grady: Spokesman of the New South* (New York, 1943), p. 253.
12. *Harper's Weekly*, XXI (July 7, 1877), 519.
13. Nixon, *Grady*, p. 110.
14. Atlanta *Constitution*, January 4, 1880.
15. *Ibid.*, September 20, 1881.
16. *Ibid.*, November 4, 1881.
17. *Ibid.*, May 18, 1884.
18. Nixon, *Grady*, pp. 238–9.
19. *Ibid.*, pp. 243–4.
20. Joel Chandler Harris, ed., *Life of Henry W. Grady, Including His Writings and Speeches* (New York, 1890), p. 83. Grady took considerable license in his opening paragraph. There is no record of a speech by Hill at Tammany Hall in 1866. Hill did address the Young Men's Democratic Union in New York City on October 6, 1868, but that speech does not contain the language attributed to Hill by Grady. The reconciliation theme is dominant, but Hill's tone was considerably more belligerent than Grady's as he scolded the North for unreasonable Reconstruction policies and urged the defeat of Grant in the November elections. The text of the speech appears in B. H. Hill, Jr., *Senator*

Benjamin H. Hill, pp. 320–31. The phrase closest to that used by Grady appears toward the end of the speech: "The South yields secession, and yields slavery, and *yields them for equal reunion*" (p. 330).

21. Harris, ed., *Grady*, pp. 85–6.
22. *Ibid.*, p. 87.
23. *Ibid.*, pp. 87–8.
24. *Ibid.*, pp. 88–93.
25. Nixon, *Grady*, p. 253.
26. Harris, ed., *Grady*, p. 200.
27. *Ibid.*, dedication page.
28. Robert Bingham, *The New South: An Address . . . in the Interest of National Aid to Education* (n.p., 1884), p. 4.
29. Charles Dudley Warner, "Impressions of the South," *Harper's New Monthly Magazine*, LXXI (September 1885), 548.
30. Charles Dudley Warner, "The South Revisited," *Harper's New Monthly Magazine*, LXXIV (March 1887), 640.
31. "Topics of the Times," *Century Magazine*, XXX (October 1885), 964.
32. Atticus G. Haygood, *Our Brother in Black: His Freedom and His Future* (New York, 1881), p. 27.
33. Harold F. Williamson, *Edward Atkinson: The Biography of an American Liberal* (Boston, 1934), p. 176.
34. Arthur S. Link, ed., *The Papers of Woodrow Wilson* (Princeton, 1966–), I, 618.
35. Arthur Krock, ed., *Editorials of Henry Watterson* (New York, 1923), p. 41.
36. Burton J. Hendrick, *The Training of an American: The Earlier Life and Lettters of Waiter H. Page, 1855–1913* (Boston, 1928), p. 34.
37. Arlin Turner, *George W. Cable: A Biography* (Durham, 1956), pp. 247–8.
38. Harris, ed., *Grady*, pp. 180–98.
39. Isaac F. Marcosson, *"Marse Henry": A Biography of Henry Watterson* (New York, 1951), pp. 83–4.
40. Watterson, *Compromises of Life*, pp. 289–93.
41. Henry Watterson, "Oddities of Southern Life," *Century Magazine*, XXIII (April 1882), 885.
42. Richard H. Edmonds, *Unparalleled Industrial Progress* (n.p., n.d.), p. 673.

43. Yoshimitsu Ide, "The Significance of Richard Hathaway Edmonds and His *Manufacturers' Record* in the New South" (unpublished doctoral dissertation, University of Florida, 1959), pp. 54–5.

44. Buck, *Road to Reunion*, pp. 186–7.

45. [E. L. Godkin], "The White Side of the Southern Question," *The Nation*, XXXI (August 19, 1880), 126.

46. Atlanta *Constitution*, January 15, 1887.

47. Daniel A. Tompkins, *Fourth of July Address at Gastonia, N.C.* (n.p., 1902), pp. 2–5.

48. Walter Hines Page, "The Rebuilding of Old Commonwealths," *Atlantic Monthly*, LXXXIX (May 1902), 651–2.

49. Samuel C. Mitchell, "The Nationalization of Southern Sentiment," *South Atlantic Quarterly*, VII (April 1908), 110–12.

50. Atlanta *Constitution*, June 19, 1887.

51. Richard H. Edmonds, *Facts About the South* (Baltimore, 1907), p. 43.

52. Harris, ed., *Grady*, p. 88.

53. James Phelan, *The New South: The Democratic Position on the Tariff; Speech . . . Delivered at Covington, Tenn.* (Memphis, 1886), p. 2.

54. *Ibid.*, pp. 1–6.

55. David A. Robertson, "Amory Dwight Mayo," *Dictionary of American Biography*, XII, 461–2.

56. Mayo, "New South?", pp. 200–8.

57. Judson C. Ward, ed., *The New South: Thanksgiving Sermon, 1880, by Atticus G. Haygood*, in *Emory University Publications, Sources and Reprints*, Series VI (1950), No. 3, pp. v–xi. The best biography of Haygood is Harold W. Mann, *Atticus Greene Haygood: Methodist Bishop, Editor, and Educator* (Athens, Ga., 1965).

58. Ward, ed., *Haygood Thanksgiving Sermon*, p. vii.

59. *Ibid.*, p. viii.

60. *Ibid.*, pp. 1–12.

61. The most recent biography of Curry is Jessie Pearl Rice, *J. L. M. Curry: Southerner, Statesman and Educator* (New York, 1959), but Edwin Anderson Alderman and Armistead Churchill Gordon, *J. L. M. Curry, A Biography* (New York, 1911) remains useful and is particularly valuable for the number of contemporary documents reproduced in it.

62. J. L. M. Curry, *Address Delivered Before the Association*

of *Confederate Veterans, Richmond, Virginia, July 1, 1896* (Richmond, 1896), pp. 26–7.

63. J. L. M. Curry, "Citizenship and Education," *Education*, V (September 1884), 86.

64. J. L. M. Curry, "Annual Report . . . 1881," in *Proceedings of the Trustees of the Peabody Education Fund, 1881–1887* (Cambridge, Mass., 1888), III, 9; J. L. M. Curry, "Address in Response to an Invitation from the Senate and House of Representatives of Alabama, February 6th, 1885," *ibid.*, III, 266.

65. "From the Address of Dr. Curry to the Legislature of Alabama, 1 February, 1889," in *Proceedings of the Trustees of the Peabody Education Fund, 1887–1892* (Cambridge, Mass., 1893), IV, 152.

66. Atlanta *Constitution*, November 17, 1882.

67. *Manufacturers' Record*, January 4, 1900.

68. Bingham, *New South*, p. 22.

69. Burton J. Hendrick, *The Life and Letters of Walter H. Page*, 3 vols. (New York, 1922–5), I, 74–9.

70. *Ibid.*, I, 79; Charles Grier Sellers, Jr., "Walter Hines Page and the Spirit of the New South," *North Carolina Historical Review*, XXIX (October 1952), 494.

71. Mark Twain, *Life on the Mississippi* (Boston, 1883), p. 412.

72. *Manufacturers' Record*, November 3, 1888.

73. *Ibid.*, August 14, 1886.

74. William D. Kelley, *The Old South and the New* (New York, 1888), p. 95.

75. W. H. Wallace, *Three Essentials to Success: Money, Reputation, Character* (Newberry, S.C., 1887), p. 3.

76. *Manufacturers' Record*, June 23, 1888.

77. Watterson, "Oddities of Southern Life," p. 885.

78. Atlanta *Constitution*, September 23, 1881; Chapel Hill *Ledger*, September 27, 1879; Edmonds, *Tasks of Young Men of the South*, p. 2.

79. Atkinson, *Address for Promotion of Cotton Exhibition*, p. 13.

80. Quoted in Nixon, *Grady*, p. 183.

81. Atlanta *Constitution*, April 9, 1882; Harris, ed., *Grady*, p. 88; Atlanta *Constitution*, May 25, 1887.

82. Quoted in Ide, "Edmonds," p. 302.

83. Atlanta *Constitution*, August 15, 1880.

84. Wallace, *Three Essentials to Success*, pp. 4–5.
85. *Ibid.*, p. 4.
86. William S. Speer, *The Law of Success* (Nashville, 1885), p. 20.
87. Atlanta *Constitution*, July 23, 1881.
88. *Manufacturers' Record*, October 22, 1887.
89. Richard Hofstadter, *Social Darwinism in American Thought*, rev. ed. (Boston, 1955).
90. Quoted in C. Vann Woodward, *Origins of the New South, 1877–1913* (Baton Rouge, 1951), p. 148.
91. Howard Bunyan Clay, "Daniel Augustus Tompkins: An American Bourbon" (unpublished doctoral dissertation, University of North Carolina, 1950), pp. i, 318.
92. John C. Calhoun Newton, *The New South and the Methodist Episcopal Church, South* (Baltimore, 1887), p. 27.
93. Sellers, "Page and the Spirit of the New South," 497–8.
94. Nixon, *Grady*, p. 310.
95. Edmonds, *Tasks of Young Men of the South*, p. 3.
96. Mayo, "New South?", 204.
97. Edmonds, *Facts About the South*, p. 61; Richard H. Edmonds, *The Old South and the New* (n.p., 1903), p. 1.
98. Holland Thompson, *The New South* (New Haven, 1919), p. 7.
99. Henry W. Grady, *The New South*, ed. Oliver Dyer (New York, 1890), p. 166.
100. Edmonds, *Facts About the South*, p. 3.
101. Harris, ed., *Grady*, p. 119.
102. Ide, "Edmonds," p. 24.
103. Joseph G. Brown, *The New South* (Raleigh, 1902), p. 4.
104. Kelley, *Old South and New*, pp. 157–8.
105. Newton, *New South*, p. vi.
106. Broadus Mitchell, *The Rise of the Cotton Mills in the South* (Baltimore, 1921), p. 77.
107. Edmonds, *Tasks of Young Men of the South*, p. 9.

4   The Innocent South

1. *Manufacturers' Record*, March 14, 1891.
2. Joel Chandler Harris, ed., *Life of Henry W. Grady, Including His Writings and Speeches* (New York, 1890), p. 307.

3. *Ibid.*, p. 100.
4. Thomas U. Dudley, "How Shall We Help the Negro?" *Century Magazine*, XXX (June 1885), 277.
5. Frederick Jackson Turner, *The Frontier in American History* (New York, 1920), pp. 281–2.
6. Reinhold Niebuhr, *The Irony of American History* (New York, 1952), p. 24.
7. C. Vann Woodward, *The Burden of Southern History* (Baton Rouge, 1960), pp. 19–20.
8. For a good collection of foreign commentaries, see Henry Steele Commager, *America in Perspective: The United States Through Foreign Eyes* (New York, 1947).
9. Gunnar Myrdal, *An American Dilemma: The Negro Problem and Modern Democracy*, 2 vols. (New York, 1944), I, 1–13.
10. Works on the anti-slavery views of the Jeffersonian era are numerous. For a convenient summary, see William S. Jenkins, *Pro-Slavery Thought in the Old South* (Chapel Hill, 1935), chap. 1; Jefferson's thought is discussed in Dumas Malone, *Jefferson the Virginian* (Boston, 1948), chaps. 18–20. Robert McColley, *Slavery and Jeffersonian Virginia* (Urbana, 1964) minimizes the importance of anti-slavery thought of the period. The most recent study is Winthrop D. Jordan *White Over Black: American Attitudes Toward the Negro, 1550–1812* (Chapel Hill, 1968).
11. The standard monograph on the pro-slavery ideology is Jenkins, *Pro-Slavery Thought*. A convenient collection of pro-slavery writings appears in Eric L. McKitrick, ed., *Slavery Defended: The Views of the Old South* (Englewood Cliffs, N.J., 1963).
12. The theory of retrogression is discussed in Guion Griffis Johnson's perceptive essay, "The Ideology of White Supremacy, 1876–1910," in Fletcher Melvin Green, ed., *Essays in Southern History* (Chapel Hill, 1949), pp. 139–43. White attitudes toward the Negro, with emphasis on the South in the post-Reconstruction period, are the subject of Claude H. Nolen, *The Negro's Image in the South: The Anatomy of White Supremacy* (Lexington, Ky., 1967).
13. Philip Alexander Bruce, *The Plantation Negro as a Freeman: Observations on His Character, Condition, and Prospects in Virginia* (New York, 1889), pp. 245–6, 259.
14. Charles Colcock Jones, Jr., *Georgians During the War*

Between the States: An Address Delivered Before the Con-federate Survivors' Association (Augusta, Ga., 1889), pp. 29–31.

15. Thomas Nelson Page, "A Southerner on the Negro Question," *North American Review*, CLIV (April 1892), 403, 413.

16. Thomas Nelson Page, *The Negro: The Southerner's Problem* (New York, 1904), p. 253.

17. John C. Calhoun Newton, *The New South and the Methodist Episcopal Church, South* (Baltimore, 1887), pp. 31–40.

18. Atticus G. Haygood, *Our Brother in Black: His Freedom and His Future* (New York, 1881), pp. 128–30.

19. Henry W. Grady, *The New South*, ed. Oliver Dyer (New York, 1890), p. 232.

20. Atlanta *Constitution*, May 18, 1883.

21. Harris, ed., *Grady*, p. 95.

22. Arthur Krock, ed., *The Editorials of Henry Watterson* (New York, 1923), p. 313; William D. Kelley, *The Old South and the New* (New York, 1888), p. 111.

23. *Manufacturers' Record*, May 14, 1887.

24. *Ibid.*, August 16, 1890.

25. George W. Cable, "The Freedman Case in Equity," *Century Magazine*, XXIX (January 1885), 409–18. On Cable's life see Arlin Turner, *George W. Cable, A Biography* (Durham, 1956).

26. Henry W. Grady, "In Plain Black and White: A Reply to Mr. Cable," *Century Magazine*, XXIX (April 1885), 909–17.

27. Harris, ed., *Grady*, pp. 91–2.

28. Haygood, *Our Brother in Black*, pp. 43–4.

29. Henry Watterson, *"Marse Henry": An Autobiography*, 2 vols. (New York, 1919), I, 143–4.

30. Haygood, *Our Brother in Black*, pp. 73–81.

31. James G. Blaine *et al.*, "Ought the Negro to be Disfranchised? Ought He to have been Enfranchised?" *North American Review*, CXXVIII (March 1879), 231.

32. *Ibid.*, p. 241.

33. *Ibid.*, pp. 241–2, 231.

34. Atlanta *Constitution*, January 16, 1880.

35. Grady, "In Plain Black and White," 909–17.

36. Walter B. Hill, "Uncle Tom Without a Cabin," *Century Magazine*, XXVII (April 1884), 864.

37. Haygood, *Our Brother in Black*, pp. 74–5. Page spoke of the "wretched mess" that Reconstruction had made "of the principle of a fair ballot" in his introduction to Booker T. Washington, *Up From Slavery* (Garden City, 1924), p. xv; and in a private letter discussing the Fifteenth Amendment, he wrote: "I have no hesitation in saying that I regard its adoption, when it was adopted, as a grave mistake, but I should consider it a much graver mistake to repeal it now, even if it were possible to repeal it." Page to Edgar Gardner Murphy, April 15, 1900, Southern Education Papers, Dabney Series, University of North Carolina Library.

38. Harris, ed., *Grady*, p. 194.

39. *Ibid.*, p. 184.

40. Grady, *New South*, ed. Dyer, p. 232.

41. Page, "Introduction," in Washington, *Up From Slavery*, pp. x–xxii.

42. This brief summary of the political and economic role of the Redeemers is based on the analysis in C. Vann Woodward, *Origins of the New South, 1877–1913* (Baton Rouge, 1951). Earlier interpretations of the period are discussed in Paul M. Gaston, "The 'New South,'" in Arthur S. Link and Rembert W. Patrick, eds., *Writing Southern History: Essays in Historiography in Honor of Fletcher M. Green* (Baton Rouge, 1965), pp. 316–29.

43. Henry Watterson, "The Solid South," *North American Review*, CXXVIII (January 1879), 53–4.

44. Harris, ed., *Grady*, p. 90. For local consumption Grady expressed the same idea more bluntly: "Remove the outside pressure; eliminate the idea that the north, taking advantage of its power and influence, is bent on placing the negro in positions he is not yet able to fill; leave the south to deal with the situation as it exists, and there will be no limit to the kindness and friendliness with which the negro will be treated and advanced." Atlanta *Constitution*, January 3, 1889.

45. Harris, ed., *Grady*, p. 90; Atlanta *Constitution*, November 8, 1884.

46. Grady, *New South*, ed. Dyer, pp. 239–44.

47. Harris, ed., *Grady*, p. 100.

48. Arlin Turner, ed., *The Negro Question: A Selection of Writings on Civil Rights in the South by George W. Cable* (Garden City, 1958), p. 110.

49. Johnson, "Ideology of White Supremacy," pp. 143–6.
50. Robert Bingham, *The New South: An Address in the Interest of National Aid to Education* (n.p., 1884), p. 13.
51. Turner, ed., *The Negro Question*, p. 130.
52. Turner, *Cable*, pp. 259–60.
53. Turner, ed., *The Negro Question*, pp. 60–4.
54. Harris, ed., *Grady*, pp. 100–1.
55. *Ibid.*, p. 103.
56. Raymond B. Nixon, *Henry W. Grady: Spokesman of the New South* (New York, 1943), p. 289.
57. Harris, ed., *Grady*, pp. 101–2.
58. Daniel A. Tompkins, *Manufactures* (Charlotte, 1900), p. 22.
59. Bingham, *New South*, p. 13.
60. Yoshimitsu Ide, "The Significance of Richard Hathaway Edmonds and his *Manufacturers' Record* in the New South" (unpublished doctoral dissertation, University of Florida, 1959), p. 142.
61. Haygood, *Our Brother in Black*, p. 232.
62. Atlanta *Constitution*, January 12, 1885.
63. *Ibid.*, June 16, 1887.
64. Harris, ed., *Grady*, pp. 291–2.
65. Atlanta *Constitution*, January 1, 1885.
66. Harris, ed., *Grady*, p. 289.
67. J. C. Price, "Does the Negro Seek Social Equality?", *The Forum*, X (January 1891), 558–62.
68. Turner, ed., *The Negro Question*, pp. 78–9.
69. *Ibid.*, p. 124.
70. *Ibid.*, p. 109.
71. Lewis H. Blair, *The Prosperity of the South Dependent upon the Elevation of the Negro* (Richmond, 1889), p. iv.
72. Amory Dwight Mayo, "The Progress of the Negro," *The Forum*, X (November 1890), 338–9.
73. Turner, ed., *The Negro Question*, p. 69.
74. Quoted in Johnson, "Ideology of White Supremacy," p. 155.
75. Turner, ed., *The Negro Question*, p. 88.
76. Burton J. Hendrick, *The Training of an American: The Earlier Life and Letters of Walter H. Page, 1855–1913* (Boston, 1928), p. 172.
77. Haygood, *Our Brother in Black*, p. 133.
78. Atticus G. Haygood, *Pleas for Progress* (Nashville, 1889), p. 17.

79. Haygood, *Our Brother in Black*, pp. 184–92.
80. Turner, ed., *The Negro Question*, pp. 81–2.
81. *Ibid.*, p. 95.
82. Haygood, *Our Brother in Black*, pp. 144–5.
83. Page, "Introduction," in Washington, *Up From Slavery*, pp. xvi–xvii.
84. Henry Watterson, *The Compromises of Life* (New York, 1903), pp. 289–90.
85. *Manufacturers' Record*, December 25, 1886, and October 25, 1890.
86. Atlanta *Constitution*, December 31, 1888.
87. Grady, *New South*, ed. Dyer, p. 251; Harris, ed., *Grady*, p. 300.
88. Atlanta *Constitution*, October 21, 1883.
89. *Ibid.*, January 1, 1885.
90. Grady, *New South*, ed. Dyer, p. 245.
91. Atlanta *Constitution*, October 16, 1883.
92. Grady, *New South*, ed. Dyer, pp. 245–50.
93. Harris, ed., *Grady*, pp. 294–9.
94. *Ibid.*, pp. 104–5.

5 The Vital Nexus

1. The lines are from "The Conquered Banner," the complete text of which may be found in Abram J. Ryan, *Poems: Patriotic, Religious, Miscellaneous* (Baltimore, 1881), pp. 185–7.
2. John C. Calhoun Newton, *The New South and the Methodist Episcopal Church, South* (Baltimore, 1887), pp. vi–vii.
3. James Branch Cabell, *Let Me Lie, Being in the Main an Ethnological Account of the Remarkable Commonwealth of Virginia, and the Making of its History* (New York, 1947), p. 74.
4. Robert Penn Warren, *The Legacy of the Civil War: Meditations on the Centennial* (New York, 1961), p. 15.
5. Nicholas Worth [pseud., Walter Hines Page], *The Southerner* (New York, 1909), p. 86.
6. John Randolph Tucker, *The Old South and the New South* (Columbia, S.C., 1887), p. 1.
7. Charles Colcock Jones, Jr., *Georgians During the War Between the States* (Augusta, Ga., 1889), p. 24.

8. Charles Colcock Jones, Jr., *Sons of Confederate Veterans* (Augusta, Ga., 1891), p. 8.

9. Charles Colcock Jones, Jr., *The Old South* (Augusta, Ga., 1887), p. 17.

10. Edward A. Pollard, *The Lost Cause: A New Southern History of the War of the Confederates* (New York, 1866), p. 751.

11. *Ibid.*

12. *Ibid.*, pp. 750–2.

13. Bledsoe founded the *Southern Review* in 1867 and edited it in Baltimore until his death in 1877.

14. Albert Taylor Bledsoe, "Chivalrous Southrons," *Southern Review*, VI (July 1869), 109; and "The Present Crisis," *Southern Review*, XIII (January 1873), 4. Scarcely an issue of the journal is without an attack by Bledsoe on the materialism of his age made in the name of the principles of the Old South, but see particularly "North and South," II (July 1867), 122–46; "Causes of Sectional Discontent," II (July 1867), 200–30; and "Public School Education at the North," IV (July 1868), 1–36.

15. Robert L. Dabney, "The New South," in C. R. Vaughan, ed., *Discussions by Robert L. Dabney*, 4 vols. (Mexico, Mo., 1897), IV, 1–24.

16. Randall Stewart et al., *The Literature of the South* (Chicago, 1952), p. 438.

17. Benjamin B. Kendrick and Alex M. Arnett, *The South Looks at Its Past* (Chapel Hill, 1935), p. 105.

18. Frank L. Owsley, "A Key to Southern Liberalism," *Southern Review*, III (Summer 1937), 37.

19. Herman C. Nixon in Twelve Southerners, *I'll Take My Stand: The South and the Agrarian Tradition* (New York, 1930), p. 193.

20. Robert S. Cotterill, "The Old South to the New," *Journal of Southern History*, XV (February 1949), 3.

21. William B. Hesseltine, *Confederate Leaders in the New South* (Baton Rouge, 1950), p. 35. See also the same author's *The South in American History* (New York, 1943), pp. 539–42.

22. C. Vann Woodward has challenged the conventional view, sketched above, but his initial modification has not been worked out in detail by other historians. His discussion is concerned with the way in which the New South spokesmen contributed to the mythical image of the Old South but

does not address itself to the second facet of the New South attitude; that is, the interpretation of antebellum history in a way that makes the New South school out to be the keepers of the authentic Southern tradition. Consult C. Vann Woodward, *Origins of the New South, 1877–1913* (Baton Rouge, 1951), pp. 154–8.

23. William D. Kelley, *The Old South and the New* (New York, 1888), pp. 2, 121, 158–9.
24. Howard Bunyan Clay, "Daniel Augustus Tompkins: An American Bourbon" (unpublished doctoral dissertation, University of North Carolina, 1950), pp. 1–4, 60.
25. Alexander K. McClure, *The South: Its Industrial, Financial, and Political Condition* (Philadelphia, 1886), p. 31.
26. Atticus G. Haygood, *Our Brother in Black: His Freedom and His Future* (New York, 1881), pp. 41–2.
27. Newton, *New South*, p. vi.
28. Daniel A. Tompkins, *Manufactures* (Charlotte, 1900), p. 4.
29. Daniel A. Tompkins, "The Manufacture of Cotton in the South," *Manufacturers' Record*, March 24, 1884.
30. Daniel A. Tompkins, *Fourth of July Address at Gastonia, N.C.* (n.p., 1902), p. 1 and *passim*.
31. Richard H. Edmonds, *The Old South and the New* (n.p., 1903), p. 12.
32. *Ibid.*, pp. 3–5.
33. Richard H. Edmonds, *Tasks of Young Men of the South* (n.p., 1903), p. 4.
34. Richard H. Edmonds, *Facts About the South* (Baltimore, 1907), p. 43.
35. Edmonds, *Tasks of Young Men of the South*, p. 1.
36. Edmonds, *Facts About the South*, p. 43.
37. Yoshimitsu Ide, "The Significance of Richard Hathaway Edmonds and his *Manufacturers' Record* in the New South" (unpublished doctoral dissertation, University of Florida, 1959), pp. 56–7.
38. Edmonds, *Facts About the South*, p. 60.
39. Henry W. Grady, *The New South*, ed. Oliver Dyer (New York, 1890), p. 146.
40. Amory Dwight Mayo, "Is There a New South?" *Social Economist*, V (October 1893), 207; Joseph G. Brown, *The New South* (Raleigh, 1902), p. 13.
41. Page, *The Southerner*, especially pp. 46–7. The "Mummy Letters" are discussed above, pp. 61–2.
42. Burton J. Hendrick, *The Training of an American: The*

Earlier Life and Letters of Walter H. Page, 1855–1913 (Boston, 1928), p. 116.

43. Walter Hines Page, "Study of an Old Southern Borough," *Atlantic Monthly*, XLVII (May 1881), 658.

44. Woodward, *Origins of the New South*, p. 158.

45. Joel Chandler Harris, *Uncle Remus: His Songs and His Sayings* (New York, 1881 [i.e., 1880]); Thomas Nelson Page, "Marse Chan," *Century Magazine*, XXVII (April 1884), 932–42.

46. William R. Taylor, *Cavalier and Yankee: The Old South and American National Character* (New York, 1961), p. 82.

47. *Ibid.*, p. 92.

48. Thomas Roderick Dew, *Review of the Debate in the Virginia Legislature of 1831 and 1832* (Richmond, 1832); George Fitzhugh, *Sociology for the South; or, the Failure of Free Society* (Richmond, 1854); George Fitzhugh, *Cannibals All! or, Slaves Without Masters* (Richmond, 1857). The standard monograph on the pro-slavery philosophy is William S. Jenkins, *Pro-Slavery Thought in the Old South* (Chapel Hill, 1935).

49. John Pendleton Kennedy, *Swallow Barn; or, a Sojourn in the Old Dominion* (Philadelphia, 1832).

50. Francis Pendleton Gaines, *The Southern Plantation: A Study in the Development and the Accuracy of a Tradition* (New York, 1924), p. 23.

51. *Ibid.*, p. 30.

52. Julia Collier Harris, ed., *Joel Chandler Harris, Editor and Essayist: Miscellaneous Literary, Political, and Social Writings* (Chapel Hill, 1931), pp. 116–17.

53. Edmund Wilson, *Patriotic Gore: Studies in the Literature of the American Civil War* (New York, 1962), p. 438.

54. Joyce Appleby, "Reconciliation and the Northern Novelist, 1865–1880," *Civil War History*, X (June 1964), 117–29. See also Robert A. Lively, *Fiction Fights the Civil War: An Unfinished Chapter in the Literary History of the American People* (Chapel Hill, 1957).

55. The articles appeared in book form shortly after they were published in the magazine: Edward King, *The Great South: A Record of Journeys* (Hartford, Conn., 1875).

56. "Southern Literature," *Scribner's Monthly*, XXII (September 1881), 785–6. See also Herbert F. Smith, "Joel Chandler Harris's Contributions to Scribner's Monthly and Cen-

tury Magazine, 1880–1887," *Georgia Historical Quarterly*, XLVII (June 1963), 169–79; and Charles W. Coleman, Jr., "The Recent Movement in Southern Literature," *Harper's New Monthly Magazine*, LXXIV (May 1887), 837–55.

57. R. W. Gilder to Joel Chandler Harris, March 5, 1891, Harris Papers, Emory University.

58. Albion W. Tourgee, "The South as a Field for Fiction," *The Forum*, VI (December 1888), 404–7.

59. Gaines, *The Southern Plantation*, p. 82.

60. Ethel Moore, "Reunion of Tennesseans: Address of Welcome by Miss Ethel Moore," *Confederate Veteran*, VI (October 1898), 482.

61. Gaines, *The Southern Plantation*, pp. 63–6.

62. Thomas Nelson Page, *Red Rock: A Chronicle of Reconstruction* (New York, 1898), p. viii.

63. Joel Chandler Harris, ed., *Life of Henry W. Grady, Including His Writings and Speeches* (New York, 1890), p. 88.

64. Grady, *New South*, ed. Dyer, pp. 148–60, 260.

65. Harris, ed., *Grady*, p. 195.

66. Edmonds, *Old South and New*, p. 11.

67. Edmonds, *Tasks of Young Men of the South*, p. 12.

68. Brown, *The New South*, p. 3.

69. Booker T. Washington, *Up From Slavery* (Garden City, 1901), pp. 1–12.

70. *Ibid.*, pp. 12–14.

71. Irwin Russell, *Christmas Night in the Quarters and Other Poems* (New York, 1917), p. 67.

72. Washington, *Up From Slavery*, pp. 80–7.

73. Taylor, *Cavalier and Yankee*, p. 18

74. C. Vann Woodward, "A Southern Critique for the Gilded Age," in *The Burden of Southern History* (Baton Rouge, 1960), pp. 109–40. The three works discussed by Woodward are Melville's poem, *Clarel* (1876); Adams's novel *Democracy* (1880); and James's novel *The Bostonians* (1886).

75. Gaines, *The Southern Plantation*, pp. 2–3.

76. Gunnar Myrdal, *An American Dilemma: The Negro and Modern Democracy*, 2 vols. (New York, 1944), II, 1375.

77. The text is available in Robert Lemuel Wiggins, *The Life of Joel Chandler Harris: From Obscurity in Boyhood to Fame in Early Manhood, with Short Stories and Other*

Early Literary Work not Heretofore Published in Book Form (Nashville, 1918), pp. 263–8.

78. Harris, *Uncle Remus: His Songs and His Sayings*, pp. 175–85.
79. *Ibid.*, p. 184; Wiggins, *Harris*, p. 267.
80. John Stafford, "Patterns of Meaning in *Nights With Uncle Remus*," *American Literature*, XVIII (May 1946), 94–5.
81. Joel Chandler Harris, *Free Joe and Other Georgian Sketches* (New York, 1887), pp. 72–98.
82. See Stafford, "Patterns of Meaning," p. 97; Paul H. Buck, *The Road to Reunion, 1865–1900* (Boston, 1937), chap. 8; and John Donald Wade, "Profits and Losses in the Life of Joel Chandler Harris," *American Review*, I (April 1933), 28–9.
83. Sterling A. Brown, "Negro Character as Seen by White Authors," *Journal of Negro Education*, II (April 1933), 188.
84. Stafford, "Patterns of Meaning," 98–103, 108.
85. The lines are from Irwin Russell's "Christmas Night in the Quarters," the text of which may be found in his *Christmas Night in the Quarters*, pp. 3–24.
86. Virginia Frazer Boyle, "A Kingdom for Micajah," *Harper's New Monthly Magazine*, C (March 1900), 35.
87. Tourgee, "South as a Field for Fiction," 409.
88. Thomas Nelson Page, *In Ole Virginia; or, Marse Chan and Other Stories* (New York, 1887), pp. 1–38, 39–77.
89. Harry Stillwell Edwards, " 'Ole Miss' and Sweetheart," *Harper's New Monthly Magazine*, LXXVII (July 1888), 288–96.
90. Page, *In Ole Virginia*, p. 10.
91. Francis Hopkinson Smith, *Colonel Carter of Cartersville* (Boston, 1891), p. 61.
92. Howard Weeden, *Bandanna Ballads* (New York, 1899), p. 10.
93. Tourgee, "South as a Field for Fiction," 409.
94. John M. Webb, "Militant Majorities and Racial Minorities," *Sewanee Review*, LXV (Spring 1957), 335.
95. Tompkins, *Manufactures*, p. 22.
96. Smith, *Colonel Carter*, p. 99.
97. See, for example, *Confederate Veteran*, VI (October 1898), 493–8.
98. Woodward, *Origins of the New South*, p. 158.

99. Quoted in *ibid.*, p. 157.
100. Grady, *New South*, ed. Dyer, p. 147.
101. Cabell, *Let Me Lie*, p. 74.

6   The Emperor's New Clothes

1. Henry W. Grady, *The New South*, ed. Oliver Dyer (New York, 1890), pp. 267–8.
2. Lewis H. Blair, *The Prosperity of the South Dependent upon the Elevation of the Negro* (Richmond, 1889), p. 1.
3. Hans Christian Andersen, "The Emperor's New Clothes," in *Andersen's Fairy Tales*, trans. Mrs. E. V. Lucas and Mrs. H. B. Pauli (New York, 1945), pp. 267–8.
4. Judson C. Ward, ed., *The New South: Thanksgiving Sermon, 1880, by Atticus G. Haygood*, in *Emory University Publications, Sources and Reprints*, Series VI (1950), No. 3, p. 12.
5. Joel Chandler Harris, ed., *Life of Henry W. Grady, Including His Writings and Speeches* (New York, 1890), p. 88.
6. Wilbur Fisk Tillett, "The White Man of the New South," *Century Magazine*, XXXIII (March 1887), 769–70.
7. Charles Dudley Warner, "Society in the New South," *New Princeton Review*, I (January 1886), 1.
8. Charles Dudley Warner, "The South Revisited," *Harper's New Monthly Magazine*, LXXIV (March 1887), 638.
9. Quoted in William D. Kelley, *The Old South and the New* (New York, 1888), p. 91.
10. Marion J. Verdery, " 'The New South'—Financially Reviewed," *North American Review*, CXLIV (February 1887), 161–2.
11. Atlanta *Constitution*, July 7, 1881; August 30, 1882; and September 13, 1883.
12. *Ibid.*, December 6, 1884; July 17, 1885; July 12, 1886; and December 14, 1886.
13. Harris, ed., *Grady*, p. 182.
14. *Ibid.*, pp. 204–5.
15. Grady, *New South*, ed. Dyer, p. 268.
16. The first quote is from Richard H. Edmonds, *Facts About the South* (Baltimore, 1907), pp. 60–1, a short book that brought together many previously published pieces. The second quote is from Richard H. Edmonds, *The South's*

Redemption: From Poverty to Prosperity (Baltimore, 1890), p. 5.

17. *Manufacturers' Record*, December 18, 1886; February 11, 1888; March 3, 1888; June 30, 1888; and June 28, 1890.

18. Henry Watterson, *The Compromises of Life* (New York, 1903), p. 289; Daniel A. Tompkins, *The Unification and Enlargement of American Interests* (Charlotte, N.C., 1900), pp. 2–3.

19. Harris, ed., *Grady*, p. 87.

20. Paul H. Buck, *The Road to Reunion, 1865–1900* (Boston, 1937), is the best study of the reconciliation of North and South. While parts of Buck's interpretation have been challenged, his discussion of the common ground occupied by the New South spokesmen and their industrialist friends in the North is excellent.

21. Warner, "Society in the New South," p. 12.

22. Harris, ed., *Grady*, p. 88.

23. Grady, *New South*, ed. Dyer, pp. 181–4.

24. Kelley, *Old South and New*, p. 4.

25. Joseph G. Brown, *The New South; Address Delivered at the Convention of the American Bankers' Association at New Orleans, November 11, 1902* (Raleigh, 1902), p. 13; Charles Morris, *The Old South and the New . . . from the Earliest Times to the Jamestown Exposition* (n.p., 1907), dedication page.

26. Nicholas Worth [pseud., Walter Hines Page], *The Southerner* (New York, 1909), p. 17.

27. In a letter of advice on how to write about the civilization of the South, Page said that "the New-South point of view and the old-South point of view both have great perils. Couldn't you plunge in, in the middle?" W. H. Page to William P. Trent, September 5, 1896, Page Papers, Houghton Library, Harvard University.

28. Edmonds, with 432 shares, was the largest stockholder in 1895; Page held 360 shares. List of stockholders of *Manufacturers' Record*, May 23, 1895. Page Papers, Houghton Library, Harvard University.

29. Burton J. Hendrick, *The Training of an American: The Earlier Life and Letters of Walter H. Page, 1855–1913* (Boston, 1928), pp. 392–3.

30. For an interesting and perceptive account of Blair's activities, see Charles E. Wynes, "Lewis Harvie Blair, Virginia

Reformer: The Uplift of the Negro and Southern Prosperity," *Virginia Magazine of History and Biography*,
LXXII (January 1964), 3–18. Blair's book has been recently reissued with a revised title: *A Southern Prophecy:
The Prosperity of the South Dependent upon the Elevation
of the Negro*, ed. C. Vann Woodward (Boston, 1964).

31. Blair, *Prosperity of the South*, p. 3.
32. *Ibid.*, pp. 3–4.
33. *Ibid.*, p. 4.
34. *Manufacturers' Record*, January 29, 1887.
35. *Ibid.*, March 24, 1888.
36. Quoted in Yoshimitsu Ide, "The Significance of Richard
Hathaway Edmonds and His *Manufacturers' Record* in the
New South" (unpublished doctoral dissertation, University
of Florida, 1959), pp. 325–6.
37. Blair, *Prosperity of the South*, p. 7.
38. *Ibid.*, p. v.
39. *Ibid.*, pp. 14–15. Recent estimates of per capita income
in the late nineteenth century help Blair's case. In 1880
Georgia's estimated per capita income was $86; in 1900
it was precisely the same: $86. See below, footnote 41.
40. C. Vann Woodward, *Origins of the New South, 1877–
1913* (Baton Rouge, 1951), pp. 111, 318.
41. Everett S. Lee et al., *Population Redistribution and Economic Growth, United States, 1870–1950* (Philadelphia,
1957), pp. 349, 753. Changes in estimated per capita income
in each of the Southern states were as follows:

	Per Capita Income		
State	1880	1900	Increase
Alabama	$82	$ 88	7.3%
Arkansas	79	89	12.5
Florida	79	112	41.8
Georgia	86	86	—
Kentucky	107	120	12.1
Louisiana	138	128	−7.2
Mississippi	82	84	2.4
North Carolina	64	72	12.5
South Carolina	72	74	2.8
Tennessee	81	101	24.7
Texas	98	138	40.8
Virginia	85	110	29.4
West Virginia	89	117	31.5

42. H. H. Winsborough, "The Changing Regional Character of the South," in John C. McKinney and Edgar T. Thompson, eds., *The South in Continuity and Change* (Durham, 1965), p. 38.
43. Woodward, *Origins of the New South*, p. 311.
44. William H. Nicholls, *Southern Tradition and Regional Progress* (Chapel Hill, 1960), p. 24.
45. Woodward, *Origins of the New South*, chap. 11.
46. *Ibid.*, p. 304.
47. David M. Potter, *People of Plenty: Economic Abundance and the American Character* (Chicago, 1954), p. 84.
48. *Ibid.*, pp. 85–9.
49. Nicholls, *Southern Tradition and Regional Progress*, p. 27.
50. Harris, ed., *Grady*, p. 303.
51. Quoted in Booker T. Washington, *Up From Slavery* (Garden City, 1900), p. 238.
52. Robert Spencer, *Booker T. Washington and the Negro's Place in American Life* (Boston, 1955), p. 116.
53. Washington, *Up From Slavery*, p. 235.
54. This and subsequent quotations from Washington's address are taken from the text as printed in E. David Washington, ed., *Selected Speeches of Booker T. Washington* (Garden City, 1932), pp. 31–6.
55. Rayford Logan's careful study of press reaction to Washington's address concludes that its enthusiastic reception is an "excellent yardstick" for measuring the "victory of 'The New South,'" since he [Washington] accepted a subordinate place for Negroes in American life"; Rayford W. Logan, *The Negro in American Life and Thought: The Nadir, 1877–1901* (New York, 1954), p. 276. Most Negroes, Logan points out, were critical of the address.
56. "The Atlanta Exposition," *Outlook*, LIII (January 11, 1896), 52.
57. "The Jubilee of the New South," *Century Magazine*, LI (January 1896), 470.
58. Quoted in Washington, *Up From Slavery*, p. 226.
59. Woodward, *Origins of the New South*, pp. 205–6. For a brief account of the rise of the Jim Crow system, and an introduction to the literature, consult C. Vann Woodward, *The Strange Career of Jim Crow*, 2nd rev. ed. (New York, 1966).
60. Washington, *Up From Slavery*, p. 318. Page, who admired

Washington, rejected the picture of the happy Negro in the New South and was puzzled by Washington's optimistic utterances. Writing from Charleston, South Carolina, he said that "so far as the negro is concerned, I'd rather be an imp in hades than a darkey in S.C. One decided advantage that the imp has is—personal safety." In the same letter he wrote that "I can't find white men here whose view of the negro has essentially changed since slavery. Booker Washington told me last week that the result of his work of which he is proudest is the fast-changing attitude of the white man—the Southern white man. But he hasn't changed here—not a whit." W. H. Page to H. E. Scudder, March 18, 1899, Page Papers, Houghton Library, Harvard University.

61. Spencer, *Booker T. Washington*, p. 199.

EPILOGUE: The Enduring Myth

1. Walter Prescott Webb, "The South's Future Prospect," in Frank E. Vandiver, ed., *The Idea of the South: Pursuit of a Central Theme* (Chicago, 1964), p. 74.
2. Walter Prescott Webb, "The South's Call to Greatness: Challenge to All Southerners," *The Graduate Journal* (University of Texas), III (Supplement, 1960), 299.
3. New York *Times*, February 19, 1969, pp. 1, 28; Charlottesville, Va., *Daily Progress*, February 19, 1969, p. 1.
4. Joseph J. Spengler, "Southern Economic Trends and Prospects," in John C. McKinney and Edgar T. Thompson, eds., *The South in Continuity and Change* (Durham, 1965), pp. 109–11.
5. National Emergency Council, *Report on Economic Conditions in the South* (Washington, 1938), p. 1.
6. *Ibid.*, p. 8.
7. George B. Tindall, *The Emergence of the New South, 1913–1945* (Baton Rouge, 1967), p. 599.
8. Quoted in Wilma Dykeman and James Stokely, *Seeds of Southern Change: The Life of Will Alexander* (Chicago, 1962), p. 111.
9. C. Vann Woodward, *The Burden of Southern History* (Baton Rouge, 1960), p. 28.

278 ~ The New South Creed

10. Ellen Glasgow, *A Certain Measure: An Interpretation of Prose Fiction* (New York, 1943), pp. 28, 135–6.
11. V. O. Key, Jr., *Southern Politics in State and Nation* (New York, 1949), p. 4.
12. Webb, "South's Call to Greatness," pp. 299, 303.
13. Will W. Alexander, "Our Conflicting Racial Policies," *Harper's Magazine*, CXC (January 1945), 172–9.
14. Quoted in C. Vann Woodward, *The Strange Career of Jim Crow*, 2nd rev. ed. (New York, 1966), p. 145.
15. Jenkins Lloyd Jones, "The New South on the Move," Richmond, Va., *Times-Dispatch*, August 7, 1966.
16. Otto Kerner et al., *Report of the National Advisory Commission on Civil Disorders* (New York, 1968), p. 1.

Selective Bibliography

The best general history of the era in which the New South movement flourished is C. Vann Woodward, *Origins of the New South, 1877–1913* (Baton Rouge: Louisiana State University Press; 1951), a work at once original and yet reflective of two decades of revisionist scholarship. Holland Thompson, *The New South* (New Haven: Yale University Press; 1919), a brief volume generally sympathetic to the New South movement, successfully evokes the optimistic mood of the New South spokesmen. Philip Alexander Bruce, *The Rise of the New South* (Philadelphia: George Barrie & Sons; 1905), is long and tedious and written from the viewpoint of a New South spokesman, but is rich in detail. The literature of the period and changing interpretations of it are discussed in two historiographical essays: Jacob E. Cooke, "The New South," in Donald Sheehan and Harold C. Syrett, eds., *Essays in American Historiography: Papers Presented in Honor of Allan Nevins* (New York: Columbia University Press; 1960), pp. 50–80, and Paul M. Gaston, "The 'New South,'" in Arthur S. Link and Rembert W. Patrick, eds., *Writing Southern History: Essays in Historiography in Honor of Fletcher M. Green* (Baton Rouge: Louisiana State University Press; 1965), pp. 316–36. There are no published books on the intellectual history of the New South movement, but Robert Darden Little, "The Ideology of the New South: A Study in the Development of Ideas, 1865–1910" (unpublished doctoral dissertation, University of Chicago, 1950), should be consulted. Dr. Little's approach is quite different from my own, but I found his study interesting and helpful.

In the classified, selective bibliography that follows I have listed the works which I found most useful, but I include here a word about the sources. As the footnotes indicate, I have relied heavily on the two major journals of the New South movement, the Atlanta *Constitution* and the *Manufacturers' Record*, in which the ideas of Henry W. Grady and Richard H. Edmonds, respectively, are fully set forth. Because I was concerned primarily with the history of a public idea I used manuscript sources only sparingly. The Walter Hines Page Papers at the Houghton Library of Harvard University turned up a few useful items, but the Henry W. Grady Papers and the Joel Chandler Harris Papers, both at Emory University, were of little value. The public discussion of the meaning of the New South movement was carried on in all types of publications. The periodical literature of the period is particularly rewarding, and I examined the files of two dozen magazines, the most useful of which were: *DeBow's Review*, for the genesis of the New South creed; and *The Century Magazine* (published as *Scribner's Monthly* before 1881), *The Atlantic Monthly*, and *Harper's New Monthly Magazine*, for the 'eighties and 'nineties. The bibliography lists the individual articles which I found to be most significant.

A bibliography for the Epilogue, in which I set forth my interpretation of the significance of the myth of the New South in the twentieth century, would run to unmanageable proportions. George B. Tindall, *The Emergence of the New South, 1913–1945* (Baton Rouge: Louisiana State University Press; 1967), is a comprehensive study that teems with bibliographical information. In Link and Patrick's *Writing Southern History* the historiographical essays by Tindall, on race relations, and by Dewey W. Grantham, Jr., on the twentieth century, are excellent guides.

A. *Memoirs, Works, Autobiographies, Biographies* (*arranged by subject*)

EDWARD ATKINSON

Williamson, Harold Francis: *Edward Atkinson: The Biography of an American Liberal, 1827–1905.* Boston: Old Corner Book Store, Inc.; 1934.

CHARLES BRANTLEY AYCOCK

Orr, Oliver H., Jr.: *Charles Brantley Aycock.* Chapel Hill: University of North Carolina Press; 1961.

GEORGE WASHINGTON CABLE

Turner, Arlin: *George W. Cable, A |Biography.* Durham: Duke University Press; 1956.
———, ed.: *The Negro Question: A Selection of Writings on Civil Rights in the South by George W. Cable.* Garden City: Doubleday & Company, Inc.; 1958.

J. L. M. CURRY

Alderman, Edwin Anderson, and Armistead Churchill Gordon: *J. L. M. Curry, A Biography.* New York: Macmillan Company; 1911.
Rice, Jessie Pearl: *J. L. M. Curry: Southerner, Statesman and Educator.* New York: King's Crown Press; 1949.

ROBERT L. DABNEY

Vaughan, C. R., ed.: *Discussions by Robert L. Dabney,* 4 vols. Mexico, Mo.: Crescent Book House; 1897.

JOSEPHUS DANIELS

Daniels, Josephus: *Editor in Politics.* Chapel Hill: University of North Carolina Press; 1941.
———: *Tar Heel Editor.* Chapel Hill: University of North Carolina Press; 1939.

FRANCIS W. DAWSON

Logan, S. Frank: "Francis W. Dawson, 1840–1889: South Carolina Editor." Unpublished master's thesis, Duke University, 1947.

HENRY W. GRADY

Grady, Henry Woodfin: *The New South,* ed. Oliver Dyer. New York: Robert Bonner's Sons; 1890.

————: *The New South and Other Addresses with Biography, Critical Opinions, and Explanatory Note*, ed. Edna Lee Turpin. New York: Maynard, Merrill & Co.; 1904.
Harris, Joel Chandler, ed.: *Life of Henry W. Grady, Including his Writings and Speeches*. New York: Cassell Publishing Company; 1890.
Nixon, Raymond B.: *Henry W. Grady: Spokesman of the New South*. New York: Alfred A. Knopf; 1943.

JOEL CHANDLER HARRIS

Harris, Julia Collier, ed.: *Joel Chandler Harris, Editor and Essayist: Miscellaneous Literary, Political, and Social Writings*. Chapel Hill: University of North Carolina Press; 1931.
————: *The Life and Letters of Joel Chandler Harris*. Boston: Houghton Mifflin Company; 1918.
Wiggins, Robert Lemuel: *The Life of Joel Chandler Harris: From Obscurity in Boyhood to Fame in Early Manhood with Short Stories and other Early Literary Work not heretofore Published in Book Form*. Nashville: Publishing House Methodist Episcopal Church, South; 1918.

ATTICUS GREENE HAYGOOD

Dempsey, Elam Franklin: *Atticus Greene Haygood*. Nashville: Parthenon Press, Methodist Publishing House; 1940.
Mann, Harold W.: *Atticus Greene Haygood: Methodist Bishop, Editor, and Educator*. Athens: University of Georgia Press; 1965.
Ward, Judson C., ed.: *The New South: Thanksgiving Sermon, 1880, by Atticus G. Haygood*, in *Emory University Publications, Sources and Reprints*, Series VI, Number 3. Atlanta, 1950.

BENJAMIN H. HILL

Hill, Benjamin Harvey, Jr.: *Senator Benjamin H. Hill, His Life, Speeches and Writings*. Atlanta: H. C. Hudgins & Co.; 1891.
Pearce, Haywood, Jr.: *Benjamin H. Hill: Secession and Reconstruction*. Chicago: University of Chicago Press; 1928.

WILLIAM DARRAH KELLEY

Kelley, William Darrah: *Speeches, Addresses and Letters*. Philadelphia: Henry Carey Baird; 1872.

LUCIUS Q. C. LAMAR

Cate, Wirt A.: *Lucius Q. C. Lamar*. Chapel Hill: University of North Carolina Press; 1935.

Mayes, Edward: *Lucius Q. C. Lamar: His Life, Times, and Speeches, 1825–1893.* Nashville: Publishing House of the Methodist Episcopal Church, South; 1896.

SIDNEY LANIER

Anderson, Charles R. et al., eds.: *The Centennial Edition of the Works of Sidney Lanier,* 10 vols. Baltimore: Johns Hopkins Press; 1945.
Mims, Edwin: *Sidney Lanier.* Boston: Houghton Mifflin Company; 1905.
Starke, Aubrey: *Sidney Lanier: A Biographical and Critical Study.* Chapel Hill: University of North Carolina Press; 1933.

WALTER HINES PAGE

Hendrick, Burton J.: *The Life and Letters of Walter H. Page,* 3 vols. New York: Doubleday, Page & Company; 1922–5.
————: *The Training of an American: The Earlier Life and Letters of Walter H. Page, 1855–1913.* Boston: Houghton Mifflin Company; 1928.

DANIEL AUGUSTUS TOMPKINS

Clay, Howard Bunyan: "Daniel Augustus Tompkins: An American Bourbon." Unpublished doctoral dissertation, University of North Carolina, 1950.
Winston, George Tayloe: *A Builder of the New South, Being the Life Work of Daniel Augustus Tompkins.* Garden City: Doubleday, Page & Company; 1920.

HOKE SMITH

Grantham, Dewey W., Jr.: *Hoke Smith and the Politics of the New South.* Baton Rouge: Louisiana State University Press; 1958.

ALBION WINEGAR TOURGEE

Olsen, Otto H.: *Carpetbagger's Crusade: The Life of Albion Winegar Tourgee.* Baltimore: Johns Hopkins Press; 1965.

BOOKER T. WASHINGTON

Mathews, Basil: *Booker T. Washington: Educator and Interracial Interpreter.* Cambridge: Harvard University Press; 1948.
Spencer, Robert: *Booker T. Washington and the Negro's Place in American Life.* Boston: Little, Brown and Company; 1955.
Washington, Booker T.: *Up From Slavery.* Garden City: Doubleday, Page & Company; 1900.

Washington, E. David, ed.: *Selected Speeches of Booker T. Washington*. Garden City: Doubleday, Doran & Company, Inc.; 1932.

TOM WATSON

Woodward, C. Vann: *Tom Watson: Agrarian Rebel*. New York: Macmillan Company; 1938.

HENRY WATTERSON

Krock, Arthur, ed.: *The Editorials of Henry Watterson*. New York: George H. Doran Company; 1923.
Marcosson, Isaac: *"Marse Henry": A Biography of Henry Watterson*. New York: Dodd, Mead & Company; 1951.
Wall, Joseph Frazier: *Henry Watterson: Reconstructed Rebel*. New York: Oxford University Press; 1956.
Watterson, Henry: *The Compromises of Life*. New York: Fox, Duffield & Company; 1903.
———: *"Marse Henry": An Autobiography*, 2 vols. New York: George H. Doran Company; 1919.

HOWARD WEEDEN

Roberts, Frances C., and Sarah Huff Fisk: *Shadows on the Wall: The Life and Works of Howard Weeden*. Northport, Ala.: Colonial Press; 1962.

B. *Contemporary Books and Pamphlets*

Atkinson, Edward: *Address Given in Atlanta . . . for the Promotion of International Cotton Exhibition*. Boston: A. Williams and Company; 1881.
Bingham, Robert: *The New South: An Address . . . in the Interest of National Aid to Education*. N.p.; 1884.
Blair, Lewis H.: *The Prosperity of the South Dependent upon the Elevation of the Negro*. Richmond: Everett Waddey; 1889.
Brown, Joseph G.: *The New South—Address Delivered at the Convention of the American Bankers' Association at New Orleans, November 11, 1902*. Raleigh: Edwards & Broughton Printers and Binders; 1902.
Bruce, Philip Alexander: *The Plantation Negro as a Freeman:*

Observations on his Character, Condition, and Prospects in Virginia. New York: G. P. Putnam's Sons; 1889.

Cooke, John Esten: *The Heir of Gaymount, A Novel.* New York: Van Evrie, Horton & Co.; 1870.

Curry, J. L. M.: *Address Delivered Before the Association of Confederate Veterans, Richmond, Virginia, July 1, 1896.* Richmond: B. F. Johnson; 1896.

Edmonds, Richard Hathaway: *Facts About the South.* Baltimore: Manufacturers' Record Publishing Co.; 1907.

————: *The Old South and the New.* N.p.; 1903.

————: *The South's Redemption: From Poverty to Prosperity.* Baltimore: Manufacturers' Record Publishing Company; 1890.

————: *Tasks of Young Men of the South.* N.p.; 1903.

————: *Unparalleled Industrial Progress.* Np., n.d.

Harris, Joel Chandler: *Daddy Jake the Runaway and Short Stories Told After Dark.* New York: Century Co.; 1889.

————: *Free Joe and Other Georgian Sketches.* New York: Charles Scribner's Sons; 1887.

————: *Nights With Uncle Remus: Myths and Legends of the Old Plantation.* Boston: Houghton, Mifflin and Company; 1883.

————: *Uncle Remus: His Songs and His Sayings.* New York: D. Appleton and Company, 1881 [i.e., 1880].

Haygood, Atticus Greene: *Our Brother in Black: His Freedom and His Future.* New York: Phillips & Hunt; 1881.

————: *Pleas for Progress.* Nashville: Methodist Episcopal Church, South; 1889.

Hillyard, M. B.: *The New South.* Baltimore: Manufacturers' Record Co.; 1887.

Johnston, William Preston: *Problems of Southern Civilization: An Address Delivered Before the Polytechnic Institute of Alabama.* N.p., n.d.

Jones, Charles Colcock, Jr.: *The Battle of Honey Hill: An Address Delivered Before the Confederate Survivors' Association.* Augusta, Ga.: Chronicle Printing Establishment; 1885.

————: *Brigadier General Robert Toombs: An Address Delivered Before the Confederate Survivors' Association.* Augusta, Ga.: Chronicle Office; 1886.

————: *The Evacuation of Battery Wagner and the Battle of Ocean Pond: An Address Before the Confederate Survivors' Association.* Augusta, Ga.: Chronicle Publishing Company; 1888.

————: *Funeral Oration Pronounced in the Opera House in Augusta Georgia . . . upon the Occasion of the Memorial Services in Honor of Jefferson Davis.* Augusta, Ga.: Chronicle Printing Establishment; 1889.

————: *Georgians During the War Between the States: An Address Delivered Before the Confederate Survivors' Association.* Augusta, Ga.: Chronicle Publishing Company; 1889.

————: *The Old South: Address Delivered Before the Confederate Survivors' Association.* Augusta, Ga.: Chronicle Publishing Co.; 1887.

————: *The Siege and Evacuation of Savannah, Georgia in December 1864: An Address Delivered Before the Confederate Survivors' Association.* Augusta, Ga.: Chronicle Publishing Company; 1890.

————: *Sons of Confederate Veterans: An Address Delivered Before the Confederate Survivors' Association.* Augusta, Ga.: Chronicle Publishing Company; 1891.

Kelley, William Darrah: *The Old South and the New.* New York: G. P. Putnam's Sons; 1888.

King, Edward: *The Great South, A Record of Journeys . . .* Hartford: American Publishing Company; 1875.

McClure, Alexander Kelly: *The South: Its Industrial, Financial, and Political Condition.* Philadelphia: J. B. Lippincott Company; 1886.

Morris, Charles: *The Old South and the New . . . from the Earliest Times to the Jamestown Exposition.* N.p.; 1907.

Newton, John C. Calhoun: *The New South and the Methodist Episcopal Church, South.* Baltimore: King Brothers; 1887.

Page, Thomas Nelson: *The Negro: The Southerner's Problem.* New York: C. Scribner's Sons; 1904.

————: *In Ole Virginia; or Marse Chan and Other Stories.* New York: Charles Scribner's Sons; 1887.

————: *Red Rock: A Chronicle of Reconstruction.* New York: Charles Scribner's Sons; 1898.

Phelan, James: *The New South. The Democratic Position on the Tariff: Speech Delivered at Covington, Tenn.* Memphis: S. C. Toof & Co.; 1886.

Pollard, Edward A: *The Lost Cause: A New Southern History of the War of the Confederates.* New York: E. B. Treat & Co., Publishers, 1866.

Russell, Irwin: *Christmas-Night in the Quarters and Other Poems.* New York: Century Co.; 1917.

Ryan, Abram J.: *Poems: Patriotic, Religious, Miscellaneous.* Baltimore: John B. Piet; 1881.

Smith, Francis Hopkinson: *Colonel Carter of Cartersville.* Boston: Houghton Mifflin Company; 1891.

Speer, William S.: *The Law of Success.* Nashville: Southern Methodist Publishing House; 1885.

Switzler, Col. William F.: *The Old South and the New: Speech Delivered in Charleston . . . at the Opening of the Industrial Exhibition.* Columbia, Mo.: Statesman Office Book and Job Print; 1885.

Tompkins, Daniel Augustus: *Fourth of July Address at Gastonia, N. C.* N.p.; 1902.

———: *Manufactures: An Address Made at the First Annual Dinner of the Progressive Association of Edgecombe County.* Charlotte: Observer Printing and Publishing House; 1900.

———: *The Tariff: An Address Made Before the Annual Convention of the American Manufacturers Association.* Richmond, 1909.

———: *The Unification and Enlargement of American Interests.* Charlotte, 1900.

Tourgee, Albion Winegar: *A Fool's Errand, By One of the Fools: The Famous Romance of American History.* New York: Fords, Howard & Hulbert; 1879.

Trammell, William Dugas: *Ça Ira, A Novel.* New York: United States Publishing Co.; 1874.

Trenholm, William Lee: *The South: An Address on the Third Anniversary of the Charleston Board of Trade.* Charleston: Walker, Evans & Cogswell; 1869.

Tucker, John Randolph: *The Old South and the New South: Baccalaureate Address Before the South Carolina College.* Columbia: Presbyterian Publishing House; 1887.

Twain, Mark: *Life on the Mississippi.* Boston: J. R. Osgood and Company; 1883.

Wallace, W. H.: *Three Essentials to Success: Money, Reputation, Character; Annual Address Before the Eutonian Literary Society of Clinton Academy, S. C.* Newberry, S.C.: Wallace & Kinard Printers; 1887.

Weeden, Howard: *Bandanna Ballads.* New York: Doubleday & McClure Company; 1899.

———: *Songs of the Old South.* New York: Doubleday, Page & Company; 1900.

Worth, Nicholas (pseud., Walter Hines Page): *The Southerner.* New York: Doubleday, Page & Company; 1909.

C. *Contemporary Periodical Articles*

Allston, Col. Ben: "Address by Col. Ben Allston. Delivered Before the Winyah Indigo Society, South Carolina, at its One Hundred and Fourteenth Anniversary, May 7, 1869," *DeBow's Review*, VI (August 1869), 669–71.

Atkinson, Edward: "Significant Aspects of the Atlanta Cotton Exposition," *Century Magazine*, XXIII (February 1882), 563–74.

————: "The Solid South?" *International Review*, X (March 1881), 197–209.

Atkinson, W. Y.: "The Atlanta Exposition," *North American Review*, CLXI (October 1895), 385–93.

"The Atlanta Exposition," *Outlook*, LIII (January 11, 1896), 52.

Blaine, James G., L. Q. C. Lamar, Wade Hampton, James A. Garfield, Alexander H. Stephens, Wendell Phillips, Montgomery T. Blair, and Thomas A. Hendricks: "Ought the Negro to be Disfranchised? Ought He to have been Enfranchised?" *North American Review*, CXXVIII (March 1879), 225–83.

Bledsoe, Albert Taylor: "Causes of Sectional Discontent," *Southern Review*, II (July 1867), 200–30.

————: "Chivalrous Southrons," *Southern Review*, VI (July 1869), 96–128.

————: "North and South," *Southern Review*, II (July 1867), 122–46.

————: "The Present Crisis," *Southern Review*, XIII (January 1873), 1–40.

————: "Public School Education at the North," *Southern Review*, IV (July 1868), 1–36.

Boyle, Virginia Frazer: "A Kingdom for Micajah," *Harper's New Monthly Magazine*, C (March 1900), 527–35.

Bruce, Philip Alexander: "Social and Economic Revolution in the Southern States," *Contemporary Review*, LXXVIII (July 1900), 58–73.

Burwell, W. M.: "The Book of Numbers," *DeBow's Review*, VII (October 1870), 800–10.

————: "To the Patrons of DeBow's Review," *DeBow's Review*, V (March 1868), 332–3.

Cabell, E. C.: "White Emigration to the South," *DeBow's Review*, I (January 1866), 91–4.

Cable, George W.: "The Freedman's Case in Equity," *Century Magazine*, XXIX (January 1885), 409–18.

———: "The Silent South," *Century Magazine*, XXX (September 1885), 674–91.

Coleman, Charles W., Jr.: "The Recent Movement in Southern Literature," *Harper's New Monthly Magazine*, LXXIV (May 1887), 837–55.

Curry, J. L. M.: "Citizenship and Education," *Education*, V (September 1884), 78–90.

———: "The South: Her Condition and Needs," *Galaxy*, XXIII (April 1877), 544–53.

DeBow, J. D. B.: "The Future of the South," *DeBow's Review*, I (January 1866), 6–14.

———: "Manufactures, The South's True Remedy," *DeBow's Review*, III (February 1867), 172–8.

———: "The Future of South Carolina—Her Inviting Resources," *DeBow's Review*, II (July 1866), 38–49.

Delavique, John C.: "Cotton," *DeBow's Review*, IV (December 1867), 562–71.

DeLeon, Edwin: "The New South," *Harper's New Monthly Magazine*, XLVIII (1874), 270–80, 406–22; XLIX (1874), 555–68.

———: "The New South: What it is Doing, and What it Wants," *Putnam's Magazine*, XV (April 1870), 458–64.

———: "Ruin and Reconstruction of the Southern States," *Southern Magazine*, XIV (1874), 17–41, 287–309, 453–82, 561–90.

———: "The Southern States Since the War," *Fraser's Magazine*, XC (1874), 153–63, 346–66, 620–37.

Dudley, Thomas U.: "How Shall We Help the Negro?" *Century Magazine*, XXX (June 1885), 273–80.

Edwards, Harry Stillwell: "De Valley An' De Shadder," *Century Magazine*, XXXV (January 1888), 468–77.

———: " 'Ole Miss' and Sweetheart," *Harper's New Monthly Magazine*, LXXVII (July 1888), 288–96.

"Exodus," *DeBow's Review*, V (November 1868), 979–83.

Gilman, S. H.: "Cotton Manufacturing in or Near the Cotton Fields of Texas Compared with the Same at Any Point Distant Therefrom," *DeBows Review*, V (September 1868), 837–40.

Godkin, E. L.: "The Political Outlook," *Scribner's Monthly*, XIX (February 1880), 613–20.

———: "The White Side of the Southern Question," *The Nation*, XXXI (August 19, 1880), 126–7.

"Governor Hampton at Auburn," *Harper's Weekly*, XXI (July 7, 1877), 519.

Grady, Henry W.: "In Plain Black and White: A Reply to Mr. Cable," *Century Magazine*, XXIX (April 1885), 909–17.

" 'The Great South' Series of Papers," *Scribner's Monthly*, IX (December 1874), 248–9.

Gunton, Matthew: "Is There a New South? Reply to Mr. Mayo," *Social Economist*, V (December 1893), 358–65.

Hill, Daniel Harvey: "Education," *The Land We Love*, I (May and June 1866), 1–11 and 83–91.

————: "Industrial Combinations," *The Land We Love*, V (May 1868), 25–34.

————: "The Old South," *Southern Historical Society Papers*, XVI (1888), 423–43.

Hill, Walter B.: "Uncle Tom Without a Cabin," *Century Magazine*, XXVII (April 1884), 859–64.

"The Industrial Policy of the South," *DeBow's Review*, VI (November 1869), 928–9.

James, Charles J.: "Cotton Manufactures—Great Field for the South," *DeBow's Review*, I (May 1866), 504–15.

Johnston, John W.: "The Emancipation of the Southern Whites," *Manufacturers' Record*, July 9, 1887.

"The Jubilee of the New South," *Century Magazine*, LI (January 1896), 470.

Lanier, Henry W.: "The New South's Industrial Future," *Outlook*, LIX (June 25, 1898), 477–9.

Lanier, Sidney: "The New South," *Scribner's Monthly*, XX (October 1880), 840–51.

Logan, T. M.: "The Southern Industrial Prospect," *Harper's New Monthly Magazine*, LII (March 1876), 589–93.

Maury, Matthew Fontaine: "The American Colony in Mexico," *DeBow's Review*, I (June 1866), 623–30.

Mayo, Amory Dwight: "Is There a New South?" *Social Economist*, V (October 1893), 200–8.

————: "The Progress of the Negro," *Forum*, X (November 1890), 335–45.

Merrill, A. P.: "Southern Labor," *DeBow's Review*, VI (July 1869), 586–92.

Mitchell, Samuel C.: "The Nationalization of Southern Sentiment," *South Atlantic Quarterly*, VII (April 1908), 107–13.

Moore, Ethel: "Reunion of Tennesseans: Address of Welcome by Miss Ethel Moore," *Confederate Veteran*, VI (October 1898), 482.

Moore, H. T.: "The Industrial Interests of the South," *DeBow's Review*, V (February 1868), 147–55.

"North and South," *Century Magazine*, XXX (October 1885), 964.

Oswald, Felix L.: "The New South," *Chautauquan*, XV (August 1892), 541–53.

Page, Thomas Nelson: "A Southerner on the Negro Question," *North American Review*, CLIV (April 1892), 401–13.

Page, Walter Hines: "The Rebuilding of Old Commonwealths," *Atlantic Monthly*, LXXXIX (May 1902), 651–61.

————: "Study of an Old Southern Borough," *Atlantic Monthly*, XLVII (May 1881), 648–58.

Patton, Robert M.: "The New Era of Southern Manufactures," *DeBow's Review*, III (January 1867), 56–69.

Pollard, Edward A.: "The Real Condition of the South," *Lippincott's Magazine*, VI (December 1870), 612–20.

Preston, Margaret J.: "The Gospel of Labor (What the South Says to Her Children)," *Southern Magazine*, IX (December 1871), 733–4.

Price, J. C.: "Does the Negro Seek Social Equality?" *Forum*, X (January 1891), 558–64.

Reeves, W. N.: "The Unemployed—Send Them South," *Outlook*, IL (February 10, 1894), 286.

Shaler, N. S.: "The Economic Future of the New South," *Arena*, II (August 1890), 257–68.

Smalley, Eugene V.: "The New Orleans Exposition," *Century Magazine*, XXX (May and June 1885), 3–14 and 185–99.

Smith, Hoke: "The Resources and Development of the South," *North American Review*, CLIX (August 1894), 129–36.

"Southern Literature," *Scribner's Monthly*, XXII (September 1881), 785–6.

"Studies in the South," *Atlantic Monthly*, LI (January 1883), 87–99.

Tillett, Wilbur Fisk: "The White Man of the New South," *Century Magazine*, XXXIII (March 1887), 769–76.

Tompkins, Daniel Augustus: "Southern Prosperity," *Manufacturers' Record*, June 4, 1887.

Tourgee, Albion Winegar: "The South as a Field for Fiction," *Forum*, VI (December 1888), 404–13.

Trammell, William Dugas: Review of *"Address Delivered Before the Alumni Society of the University of Georgia* by Benjamin H. Hill," *Southern Magazine*, X (June 1872), 751–61.

Trent, William Peterfield: "Dominant Forces in Southern Life," *Atlantic Monthly*, LXXIX (January 1897), 42–53.

Verdery, Marion J.: " 'The New South'—Financially Reviewed," *North American Review*, CXLIV (February 1887), 161–8.

Wagener, John A.: "European Immigration," *DeBow's Review*, IV (July and August 1867), 94–105.

Warner, Charles Dudley: "Impressions of the South," *Harper's New Monthly Magazine*, LXXI (September 1885), 546–51.

——: "Society in the New South," *New Princeton Review*, I (January 1886), 1–14.

——: "The South Revisited," *Harper's New Monthly Magazine*, LXXIV (March 1887), 634–40.

Washington, Booker T.: "The Case of the Negro," *Atlantic Monthly*, LXXXIV (November 1899), 577–87.

——: "Signs of Progress Among the Negroes," *Century Magazine*, LIX (January 1900), 472–8.

Watterson, Henry: "Oddities of Southern Life," *Century Magazine*, XXIII (April 1882), 884–95.

——: "The Reunited Union," *North American Review*, CXL (January 1885), 22–9.

——: "The Solid South," *North American Review*, CXXVIII (January 1879), 47–58.

Yerger, E. N.: "The True Strength of the Southern States," *Southern Magazine*, XI (May 1875), 520–5.

D. *Secondary Works: Books*

Brandfon, Robert L.: *Cotton Kingdom of the New South: A History of the Yazoo Mississippi Delta from Reconstruction to the Twentieth Century*. Cambridge: Harvard University Press; 1967.

Brookes, Stella Brewer: *Joel Chandler Harris—Folklorist*. Athens: University of Georgia Press; 1950.

Brown, Sterling: *The Negro in American Fiction*. Washington: Association in Negro Folk Education; 1937.

Buck, Paul Herman: *The Road to Reunion, 1865–1900*. Boston: Little, Brown and Company; 1937.

Cash, W. J.: *The Mind of the South*. New York: Alfred A. Knopf, Inc.; 1941.

Clark, Thomas D.: *The Emerging South*. New York: Oxford University Press; 1961.

Clark, Victor S.: *History of Manufactures in the United States, 1860–1914.* Washington: Carnegie Institution of Washington; 1928.

Commager, Henry Steele: *The American Mind: An Interpretation of American Thought and Character Since the 1880's.* New Haven: Yale University Press; 1950.

Cooper, William J., Jr.: *The Conservative Regime: South Carolina, 1877–1890.* Baltimore: Johns Hopkins Press; 1968.

Gaines, Francis Pendleton: *The Southern Plantation: A Study in the Development and the Accuracy of a Tradition.* New York: Columbia University Press; 1924.

Going, Allen Johnston: *Bourbon Democracy in Alabama, 1874–1890.* University: University of Alabama Press; 1951.

Goldman, Eric F.: *Rendezvous With Destiny: A History of Modern American Reform.* New York: Alfred A. Knopf; 1952.

Gossett, Thomas T.: *Race: The History of an Idea in America.* Dallas: Southern Methodist University Press; 1963.

Green, Fletcher Melvin, ed.: *Essays in Southern History.* Chapel Hill: University of North Carolina Press; 1949.

Greenhut, Melvin L., and W. Tate Whitman, eds.: *Essays in Southern Economic Development.* Chapel Hill: University of North Carolina Press; 1964.

Hesseltine, William Best: *Confederate Leaders in the New South.* Baton Rouge: Louisiana State University Press; 1950.

Hofstadter, Richard: *Social Darwinism in American Thought,* rev. edn. Boston: Beacon Press; 1955.

Ide, Yoshimitsu: "The Significance of Richard Hathaway Edmonds and His *Manufacturers' Record* in the New South." Unpublished doctoral dissertation, University of Florida, 1959.

Kendrick, Benjamin Burke, and Alex Mathews Arnett: *The South Looks at Its Past.* Chapel Hill: University of North Carolina Press; 1935.

Kirwan, Albert D.: *Revolt of the Rednecks: Mississippi Politics, 1876–1925.* Lexington: University of Kentucky Press; 1951.

Lee, Everett S., et al.: *Population Redistribution and Economic Growth, United States, 1870–1950.* Philadelphia: American Philosophical Society; 1957.

Lewinson, Paul: *Race, Class, and Party: A History of Negro Suffrage and White Politics in the South.* New York: Oxford University Press; 1932.

Lively, Robert A.: *Fiction Fights the Civil War: An Unfinished Chapter in the Literary History of the American People.* Chapel Hill: University of North Carolina Press; 1957.

Logan, Frenise A.: *The Negro in North Carolina, 1876–1894.* Chapel Hill: University of North Carolina Press; 1964.

Logan, Rayford W.: *The Negro in American Life and Thought: The Nadir, 1877–1901.* New York: Dial Press, Inc.; 1954.

McKinney, John C., and Edgar T. Thompson, eds.: *The South in Continuity and Change.* Durham: Duke University Press; 1965.

Meier, August: *Negro Thought in America, 1880–1915: Racial Ideologies in the Age of Booker T. Washington.* Ann Arbor: University of Michigan Press; 1963.

Mitchell, Broadus: *The Rise of the Cotton Mills in the South.* Baltimore: Johns Hopkins Press; 1921.

———, and George Sinclair Mitchell: *The Industrial Revolution in the South.* Baltimore: Johns Hopkins Press; 1930.

Moger, Allen Wesley: *The Rebuilding of the Old Dominion: A Study in Economic, Social, and Political Transition from 1880 to 1902.* Ann Arbor, Mich.: Edwards Brothers, Inc.; 1940.

Murray, Henry A., ed.: *Myth and Mythmaking.* New York: George Braziller; 1960.

Myrdal, Gunnar: *An American Dilemma: The Negro Problem and Modern Democracy,* 2 vols. New York: Harper & Brothers; 1944.

National Emergency Council: *Report on Economic Conditions of the South.* Washington: Government Printing Office; 1938.

Nicholls, William H.: *Southern Tradition and Regional Progress.* Chapel Hill: University of North Carolina Press; 1960.

Nolen, Claude H.: *The Negro's Image in the South: The Anatomy of White Supremacy.* Lexington: University of Kentucky Press; 1967.

North, Douglas C.: *The Economic Growth of the United States, 1790–1860.* Englewood Cliffs, N.J.: Prentice-Hall, Inc.; 1961.

Odum, Howard W., et al.: *Southern Pioneers in Social Interpretation.* Chapel Hill: University of North Carolina Press; 1925.

Perloff, Harvey S., et al.: *Regions, Resources, and Economic Growth.* Baltimore: Johns Hopkins Press; 1960.

Potter, David: *People of Plenty: Economic Abundance and the American Character.* Chicago: University of Chicago Press; 1954.

Rose, Willie Lee: *Rehearsal for Reconstruction: The Port Royal Experiment.* Indianapolis: Bobbs-Merrill Co.: 1964.

Shugg, Roger: *Origins of the Class Struggle in Louisiana:*

A Social History of White Farmers and Laborers During Slavery and After, 1840–1875. Baton Rouge: Louisiana State University Press; 1939.

Simkins, Francis Butler: *The Everlasting South.* Baton Rouge: Louisiana State University Press; 1963.

Sitterson, J. Carlyle, ed.: *Studies in Southern History.* Chapel Hill: University of North Carolina Press; 1957.

Stewart, Randall, et al.: *The Literature of the South.* Chicago: Scott, Foresman and Company; 1952.

Stover, John F.: *The Railroads of the South, 1865–1900.* Chapel Hill: University of North Carolina Press; 1955.

Taylor, William R.: *Cavalier and Yankee: The Old South and American National Character.* New York: George Braziller; 1961.

Tindall, George Brown: *South Carolina Negroes, 1877–1900.* Columbia: University of South Carolina Press; 1952.

Turner, Frederick Jackson: *The Frontier in American History.* New York: Henry Holt; 1920.

Twelve Southerners: *I'll Take My Stand: The South and the Agrarian Tradition.* New York: Harper & Brothers Publishers; 1930.

Vandiver, Frank E., ed.: *The Idea of the South: Pursuit of a Central Theme.* Chicago: University of Chicago Press; 1964.

Wharton, Vernon Lane: *The Negro in Mississippi, 1865–1890.* Chapel Hill: University of North Carolina Press; 1947.

Wilson, Edmund: *Patriotic Gore: Studies in the Literature of the American Civil War.* New York: Oxford University Press; 1962.

Woodward, C. Vann: *The Burden of Southern History.* Baton Rouge: Louisiana State University Press; 1960.

———: *Reunion and Reaction: The Compromise of 1877 and the End of Reconstruction.* Boston: Little, Brown and Company; 1951.

———: *The Strange Career of Jim Crow,* 2nd rev. edn. New York: Oxford University Press; 1966.

Wyllie, Irving G.: *The Self-Made Man in America: The Myth of Rage to Riches.* New Brunswick, N.J.: Rutgers University Press; 1954.

Wynes, Charles E.: *Race Relations in Virginia, 1870–1902.* Charlottesville: University of Virginia Press; 1961.

E. Secondary Works: Articles

Appleby, Joyce: "Reconciliation and the Northern Novelist, 1865–1880," *Civil War History*, X (June 1964), 117–29.

Atchison, Ray M.: "*The Land We Love:* A Southern Post-Bellum Magazine of Agriculture, Literature, and Military History," *North Carolina Historical Review*, XXXVII (October 1960), 506–15.

Baskette, Floyd K.: "Atticus G. Haygood's Thanksgiving Sermon," *Emory University Quarterly*, II (March 1946), 21–9.

Belissary, Constantine G.: "The Rise of Industry and the Industrial Spirit in Tennessee, 1865–1885," *Journal of Southern History*, XIX (May 1953), 193–215.

Berthoff, Rowland T.: "Southern Attitudes Toward Immigration, 1865–1914," *Journal of Southern History*, XVII (August 1951), 328–60.

Brown, Sterling A.: "Negro Character as Seen by White Authors," *Journal of Negro Education*, II (April 1933), 179–203.

Cotterill, Robert Spencer: "The Old South to the New," *Journal of Southern History*, XV (February 1949), 3–8.

Daumer, Louise: "Myth and Humor in the Uncle Remus Fables," *American Literature*, XX (May 1948), 129–43.

English, Thomas H.: "The Twice-Told Tale and Uncle Remus," *Georgia Review*, II (Winter 1948), 447–60.

Flory, Claude R.: "Paul Hamilton Hayne and the New South," *Georgia Historical Quarterly*, XLVI (December 1962), 388–94.

Johnson, Charles S.: "The Social Philosophy of Booker T. Washington," *Opportunity*, VI (April 1928), 102–5, 115.

Johnson, Guy B.: "Negro Racial Movements and Leadership in the United States," *American Journal of Sociology*, XLII (July 1937), 57–71.

Link, Arthur S.: "The Progressive Movement in the South, 1870–1914," *North Carolina Historical Review*, XXIII (April 1946), 172–95.

Owsley, Frank L.: "A Key to Southern Liberalism," *Southern Review*, III (Summer 1937), 28–38.

————: "The Old South and the New," *American Review*, VI (February 1936), 475–85.

Phillips, Ulrich B.: "The Central Theme of Southern History," *American Historical Review*, XXXIV (October 1928), 30–43.

Potter, David M.: "An Appraisal of Fifteen Years of the *Journal of Southern History*, 1935–1949," *Journal of Southern History*, XVI (February 1950), 25–32.

———: "The Enigma of the South," *Yale Review*, LI (Autumn 1961), 142–51.

———: "On Understanding the South: A Review Article," *Journal of Southern History*, XXX (November 1964), 451–62.

Rutman, Darrett B.: "Philip Alexander Bruce: A Divided Mind of the South," *Virginia Magazine of History and Biography*, LXVIII (October 1960), 387–407.

Sellers, Charles Grier, Jr.: "Walter Hines Page and the Spirit of the New South," *North Carolina Historical Review*, XXIX (October 1952), 481–99.

Smith, Herbert F.: "Joel Chandler Harris's Contributions to Scribner's Monthly and Century Magazine, 1880–1887," *Georgia Historical Quarterly*, XLVII (June 1963), 169–79.

Stafford, John: "Patterns of Meaning in *Nights With Uncle Remus*," *American Literature*, XVIII (May 1946), 89–108.

Stover, John F.: "Northern Financial Interests in Southern Railroads, 1865–1900," *Georgia Historical Quarterly*, XXXIX (September 1955), 205–20.

Tindall, George B., et al.: "The Status and Future of Regionalism—A Symposium," *Journal of Southern History*, XXVI (February 1960), 22–56.

Wade, John Donald: "Henry W. Grady," *Southern Review*, III (Winter 1938), 479–509.

———: "Profits and Losses in the Life of Joel Chandler Harris," *American Review*, I (April 1933), 17–35.

———: "What the South Figured, 1865–1914," *Southern Review*, III (Autumn 1937), 360–7.

Ward, Judson C., Jr.: "The New Departure Democrats of Georgia: An Interpretation," *Georgia Historical Quarterly*, XLI (September 1957), 227–36.

Webb, John M.: "Militant Majorities and Racial Minorities," *Sewanee Review*, LXV (Spring 1957), 332–47.

Webb, Walter Prescott: "The South's Call to Greatness: Challenge to All Southerners," *The Graduate Journal* (University of Texas), III (Supplement, 1960), 299–309.

Westbrook, John T.: "Twilight of Southern Regionalism," *Southwest Review*, XLII (Summer 1957), 231–4.

Whaley, W. Gordon: "The South Will Likely Fail," *The Gradu-*

ate Journal (University of Texas), III (Supplement, 1960), 311–21.

Woodward, C. Vann: "Hillbilly Realism," *Southern Review*, IV (Spring 1939), 676–81.

Wynes, Charles E.: "Lewis Harvie Blair, Virginia Reformer: The Uplift of the Negro and Southern Prosperity," *Virginia Magazine of History and Biography*, LXXII (January 1964), 3–18.

Index

Adams, Henry, 178
Alexander, Will Winton (interracial leader), 227, 234–5
Allston, Ben, 23
"American Creed," 129, 131; and legend of moral innocence, 119–21
American myths: and relationship to New South creed, 13, 219; and opulence, 45–6; and success, 83–4; and innocence, 119–21; dissipation of, 242–6; *see also* myth; New South myth (20th century)
Andersen, Hans Christian, 188
Appleby, Joyce, 170
Ashmore, Harry, 11
Atkinson, Edward, 86; advocates sectional reconciliation, 85; receives honorary degree, 91; and gospel of work, 108
Atlanta Exposition (1895), 209–12
Aycock, Charles Brantley, 108

Badeau, Captain Adam, as editor of *The New South*, 18–19
Bailey, Josiah, 223
Bingham, Robert: and sectional reconciliation, 91; and public education, 105; and the Negro question, 136, 138

Blair, Lewis Harvie, 142, 187–8, 218; critic of New South myth, 199–202
Bledsoe, Albert Taylor, 156–7
Brown v. Board of Education, 236
Brown, Joseph G., 115; on myth of the Old South, 175
Brown, Sterling A., 182
Bruce, Philip Alexander, 123–4
Buck, Paul Herman, 83–4, 96–7, 274
Burwell, William M., as editor of *DeBow's Review*, 28
Byrnes, James F., 236

Cabell, James Branch, 151, 186, 229
Cable, George Washington, 218; critic of Grady's New South address, 93–4; on the Negro question, 127, 130, 135, 136–7, 139, 140, 141–2, 144–5, 148, 149
Carnegie, Andrew, 209
Cash, Wilbur J., on continuity in Southern history, 11–12
Civil Rights Cases, 148, 149
Commager, Henry Steele, 84, 115
Commission on Interracial Cooperation, 227–8
Cooke, John Esten, 251
Cotterill, Robert Spencer, 158–9

Look Away from Dixie
Frank E. Smith

The Cold War
Retrospect and Prospect
Frederick L. Schuman

Writing Southern History
Essays in Historiography in Honor of Fletcher M. Green
Edited by Arthur S. Link and Rembert W. Patrick

Romanticism and Nationalism in the Old South
Rollin G. Osterweis

The Mind of the Old South
Clement Eaton

Pitchfork Ben Tillman
Francis Butler Simkins

Hoke Smith and the Politics of the New South
Dewey W. Grantham, Jr.

Religion and the Constitution
Paul G. Kauper

American Negro Slavery
Ulrich Bonnell Phillips

The Meaning of Yalta
Big Three Diplomacy and the New Balance of Power
Edited by John L. Snell

Southern Legacy
Hodding Carter

Edmund Ruffin, Southerner
A Study in Secession
Avery O. Craven

Romance and Realism in Southern Politics
T. Harry Williams

A History of the South

*The Southern Colonies in the Seventeenth
Century, 1607–1689*
Wesley Frank Craven